Our Prayers
Sloka Book

JET Publisning House

INDIA   **USA**

TOWARDS EXCELLENCE

P
R
A
J
N
A

Title	Our Prayers
Subtitle	Sloka Book
Copyright	Jeeyar Educational Trust
Third Edition	2010
Contributor	His Holiness Chinna Jeeyar Swamiji

CONTACT US:

INDIA	**UNITED STATES**
JIVA Sriramanagaram, Shamshabad, R.R. Dist. Andhra Pradesh - 509 325 Phone: 95535 49971, 95535 499	JETUSA Inc. Jeeyar Asram, 222, Dey Road, CRANBURY, NJ 08512, USA Phone:609-297-8797

Website: www.prajna4me.org   **Email:** prajna@jetusa.org

HIS GRACE...

Dear Bhagavad Bandhus,

On this Earth there are many countries where the ancient traditions are followed in different ways. Each country has its own way of following those traditions. But, each one of those traditions carry some sort of education to their masses. Each one of those customs has a wonderful value behind it. In the name of globalization, now-a-days, many customs or the value based practices are being discouraged and also eradicated as mere superstitions. Those customs which are in use, were probably established, based upon the environmental conditions or the background of the lineages. Though a few things change here and there, the fundamental truth, as a whole, won't change such as respecting one's father, mother, teacher, elders and showing concern for nature, protecting the Earth, cattle and showing our gratitude towards all the helpful resources. So, irrespective of what continent we belong to, it is the primary duty of every one of us to learn the basic things of benevolence which are universally practiced. It is the duty of the learned to identify such practices and put them in practice, teach them to our children, who build the future world.

JET is offering its part of service in this context by promoting classes called "Prajna" for children of all ages. Children are our future world. If they learn good things, they will definitely make the future brighter. So, Prajna is coming up with a few modules for children.

The first module is aimed at understanding the daily activities and also annual festivities. Here is a text book followed by an activity book. We invite all the interested volunteers to learn its contents and provide guidance for the children. For such interested volunteers, here is a handy guide provided! These modules lead children step by step **"Towards excellence".** We appreciate feedback from the well-wishers for the effective improvement.

We offer our Mangalasasanams to all those who made good efforts in laying the steps, building these modules and to those who use them.

GUIDELINES TO USE THIS BOOK

Right of knowledge leads to Righteous deeds. The fruits thereof bestow long lasting joy to one and all. They are the "Values" in a peaceful society. Our great sages and gurus of Vedic lore have passed on such knowledge with pristine purity in a continuous flow through generations. It is for us to protect that great treasure and reap its benefits through guided practice. It is also our responsibility to pass it on to the onward generations with same purity and care. "Prajna" is an effort in this direction.

What is prajna?

"Prajna is the ability to translate good knowledge into action"

Prajna Course

Designed to mould the young minds and inspire the adults to learn the secrets of proven Vedic practices in the context of the modern scientific developments. This course module leads through basic aspects of our everyday living to make it happy and joyful.

The first module deals with

1. Basics of "Values"
2. Familiarity with Vocabulary
3. Great stories from our history
4. Introduction to Vedic approach of practices
5. Festivals and functions in family and community
6. Creativity in work.

Let us begin...

IN THIS BOOK

14.	mangala:sa:sana paraihi mada:cha:rya puro:gamaihi |	37
	sarvais cha pu:rvair a:cha:ryaihi sathkurtha:ya:sthu mangalam ||

15.	aka:la mruthyu haranam sarva vya:dhi niva:ranam |	39
	samastha pa:pa haranam vishnu pa:do:dakam subham ||

16.	yuktha:ha:ra viha:rasya yuktha che:shtasya karmasu |	40
	yuktha swapna:vabo:dhasya yo:go: bhavathi dukha ha: ||

17.	aham vaiswa:naro: bhu:thwa:	43
	pra:nina:m de:ham a:srithaha |
	pra:na:pana sama:yukthaha
	pacha:mi annam chatur vidham||

18.	jna:na:nanda mayam de:vam nirmala sphatika:kruthim |	45
	a:dha:ram sarva vidya:na:m hayagri:vam upa:smahe: ||

19.	disanthu me: de:va sada: thwadi:ya:ha	47
	daya: tharanga:nuchara:h kata:ksha:ha |
	sro:thre:shu pumsa:m amrutham ksharanthi:m
	saraswathi:m samsritha ka:ma dhe:num ||

20.	sukla:mbara dharam vishnum sasi varnam chathur bhujam |	49
	prasanna vadanam dhya:ye:th sarva vighno:pa sa:nthaye: ||

21	yasya dwirada vakthra:dya:ha pa:rishadya:h paras satham |	51
	vighnam nighnanthi sathatham vishvak se:nam tham a:sraye: ||

22.	a:pada:m apahartha:ram da:tha:ram sarva sampada:m |	53
	lo:ka:bhira:mam sri:ra:mam bhu:yo: bhu:yo: nama:myaham ||

23. jale: rakshathu va:ra:haha sthale: rakshathu va:manaha | 55
    atavya:m na:ra simhas cha sarvathah pa:thu ke:savaha ||

24. ra:maskandam hanu:mantham vainathe:yam vruko:daram | 56
    sayane: yas smare:n nithyam dusswapnam thasya nasyathi ||

25. ka:ye:na va:cha: manase:ndriyair va: 58
    buddhya:thmana: va: prakruthe:s svabha:va:th |
    karo:mi yadyath sakalam parasmai
    na:ra:yana:ye:thi samarpaya:mi ||
    srimanna:ra:yana:ye:thi samarpaya:mi
    sarvam sri: krushna:rpanam asthu

26. kasthu:ri: thilakam lala:ta phalake:, vakshasthale: kausthubham, 60
    na:sa:gre: nava maukthikam, karathale: venum, kare:
    kankanam| sarva:nge: harichandanam cha kalayan, kante: cha
    muktha:vali:m, go:pasthri: parive:shtitho: vijayathe:,
    go:pa:la chu:da:manihi ||

27. jayathu jayathu de:vo: de:vaki: nandano:yam, 63
    jayathu jayathu krushno: vrushni vamsa pradi:paha, |
    jayathu jayathu me:ghasya:malah ko:mala:ngo:
    jayathu jayathu pruthvi: bha:ra na:so: mukundaha ||

28. krushnam kamala pathra:ksham punya sravana ki:rthanam| 65
    va:sude:vam jagad yo:nim naumi na:ra:yanam harim ||

29. krushna:ya ya:dave:ndra:ya jna:na mudra:ya yo:gine: | 67
    na:tha:ya rukmini:sa:ya namo: ve:da:ntha ve:dine: ||

30.   **s**ri: ra:ghavam dasara**th**a:thmajam aprame:yam   69
      si:tha:pathim raghukula:nvaya rathna di:pam |
      a:ja:nuba:hum aravinda da**l**a:ya tha:ksham
      ra:mam ni**s**a:chara vina:**s**akaram nama:mi ||

31   vaide:hi: sahitham sura drumathale: 70
            haime: maha:mandape:
      madhye: pushpakam a:sane:
            manimaye: vi:ra:sane: susthitham |
      agre: va:chayathi prabhanjana suthe:
            thaththvam munibhyah param
      vya:khya:ntham bharatha:dibhih
            parivrutham ra:mam bhaje: sya:malam||

32   sarasija nayane:! saro:ja hasthe:!   73
      dhava**l**athara:n**s**uka gandha ma:lya **s**o:bhe:! |
      bhagavathi! hari vallabhe:! mano:jne:!
      thribhuvana bhu:thikari! prasi:da mahyam ||

33.   mano:javam ma:rutha thulya ve:gam   75
      jithe:ndriya:m buddhimatha:m varish**t**am |
      va:tha:thmajam va:nara yu:dha mukhyam
      sri: ra:ma du:tham **s**irasa: nama:mi ||

34   ullanghya sindho:s salilam sali:lam   77
      ya**s s**o:ka vanhim janaka:thmaja:ya:ha |
      a:da:ya the:naiva dada:ha lanka:m
      nama:mi tham pra:njalir a:njane:yam ||

35   a:njane:yam athi pa:tala:nanam   79
      ka:nchana:dri kamani:ya vigraham |
      pa:rija:tha tharu mu:la va:sinam
      bha:vaya:mi pavama:na nandanam ||

① STARTING PRAYER

Introduction

Let us bow to all our masters or *Gurus*, before starting the process of learning. Mother is out first guru. Then comes father. Teachers who educate us in school are next. Then comes our spiritual masters. We should bow before all of them.

o:m asmad gurubhyo: namaha |

Meanings

gurubhyaha   =   to all gurus

asmath   =   of ours

o:m   =   This humble servant, the soul

namaha   =   surrender unconditionally

2 RUSHI PRAYER

Introduction

A *Rushi* is the one who can foresee all things. We call him a *seer* or a *sage*. There are many seers who built our society. They taught us a better lifestyle and structured the family system, long long ago.

The Sages passed on the right systems to us. The powerful message of the *Rushis* is TO SHARE. I am grateful to the Rushis and I bow down before them. With love and respect, I repeat this *manthra* twice.

o:m namah parama rushibhyo:
namah parama rushibhyaha |
o:m namah parama rushibhyo:
namah parama rushibhyaha ||

Meanings

o:m	=	This humble soul
Namaha	=	unconditionally surrenders
Parama rushibhyaha	=	to the great sages

3 SA:NTHI MANTHRAM

Introduction

You have power and I have power too. Every object around us is filled with infinite power. This power supports everything because it knows everything. So, I call it God. It is not visible. It is hidden due to my ignorance. If that ignorance is removed, my energy and knowledge will shine.

I want to shine with energy and knowledge. But, how?

I want to remove my ignorance. But, how?

Only prayer can remove ignorance. I pray to that powerful and all-knowing God.

O God! Bless me with infinite knowledge and power.

o:m
> pu:rnam idam pu:rnam adaha
> pu:rna:th pu:rnam udachyathe: |
> pu:rnasya pu:rnam a:da:ya
> pu:rnam e:va:vasishyathe ||　　o:m

Meanings

idam	=	this, **indweller** of the soul
pu:rnam	=	is omnipotent, complete
adaha	=	that, **all-pervading**
pu:rnam	=	is omnipotent
pu:rna:th	=	from that omnipotent
pu:rnam	=	the planning abode called **vyu:ham**
undachyathe:	=	emanates
pu:rnam	=	the appearance of that omnipotent called **avatha:ra:s**
pu:rnasya	=	are the manifestations of omnipotent **vyu:ham**
a:da:ya	=	the one which shaped from above forms called **archa vigraha**
avasishyathe:	=	remains
purnam e:va	=	omnipotent only

4 GURU PRA:RTHANA

Introduction

The *Gurus* reveal many secrets of this world. They shape me to become great, for they are full of knowledge. I am grateful to my gurus, so I bow to them.

> gurur bramha: gurur vish**n**uhu
> gurur de:vo: mahe:**s**waraha |
> gurus sa:ksha:th para bramha
> thasmai **s**ri: gurave: namaha ||

Meanings

guruhu	=	The Master is
bramha	=	Lord *Bramha*, the four headed god
guruhu	=	the Master is
vish**n**uhu	=	Lord *Vishnu*
guruhu	=	the Master is
devaha	=	the divine
mahe:**s**waraha	=	Lord *Siva*
guruhu	=	the Master is
sa:ksha:th	=	directly
para bramha	=	the supreme Lord *Na:ra:yana* himself
namaha	=	salutations
thasmai	=	to that
sri: gurave:	=	respected Master

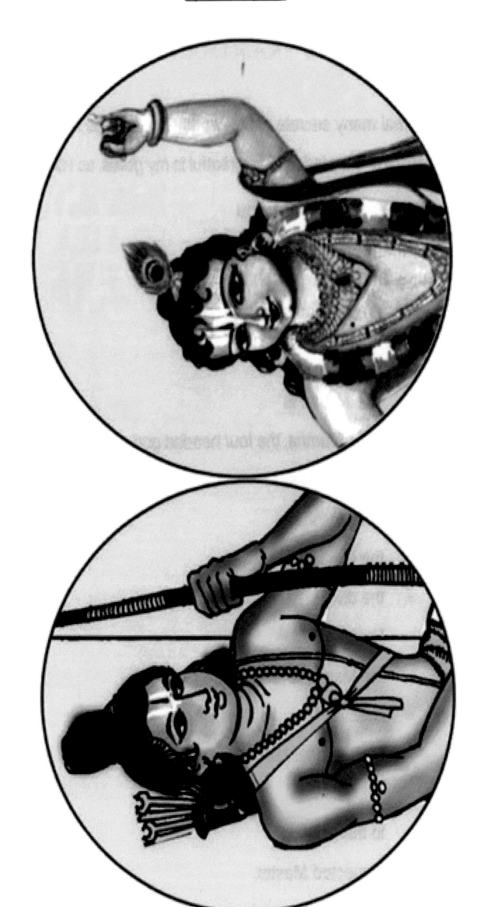

 WHILE WAKING UP FROM THE BED - 1

Introduction

To open a treasure chest, we need a key. Similarly, *manthra* is that key to improve our knowledge. We want joy and we should keep others joyful. To gain this ability, there are three *manthras*; Ra:ma, Krush**n**a and Hari.

The *manthra, Ra:ma* makes our presence joyful to all. With the *manthra, Krushna,* we make others feel the love and joy. The *manthra, Hari* removes our weakness and gives energy. Morning thoughts affect the rest of the day. Therefore, I pray for those good qualities early in the morning. This prayer keeps me energetic throughout the day. Hence, I chant this *manthra.*

    hare: ra:ma hare: ra:ma
    ra:ma ra:ma hare: hare: |
    hare: krush**n**a hare: krush**n**a
    krush**n**a krush**n**a hare: hare: ||

Meanings

hare: =   Lord *Hari,* the one who burns all sins

ra:ma   =   Lord *Ra:ma,* the one who makes everyone happy

krush**n**a =   Lord *Krushna,* the one who is the symbol of love and joy

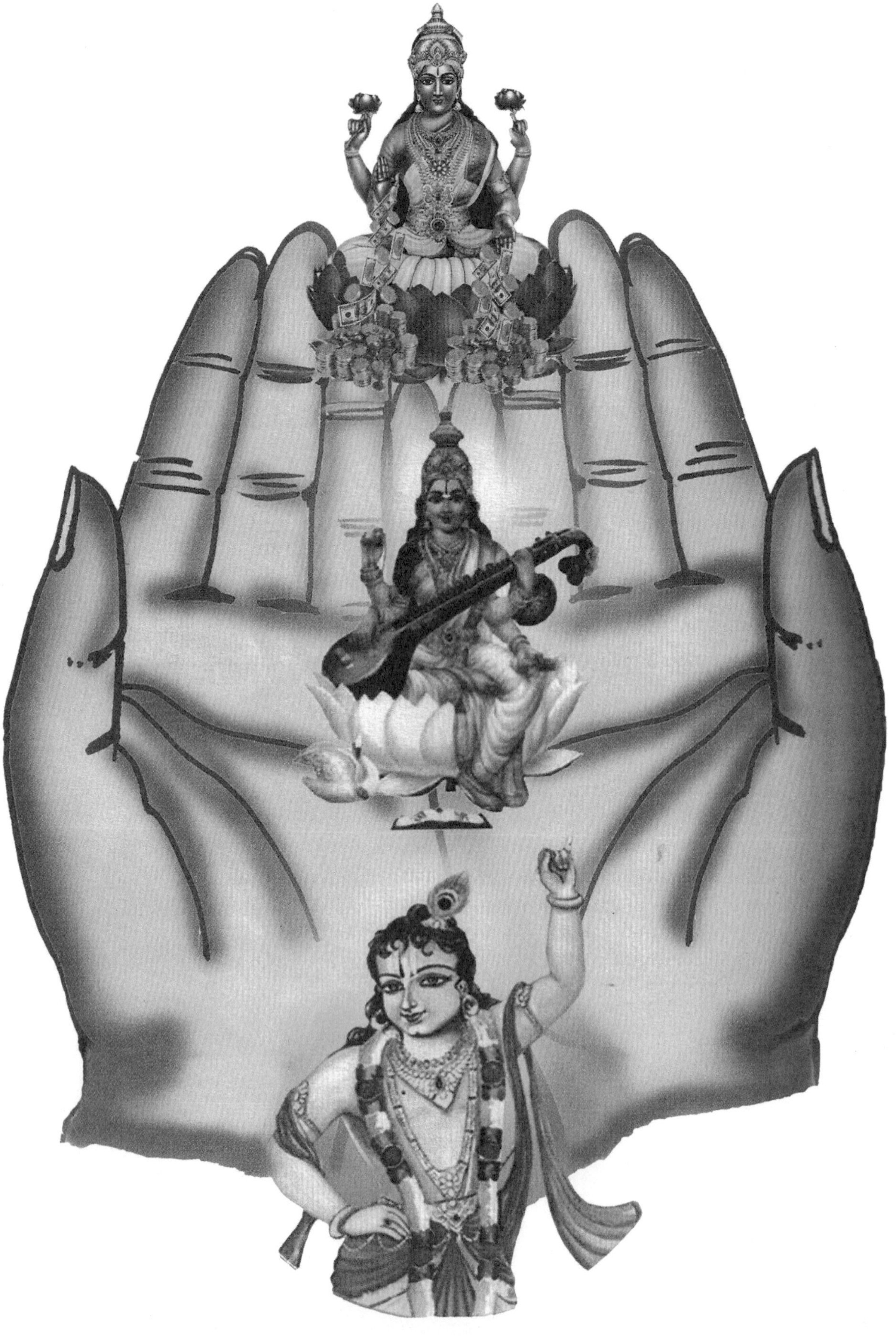

 WHILE WAKING UP FROM THE BED - 2

Introduction

We need money. Money fulfills our needs. Proper knowledge allows us to spend it well. Words we use bless us with good respect. We need to acquire all three of these. Our hands are powerful tools to do so. Money is *Lakshmi*. Knowledge is *Saraswathi* and the ability to use good words is *Go:vinda*. Let my hands become powerful tools to earn all the three. While chanting this prayer, I touch my hands.

kara:gre: vasathe: lakshmi:hi
kara madhye: saraswathi: |
kara mu:le: thu go:vindaha
prabha:the: kara dar**s**anam ||

Meanings

kara:gre:	=	on the top of the hands
lakshmi:hi	=	Goddess *Lakshmi*
vasathe:	=	resides
kara madhye:	=	in the middle of the hands
saraswathi:	=	Goddess of knowledge resides
kara mu:le: thu	=	at the base of the hands
go:vindaha	=	Lord *Vishnu* resides
prabha:the:	=	early in the morning, just after waking up
kara darsanam	=	look at the open hands

7 WHILE WAKING UP FROM THE BED - 3

<u>Introduction</u>

I love my mom because, she cares a lot for me. She has brought me to this world. She also feeds, cuddles and consoles when needed. I am very grateful to my mom.

A mother cares only for her children. But all the creatures are taken care of by a great mother, *the Mother Earth*. She cares for everybody. The Mother Earth neither gets mad nor scolds.

Oh! Beloved Mother Earth, you are The Mother of all of the mothers. I worship you always. Pardon me for stepping on you. Pardon my mistakes and bless me, so that none of my activities lead to your insult or harm. Please accept my prayer.

After praying to the mother Earth, we should prostrate to our own mother in order to show our gratitude. Everyone must prostrate to their mother regardless of being a child or an adult. If the mother is not around, then prostrate to her picture.

namasthe: priyadaththa:yai
thubhyam de:vi! Vasundhare:! |
thvam ma:tha: sarva bhu:tha:na:m
pa:da sparsam kshamaswa me: ||

Meanings

Vasundhare:	= Oh! Mother Earth, The supporter of all wealth
namaha	= salutations
the:	= the you
priya daththa:yai	= you fulfill the desires of all creatures
de:vi	= Oh! divine mother
thubhyam	= to you
namaha	= my salutations
thwam	= you are
ma:tha:	= the mother
sarva bhu:tha:na:m	= of all beings
me:	= let my
pa:da sparsam	= stepping on you
kshamaswa	= be forgiven

8 WHILE TAKING SHOWER

Introduction

Water is the origin of life. There is no life without water. Hence, water is divine. So, we worship Water. Drinking water that flows on the earth is called *Ganga*. The purity of the water makes it *Yamuna*. The force of the water is *Go:da:vari*.

The water flowing multi directional to support all water beds makes it *Saraswathi*. When water supports creatures in it, that water becomes *Narmada*. When it spreads boundless, that water becomes *Sindhu*. When divinity is visible, it is *Ka:ve:ri*. All the rivers that are with potable water are considered as the divine flow of love Mother Earth.

Oh! holy water, enrich yourself with all powers of those great rivers. Purify me. I worship your greatness.

gange:! cha yamune:! chaiva go:da:vari! sarawathi! |

narmade:! sindhu! ka:ve:ri jale:smin sannidhim kuru ||

Meanings

gange:! cha	=	Oh! Goddess of river Ganga and
yamune:!	=	Oh! river Yamuna!
go:da:vari!	=	Oh! river Go:da:vari
saraswathi!	=	Oh! river Saraswathi
narmade:!	=	Oh! river Narmada!
sindhu!	=	Oh! river Sindhu!
ka:ve:ri! cha	=	and also river Ka:ve:ri!
kuru	=	have your
sannidhim	=	divine presence
asmin	=	in this
jale: e:va	=	water only

9 AFTER APPLYING THILAKAM

Introduction

A temple is the home of god. It is always pure. We decorate it and share the joy of serving it. Our life supported by God being within our body. Thus, our body too is the home of God. But, there is a difference.

Our body is walking, moving, talking, and doing, many activities. Thus, it is a great mobile temple. Hence, we should keep it pure. We should decorate it and take proper care of it. We should keep this temple clean and healthy.

We should send good food into this temple. Like my body, everybody's body is a temple as well.

May God in this temple make this body strong. Let all the parts of my body function powerfully. I sanctify my body with the touch of His divine names.

Meanings

o:m ke:**s**ava:ya namaha	obeisance to Lord Ke:**s**ava, who is the controller of I:**s**a and Bramha
o:m na:ra:ya**n**a:ya namaha	the indweller of all animate and inanimate things.
o:m ma:dhava:ya namaha	spouse of Goddess Lakshmi
o:m go:vinda:ya namaha	the savior of all animals
o:m vish**n**ave: namaha	the omnipresent
o:m madhusu:dana:ya namaha	the destroyer of demon Madhu
o:m thrivikrama:ya namaha	the one who measured the three worlds with His divine feet, Va:mana became Thrivikrama
o:m va:mana:ya namaha	the dwarf incarnation to protect His subjects
o:m **s**ri:dhara:ya namaha	the one whose heart is abode of Goddess Lakshmi
o:m hrushi:ke:**s**a:ya namaha	the controller of all senses
o:m padma na:bha:ya namaha	the supporter of the Lotus in His Navel, from which the whole Universe emerged.
o:m da:mo:dara:ya namaha	the one who got a scar of rope around His waist, imprinted when tied Him up during the incarnation of Krush**n**a

10 THANKS TO THE SUN
SANDHYA: VANDANAM-1

<u>Introduction</u>

The Sun gives us light. Without Him, everything will become dark. He also gives us a great amount of energy, not only to me and you, but to the entire Universe. So, we should be grateful to Him.

We live with water. That water is created by the Sun through the clouds. Trees, animals, birds, and all the creatures are living with His power. Clouds rain because of the power of Sun. His energy is endless.

Oh ! Sun God, I am grateful to you. You are blessing me with pure knowledge that glows like Your rays. I offer you pure water three times to purify my body, my mind and the soul.

> e:hi su:rya ! sahasra:m**s**o: !
> the:jo: ra:**s**e: ! jagath pathe: ! |
> anukampaya ma:m bhakthya:
> gruha:**n**a:rghyam prasi:da o:m ||

* While worshipping the Sun God, chant this slokam and offer handful of water, three times. *

Meanings

sahasra + am**s**o: !	=	Oh ! Sun, having thousands of rays
the:jo: ra:**s**e: !	=	Oh ! the land of radiance
jagath pathe: !	=	Oh ! the ruler of the universe
su:rya !	=	Oh ! the nurturer
e:hi	=	reach me
anukampaya	=	shower your grace
ma:m	=	on me
bhakthya:	=	who is with devotion
gruha:**n**a	=	please accept
arghyam	=	the pure water offered by me
prasi:da	=	and bless me
o:m	=	I belong to you

11 THANKS TO THE SUN
SANDHYA: VANDANAM - 2

Introduction

Lights glow with power. A few lights burn with oil. The fuel is electricity, oil, etc. Without fuel, a lamp will not burn. The Sun is like a huge lamp that illuminates this entire world. We don't know what fuel the Sun uses, or how He glows. Will something burn without fuel? No. Then what is the power behind the Sun?

The unseen power in the Sun will never exhaust. That power in the Sun is the called Na:ra:yana, and it will support the whole life in this world.

I recognize that power as Lord Na:ra:yana sitting on a lotus, with all its greatness. I meditate upon that Lord who is dwelling in the Sun to bless me with great power.

dhye:yas sada: savithru mandala madhyavarthi:
na:ra:yanas sarasija:sana sannivishtaha,
keyu:rava:n makara kundalava:n kiri:ti ha:ri:
hiranamaya vapur dhrutha sankha chakraha II

Meanings

madhya varthi:	=	One who dwells in the middle of
mandala	=	the planet
savithru	=	Sun
na:ra:yanaha	=	the supporter of all living and nonliving entities
sannivishtaha	=	He who is sitting
a:sana	=	in the seat of
sarasija	=	lotus
ke:yu:rava:n	=	wearing shoulder rings
makara kundalava:n	=	decorated with beautiful earrings
kiri:ti:	=	one with crown on his head
ha:ri	=	one with garlands
vapuhu	=	having His divine form
hiranmaya	=	shining like gold
dhrutha	=	holding
sankha chakraha	=	conch and disc like weapons
dhye:yaha	=	is to be meditated upon
sada:	=	always

12 SUPRABHA:THAM MORNING PRAYER TO GOD

Introduction

Air is everywhere, but to feel it, we need a fan. Like air, and the all - powerful God is everywhere. A deity allows is to see and feel His presence. Turn on the fan and you can feel the air. Likewise, pray to the deity to invoke our inner strength.

I pray to You, Oh ! Almighty in this deity form. Please bless me. Let all my activities be successful. I invoke the divine energy in you.

kausalya: supraja: ra:ma pu:rva: sandhya: pravarthathe:

uththishta narasa:rdu:la karthavyam dyvamanhikam II

Meanings

rama	=	Oh ! Lord Ra:ma
supraja:ha	=	beloved child of
kausalya	=	Queen Kausalya
pu:rva:	=	eastern
sandhya:	=	Sun light
pravarthathe:	=	is emerging
uththishta	=	wake up
narasa:rdu:la	=	Oh ! tiger among the men
dyvam anhikam	=	divine morning duties
karthavyam	=	are to be performed

13 PRAYER FOR THE WELL BEING MANGALA:SA:SANAM-1

Introduction

The trees bloom with flowers and fruits. They hold on their roots. If those roots are nurtured with water, the trees grow well. The world we live in is like a tree. God is the root. Roots are invisible because they spread under the ground. But God is visible in a deity form, the *Vigraha*. Our love is like the water to feed *this holy root, the deity.* How do we show that love?

The lamp is a symbol of love. Thus, we light up the lamp to show our love to God. I sing the song of divine love with this verse...

sriyah ka:ntha:ya ka**l**ya:**n**a
nidhaye: nidhaye:r**th**ina:m |
sri: ve:nkata niva:sa:ya
sri:niva:sa:ya manga**l**am ||

Meanings

manga**l**am	=	All glory
sriyah ka:nath:ya	=	to the spouse of Goddess Sri:
ka**l**ya:**n**a nidhaye	=	to the ocean of divine qualities
nidhaye:	=	to the treasure
ar**th**ina:m	=	of seekers
sri:niva:sa:ya	=	to the abode of Lakshmi, Lord Ve:nkate:sa
niva:sa:ya	=	the resident of
sri: ve:nkata	=	Holy Tirumala

14   A PRAYER FOR THE WELL BEING MANGALA:SA:SANAM-2

Introduction

Books will support our knowledge. We learn, recollect, recapitulate and share the knowledge with help of books. Book teaches us many things, seen and unseen. Thus, a book is equivalent to my Guru. I respect and worship all books. I will never insult any form of book. I adore Books, *the source of knowledge*, with a divine song.

mangala:**s**a:sana paraihi
mada:cha:rya puro:gamaihi |
sarvai**s** cha pu:rvair a:cha:ryaihi
sathkrutha:ya:sthu mangalam ||

Meanings

mangalam   =   all glory

asthu   =   be there

sath krutha:ya   =   to the Divine Literature, which was adored

sarvaihi+cha   =   by all

pu:rvaihi+a:cha:ryaihi = Previous Masters

puro:gamaihi   =   subsequent gurus along with

math+a:cha:rya   =   my spiritual master

mangala: **s**a:sana paraihi = whose mission is to protect the literature

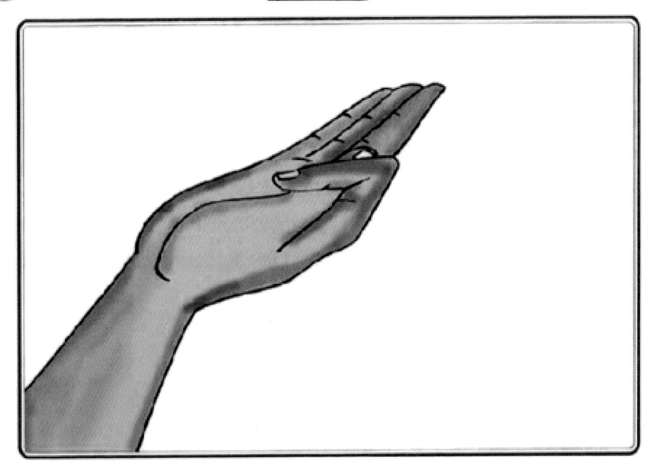

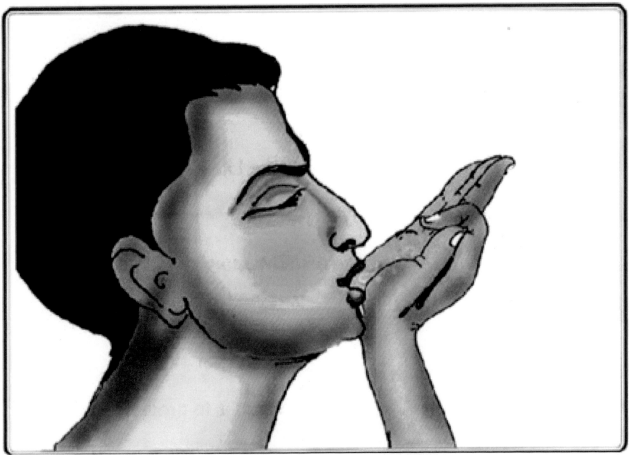

15 WHILE TAKING THI:RTHAM

Introduction

Water gets sanctified with the touch of Lord's feet. This sanctified water is called Thi:rtham. I take Thi:rtham to gain inner strength, peace and avoid any mishap. This water keeps me away from evil thoughts. It eliminates all my sins and makes me pure. Let good fortunes come to me with this sacred water.

> aka:la mruthyu haranam
> srava vya:dhi nivaranam |
> samastha pa:pa haranam
> vishnu pa:do:dakam subham ||

Meanings

vishnu pa:do:dakam	= water offered to the divine feet of Lord Vishnu, becomes Thi:rtham
subham	= gives good fortune
aka:la mruthyu haranam	= stops untimely & accidental deaths
sarva vya:dhi niva:ranam	= removes all sorts of illness and
samastha pa:pa haranam	= removes all sorts of sins

16 WHILE TAKING FOOD - 1

<u>Introduction</u>

We all wish for a comfortable life. Our thoughts and activities should be pure and perfect, so we can be trouble free to ourselves and to others. Ultimately, we must be successful in our lives.

To be successful in life, one must follow several ideals. Eating healthy food, having regular exercise and moderate entertainment are a few of them. To lead a perfect way of life, we need to eat recommended food only and not junk food. Our recreation, sleep and exercise should also be within limits. Excessive sleep, recreation, and exercise makes us lazy, anxious and restless.

If these ideals are followed, even our memory will become perfect. All our actions will be fruitful and life will become enjoyable.

I should always remember this truth while chanting this manthra...

yuktha:ha:ra viha:rasya
yuktha che:shtasya karmasu |
yuktha swapna:vabo:dhasya
yo:go: bhavathi dukhaha: ||

Meanings

yuktha	=	who regulates
a:ha:ra	=	food
viha:rasya	=	recreation
yuktha che:shtasya	=	who acts moderately
karmasu	=	in recommended duties
swapna+avabo:dhasya	=	who sleeps and wakes up
yuktha	=	moderately
yo:gaha	=	the practice or activity of such a person
bhavathi	=	becomes
duhkhaha:	=	painless

17 WHILE TAKING FOOD - 2

__Introduction__

An unseen power digests anything we eat or drink. It is an indwelling fire *Vyswa:nara.* We live as long as that supports the heat in our body. Without the *Vyswa:nara,* we cannot breathe or release waste from our body. I pray that to the unseen power *Vyswa:nara* for good digestion power, energy and a long life.

Lord Krushna said -
>   aham vy**s**wa:naro: bhu:thwa:
>   pra:**n**ina:m de:ham a:**s**rithaha |
>   pra:**n**a:pa:na sama:yukthaha
>   pacha:myannam chathur vidham ||

__Meanings__

aham	=	I
a:**s**rithaha	=	am the in-dweller of
de:ham	=	the body
pra:**n**ina:m	=	of all living creatures
bhu:thwa:	=	becoming
vy**s**wa:naraha	=	Vy**s**wa:nara, a hunger generating fire
pacha:my	=	I digest
annam	=	food
chatur vidham	=	in four varieties viz., bhakshyam, bho:jyam, cho:shyam, le:hyam
pra:**n**a+apa:na sama:yukthaha =		being with energies of the body called pra:**n**a, apa:na, vya:na, uda:na, and sama:na

 # WHILE STARTING STUDIES - 1

Introduction

We are blessed with great knowledge. We all want to improve this knowledge to lead a better life. So, we should always keep learning.

We wish that everything we gain and all the knowledge we possess should be positive. A feel of that positive thinking is called *a:nanda*, the joy. These two things 'Knowledge and Joy' are not seen. But they are very powerful and are the supports of our life. We want them crystal clear and pure. The powerful form of God that fulfills this wish is called Hayagri:va, the supporter of all knowledge. Scriptures describe Him as the Horse-necked God, (haya = horse, gri:va=neck). Let that God bless us with spotless knowledge and endless joy.

> jna:na:nanda mayam de:vam
> nirmala sphatika:kruthim |
> a:dha:ram sarva vidya:na:m
> hayagri:vam upa:smahe: ||

Meanings

upa:samhe:	=	I meditate upon
hayagri:vam	=	the horse necked
de:vam	=	bright God
jna:na mayam	=	form of joy
nirmala	=	spotless
sphatika	=	white crystal like
a:kruthim	=	form
a:dha:ram	=	a source
sarva vidya:na:m	=	of all subjects

19 WHILE STARTING STUDIES - 2

Introduction

The flow of knowledge is called Saraswathi. The words we use represent the knowledge we possess. Our words should not hurt others. They should give joy to everyone, as if nectar is sprinkled in their ears. At the same time those words should fulfill the desires of listeners. We should pray to God to bless us with that ability. Here is a precious prayer for that grace.

disanthu me: de:va sada: thwadi:ya:ha
daya: tharanga:nuchara:h kata:ksha:ha |
sro:thre:shu pumsa:m amrutham ksharanthi:m
saraswathi:m samsritha ka:ma dhe:num ||

Meanings

de:va	=	Oh ! Knowledge embodied
disanthu	=	grant
me:	=	me
sada:	=	always
kata:ksha:ha	=	the looks
thwadi:ya:ha	=	of yours
daya: tharanga+ancuhara:ha =		blended with waves of grace
saraswathi:m	=	also bless me with the flow of words
ksharanthi:m	=	that sprinkles
amrutham	=	nectar
srothre:shu	=	in to the ears
pumsa:m	=	of people
samsritha ka:madhe:num=		to fulfill their desires the divine cow ka:madhe:nu

20 BEFORE STARTING ANY WORK - 1

Introduction

I always want to be pure and perfect in my thoughts and actions. For that, I need to have my mind undisturbed by the negative forces around me.

I want to encompass everyone with friendship. For this, I need to have a pleasant appearance. I want to fulfill all my responsibilities, as though I am having four hands. I want to overcome all the obstacles. Hence, I pray to the Lord, who is possessing all the best qualities, to bless me with all those great abilities. Let us have a good start...

> **s**ukla:mbara dharam vish**n**um
> **s**a**s**i var**n**am chathur bhujam |
> prasanna vadanam dhya:ye:th
> sarva vighno:pa **s**a:nthaye ||

Meanings

sarva vighno:pa sa:nthaye:	=	for the removal of all obstacles
vishnum	=	Vishwakse:na, the all pervading hence called Vishnu
dhya:ye:th	=	should be meditated upon, who
sukla + ambara dharam	=	wears white garments
sasi varnam	=	shining like the moon
chathur bhujam	=	appears with four hands
prasanna vadanam	=	and has a pleasant face

21 BEFORE STARTING ANY WORK - 2

Introduction

To be successful in any endeavor, we need support from someone who is experienced and capable. Whoever can face any challenge and direct all his subjects towards success, is the chief among them. Vishwakse:na is such a great and powerful one. Let Vishwakse:na, the chief commander of Lord Vishnu, bless me with great expertise to overcome all the obstacles and achieve great success.

> yasya dvirada vakthra:dya:ha
> pa:rishadya:h para**s s**atham |
> vighnam nighnanthi sathatham
> Viskvak se:nam tham a:**s**raye: ||

Meanings

a:**s**raye:	=	I take refuge
tham	=	in Him
vishvakse:nam	=	The Lord Vishwakse:na
yasya	=	whose
pa:rishdya:ha	=	servants
para**s s**atham	=	are in hundreds
dvi rada vakthra:dya:ha =		each having elephant like face with two tusks
sathatham	=	always
nighnanthi	=	destroying
vighnam	=	the obstacles

22 WHILE TRAVELING - 1

Introduction

Journey is a part of life. We make many small and big journeys in our day to day life. Going to school, the office, a party, or shopping are a few examples of journeys we make. We want to come back home safe.

The way we lead our lives should be comfortable and beneficial to us and others. We need to maintain a respectable life, like **S**ri Ra:ma. Hence, I repeatedly pray to that Lord to bless my journey of life to be always safe and prosperous.

> a:pada:m apahartha:ram
> da:tha:ram sarva sampada:m |
> lo:ka:bhira:mam **s**ri:ra:mam
> bhu:yo: bhu:yo: nama:myaham ||

Meanings

aham	=	I
nama:mi	=	prostrate
sri ra:mam	=	to Lord **S**ri: Ra:ma
bhu:yaha bhu:yaha	=	again and again
apahartha:ram	=	the remover of
a:pada:m	=	agonies
da:tha:ram	=	the bestower of
sarva sampada:m	=	all sorts of wealth
lo:ka + abhi ra:mam	=	ever loved by the whole world

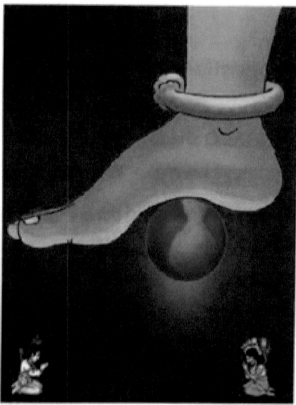

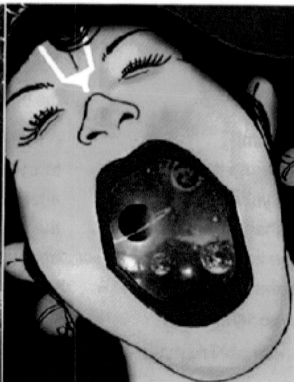

23 WHILE TRAVELING - 2

Introduction

We travel to many places on road, water, and even by air. We always want to return home safe. Even though we are travelling safely, some unexpected accidents might happen. Accidents might damage our vehicles and at times our bodies.

We do not want such things to happen. In addition to our good efforts, some sort of divine protection is needed to reach the destination safely. Hence, while starting from home, I pray for that divine power to stay with me in a form suitable to my situation and to protect me always.

jale: rakshathu va:ra:haha
sthale: rakshathu va:manaha |
atavya:m na:ra simhas cha
sarvathah pa:thu ke:savaha ||

Meanings

jale:	=	in water
va:ra:haha	=	let Lord Vara:ha
rakshathu	=	save us
sthale:	=	on the ground
va:manaha	=	let Lord Va:mana
rakshathu	=	save us
atavya:m	=	in the forest
na:rasimhaha cha	=	let the lion faced God, Lord
Narasimha also		
pa:thu	=	save us
ke:savaha	=	let Lord Ke:sava
pa:thu	=	save us
sarvathaha	=	from all corners

24 BEFORE SLEEP

Introduction

Every night before sleep, think of only good things and great people. You will have a good and peaceful sleep. If you remember three physically strong devotees. Hanuma:n, Garuda and Bhi:mase:na, you will not have any bad dreams, You will enjoy peaceful and sound sleep.

Hanuma:n, with Lord **S**ri: Ra:ma and Lakshmana on his shoulders and Garuda carrying Lord Na:ra:ya**n**a on his back, indicate that God will be with us to accept our services even when we are sleeping.

Bhi:mase:na had a fire called 'vruka' in his stomach that could digest anything he ate. Thinking of him, we can digest food well to get good sleep.

So, if we remember these three great devotees while going to bed, we will get good digestion power and a sound sleep. We will not have any bad dreams because God will be guarding us.

> ra:maskandham hanu:mantham
> vynathe:yam vruko:daram I
> **s**ayane: yas samre:n nithyam
> dussvapnam thasya na**s**yathi II

Meanings

sayane:	=	while going to bed
yaha+	=	whoever
nithyam	=	always
samre:th+	=	remembers
hanu:mantham	=	mighty Hanuma:n
ra:ma skandham	=	carrying **S**ri Ra:ma and Lakshmana on his shoulders,
vainathe:ya m	=	the eagle Garuda, son of Vinatha
vruko:daram	=	mighty Bhi:ma, who can digest anything
dus svapnam	=	bad dream
na**s**yanthi	=	disappears
thasya	=	to such person

25 AFTER COMPLETING ANY WORK

Introduction

I am able to do many activities with the help of this body and all its parts. My brain, mind, intelligence and senses are my untiring tools. All these are getting energy from one inner power named 'Na:ra:yana'.

Hence, I pay gratitude to Him and dedicate everything to Him only, without any barrier. I am not scared of Him. I always love Him.

ka:ye:na va:cha: manase:ndriyair va:
buddhya:thmana: va: prakruthe:s svabha:va:th |
karo:mi yadyath sakalam parasmy
na:ra:yana:ye:thi samarpaya:mi ||

sri:manna:ra:yana:ye:thi samarpaya:mi
Sarvam Sri: Krushna:rpanam asthu!

Meanings

yath+yath karo:mi	=	whatever I do
ka:ye:na	=	with this body
va:cha:	=	with my words
manasa:	=	with my mind
inndriyaihi+va	=	with the organs
buddhya:+	=	done deliberately
a:thmana: va:	=	or with the knowledge
swabha:va:th	=	or by the force
prakruthe:he	=	of the Nature
sakalam	=	everything
samarpaya:mi	=	I dedicate
parasmai	=	to the supreme
na:ra:yana:ya	=	Lord Nara:yana.
ithi	=	saying thus "sri:man na:ra:yana:ya"

26 REMEMBER THE FORM OF LORD SRI KRUSHNA - 1

kasthu:ri: thilakam lala:ta phalake:, vakshas**th**ale: kausthubham ,
na:sa:gre: nava maukthikam, karathale: ve**n**um, kare: kanka**n**am |
sarva:nge: harichandanam cha kalayan, kan**t**e: cha muktha:vali:m
go:pasthri: parive:shtitho: vijayathe: go:pa:la chu:da:ma**n**ihi ||

Meanings

chu:da:ma**n**ihi	=	the jewel
gopa:la	=	among the cowherd folk
vijayathe:	=	be victorious!
pari ve:shtithaha	=	one surrounded by
go:pa sthri:	=	cowherd damsel,
		the devoted women of gokula
thilakam	=	a mark called *thilakam*
kasthu:ri:	=	made of kasthu:ri: (a secretion from an animal called Kasthu:ri:, a sweet smelling black paste)
lala:ta phalake	=	on His forehead
kaushthubham	=	the rarest of the gems called *kausthubham*
vaksha s**th**ale	=	on His majestic chest
nava maukthikam	=	a new shining pearl
na:sa:gre:	=	on the tip of His nose
ve:**n**um	=	a flute
kara thale:	=	in His hand
kanka**n**am	=	a bracelet
kare:	=	on His wrist
mukhtha:vali:m cha	=	also a necklace made of pure pearl
kan**t**e:	=	on the neck,
kalayan cha	=	and also smeared with
hari chandanam	=	the sandalwood paste that removes the **tedium**
sarva:nge:	=	all over the body

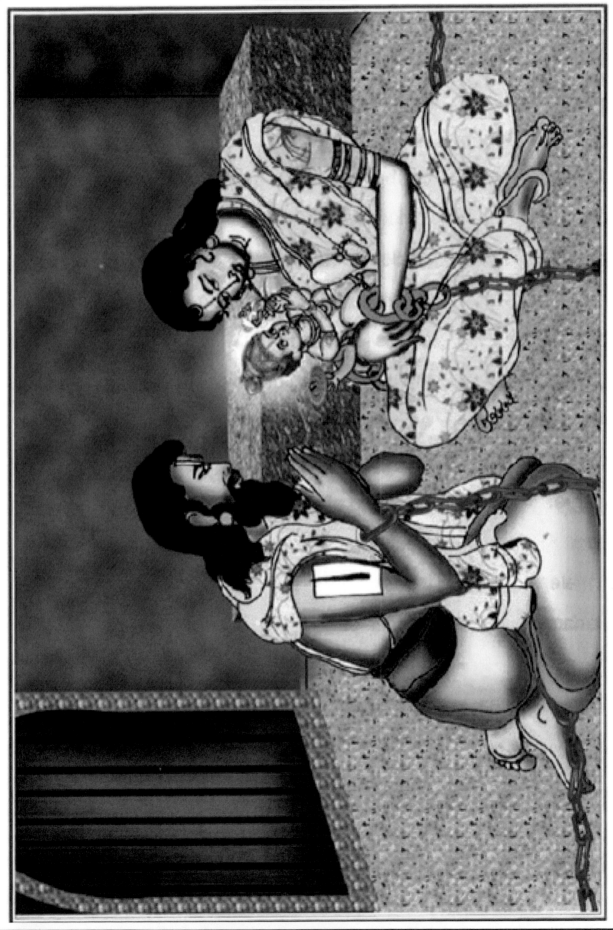

27 REMEMBER THE GLORY OF LORD SRI KRUSHNA - 2

jayathu jayathu de:vo: de:vaki: nandano:yam
jayathu jayathu krushno: vrushni vamsa pradi:paha|
jayathu jayathu me:gha **s**ya:malah ko:mala:ngo:
jayathu jayathu pru**th**vi: bha:ra na:**s**o: mukundaha ||

Meanings

ayam	=	this
de:vaha	=	divine Lord
nandanaha	=	beloved son
de:vaki:	=	of De:vaki
jayathu jayathu	=	be victorious always
krushnaha	=	Lord Krushna
pradi:paha	=	the light
vamsa	=	of dynasty
vrushni	=	of the Vrushni
jayathu jayathu	=	to be victorious all the times
ko:mala+angaha	=	let the soft and tendered body
me:gha sya:malaha	=	resembling like mysterious cloud
jayathu jayathu	=	be victorious constantly
mukundaha	=	Lord Mukunda, The bestower of Divine Abode
bha:ra na:saha	=	remover of the burden
pruthvi:	=	of The Mother Earth
jayathu jayathu	=	be victorious eternally

28 REMEMBER OUR DUTY TO LORD SRI KRUSHNA - 3

krushnam kamala pathra:ksham
punya sravana ki:rthanam |
va:sude:vam jagad yo:nim
naumi na:ra:yanam harim ||

Meanings

naumi	=	I prostrate
krushnam	=	before Lord Sri Krushna
kamala pathra+aksham	=	who possesses lovely eyes like lotus petals
punya sravana ki:rthanam	=	whose names purify the listeners & singers
va:sude:vam	=	who is omni-present and effulgent
jagath+ yo:nim	=	who is primeval cause of this universe
na:ra:yanam	=	the all supporter
harim	=	and who vanishes all the sins

29 SURRENDER TO LORD KRUSHNA - 4

krushna:ya ya:dave:ndra:ya
jna:na mudra:ya yo:gine: |
na:**th**a:ya rukmi**n**i:**sa**:ya
namo: ve:da:ntha ve:dine: ||

<u>Meanings</u>

namaha	=	I prostrate
krush**n**a:ya	=	before Lord Krushna
ya:dave:ndra:ya	=	the wealth of Ya:dava clan
jna:na mudra:ya	=	showing a posture called *jna:na mudra* with His right hand
yo:gine:	=	controller of all modes of joy
na:**th**a:ya	=	the possessor
rukmi**n**i:+ i:**sa**:ya	=	the spouse of queen Rukmini
ve:da:ntha ve:dine:	=	knower of all the essence of all the Ve:da:s

 SRI RA:MA PRA:RTHANA - 1

sri: ra:ghavam dasaratha:thmajam aprame:yam
si:tha:pathim raghukula:nvaya rathna di:pam |
a:ja:nuba:hum aravinda dala:ya tha:ksham
ra:mam nisa:chara vina:sakaram nama:mi ||

Meanings

nama:mi	= I prostrate
ra:mam	= before Ra:machandra
sri ra:ghavam	= who belongs to the great Raghu dynasty
dasaratha+a:thmajam	= the son of Dasaratha:
aprame:yam	= one who is incredible
si:tha:pathim	= the spouse of Sita
raghukula+anvaya rathna di:pam	
	= the beacon light of Raghu lineage
a:ja:nu ba:hum	= having long arms up to his knees
aravinda dala+a:yatha+aksham	= having wide eyes spread like lotus petals
nisa:chara vina:sakaram	= and one who destroys the demons

③1 SRI RA:MA PRA:RTHANA - 2

vaide:hi: sahitham sura drumathale: haime: maha:maṇdape:
madhye: pushpakam a:sane: maṇimaye: vi:ra:sane: susthitham |
agre: va:chayathi prabhanjana suthe: thaththvam munibyah param
Vya:khya:ntham bharatha:dibhih parivrutham ra:mam bhaje: sya:malam ||

Meanings

bhaje:	=	I worship
ra:mam	=	**S**ri: Ra:machandra
sya:malam	=	who is with lustrous blue complexion
sahitham	=	along with
vaide:hi:	=	Sita
sus**th**itham	=	well-positioned
vi:ra:sane:	=	in majestic posture
sura druma thale:	=	under the heavenly tree called Kalpa vrusksha
madhye:	=	which is the Centre of
maha: ma**n**dape:	=	a great hall
haime:	=	made of gold
ma**n**imaye:	=	studded with gems
pushpakam a:sane:	=	seated on a flowery throne
vya:khya:ntham	=	elaborating
param thaththvam	=	on the supremacy
munibhyaha	=	to the Sages
parivrutham	=	and surrounded
bharatha:dibhihi	=	by Bharatha, Lakshmana and Sathrughna, etc...
prabhanjana suthe:	=	while the mighty Hanuman, the son of wind-god
va:chayathi	=	chanting the holy scriptures
agre:	=	in the front

32 SRI: LAKSHMI PRA:RTHANA

sarasija nayane:! saro:ja hasthe:!
dhavalathara:nsuka gandha ma:lya **s**o:bhe:! |
bhagavathi! hari vallabhe:! mano:jne:!
thribhuvana bhu:thikari! prasi:da mahyam ||

Meanings

bhagavathi	=	Oh! The Divine mother with immaculate attributes
hari vallabhe:	=	the beloved consort of Lord Sri: Hari
mano:jne:	=	acquainted with the attitudes of Lord
sarasija nayane:	=	with dazzling eyes like lotus petals
saro:ja hasthe:	=	with tender hands like aromatic lotuses
amsuka	=	dressed in a saree
dhavala thara	=	in pure white
gandha	=	adorned with sandalwood paste
ma:lya	=	and garlands
so:bhe:	=	shining always
thri bhuvana bhu:thikari	=	Oh! Bestower of wealth to all the three worlds
prasi:da	=	show your grace
mahyam	=	on me

33 SRI A:NJANE:YA PRA:RTHANA - 1

mano:javam ma:rutha thulya ve:gam
jithe:ndriyam buddhimatha:m varishtam |
va:tha:thmajam va:nara yu:dha mukhyam
Sri: ra:ma du:tham sirasa: nama:mi ||

Meanings

nama:mi	=	I prostrate before the Mighty Hanuma:n
sirasa:	=	with bowed head
Sri ra:ma du:tham	=	the emissary of Lord Sri: Ra:ma
mano:javam	=	who can move faster than the mind
ma:rutha thulya ve:gam	=	swift like the wind
jithe:ndriyam	=	who conquered his senses
varishtam	=	the wisest
buddhimatha:m	=	among the wise
va:tha:thmajam	=	the son of wind God
mukhyam	=	the most important one
va:nara yu:dha	=	in the army of Va:nara:s

34 SRI A:NJANE:YA PRA:RTHANA - 2

ullanghya sindho:s salilam sali:lam
ya**s s**o:ka vanhim janaka:thamaja:ya:ha |
a:da:ya the:naiva dada:ha lanka:m
nama:mi tham pra:njalir a:njane:yam ||

Meanings

nama:mi	=	I prostrate
tham	=	before Hanuman, the great
a:njane:yam	=	son of Anjani
pra:njalihi	=	with folded hands in reverence
yaha	=	who
ullanghya	=	leaped across
salilam	=	the water
sindho:ho	=	of the sea
sali:lam	=	as in sport
a:da:ya	=	picked up
so:ka vanhim	=	the sorrow of fire
janaka+a:thmaja:ya:ha	=	from Sita, the daughter of Janaka
the:na+e:va	=	only with it
dada:ha	=	burnt
lanka:m	=	the city of Lanka

35 SRI A:NJANE:YA PRA:RTHANA -3

a:njane:yam athi pa:tala:nanam,
ka:nchana:dri kamani:ya vigraham |
pa:rija:tha tharu mu:la va:sinam
bha:vaya:mi pavama:na nandanam ||

Meanings

bha:vaya:mi	=	I meditate upon
pavama:na nandanam	=	the son of the Wind God
a:njane:yam	=	the son of Anjani
athi pa:tala+a:nanam	=	whose face glows in deep pink
kamani:ya vigraham	=	whose form is as fascinating as
ka:chana+adri	=	Mount Me:ru, the mountain of gold
pa:rija:tha tharu mu:la va:sinam	=	who dwells at the base of a divine tree 'Pra:rija:tha'

Jai Srimannarayana!

PRAJNA PLEDGE

Jai Srimannarayana!

O Mother Earth! I, being your best child and responsible citizen of this world, take this pledge!

I shall revere my parents, my family, my Gurus and treat everyone with love.

I shell serve my community, my country and those in need.

I pledge to protect the Nature by caring for animals, trees and the environment.

I will learn from the experiences of my ancestors and pass it on to future generations.

I, as student of Prajna, swear to abide by the universal commandments.

Worship your own and Respect all &
Serve all beings as service to God.
Jai Srimannarayana!

The New Kehila Makhzor

Edited by

Rabbi David Shneyer

Second Edition

Kehila Chadasha
Am Kolel Judaic Resource and Renewal Center
Rockville, Maryland

Kehila Chadasha and
Am Kolel Judaic Resource and Renewal Center
Rockville, Maryland.
All rights reserved.
No part of this book may be reproduced in any manner
without permission from the publisher.

ISBN 0-9743480-0-7

David Shneyer, *editor and designer*
Ralph Tryon, *production editor and typography*
Cover design by Robert Pearlman
Cover art by members of Kehila Chadasha
Editorial and production services provided by
Publication Resources, Inc.

First edition 1992
Second edition 2003

Printed in the United States of America
on recycled paper.

Introduction to the First Edition

Our people has long had a guide book for personal and collective thoughts and prayers during these Days of Awe. Throughout the ages that guide book has been known as a *makhzor*. The word *makhzor* means "cycle" and "review" and a *makhzor* has traditionally helped us reflect upon of our lives, urging us to review our relationships with others, ourselves, and the Source of Life.

Makhzorim have been around since the thirteen century. Since the mass production of texts did not exist then, the early *makhzorim* were principally used by the *khazzanim* or prayer leaders. It is noteworthy that the liturgical selections of the festival *makhzorim*, particularly those writings known as *piyyutim*, varied from region to region. Another delightful feature of these early personalized prayerbooks is that they were illustrated.

Our *makhzor*, *The New Kehila Makhzor*, is a renewal of this tradition. We, too, have included readings and artwork that reflect the creative spirit of our times. We are also guided by the importance of maintaining a strong continuity with the tradition, so that key biblical and rabbinic passages in Hebrew are included.

Maintaining the feel of an original text in translation is difficult in any language. One of the goals of this editor has been to translate the text so that it more easily reveals the value-concepts and the inner messages of the Hebrew. So many words in Hebrew are impossible to adequately translate because they are words of connotation. Words such as *Khesed* (caring), *Rakhamim* (compassion), *Kedushah* (holiness), add layers of meaning that simply cannot be defined or briefly described.

The word most pregnant with meaning is the tetragrammaton, the name for God, seen as the four letters *Yud, Hey, V(W)av, Hey*. When found together, these letters are not pronounced. They are ineffable. The rabbinic substitutes for this ancient name of the God of Israel are *Adonai* (my Lord or my Master) and *HaShem* (the Name). The actual pronunciation, according to our tradition, was lost with the destruction of the Holy Temple and the Holy of Holies where the high priest would utter the Name. Jewish mystics throughout the ages have found profound meaning in these letters without vowels. The meaning is as personal as one's breath. The letters hint at worlds past, present, and future, the eternality of life, the unity of life, the oneness within creation, and creation itself. The letters suggest the balance of male and female forces, the Power of creative tension, and the sacred potential for all.

In this *makhzor* many of the ancient and rabbinic metaphors for God have been changed in translation to reflect a more approachable relationship with the Ineffable God. The editor has used concepts of God that are gender neutral and that appreciate the deeper truth in our tradition that the Source of All encompasses both the male and the female.

Many individuals deserve thanks for helping to make this *makhzor* a reality. First among them is my wife, Diane, who reviewed concepts, edited, and proofread much of the English text and provided crucial encouragement along the way. I am grateful to Ruth Guyer for also advancing the literary cause and to David Schwartzman for researching copyright holders. Much thanks also to George and Sylvia Strumpf and the members of Kehila Chadasha who helped bring this project to completion. A special thank you to Trudi Morse for her sense of wonder and the encouragement she provided so generously.

It is my hope that this *makhzor* will serve us well. May these words and drawings and the melodies that we share, empower us to create a world that is true to the Covenants with Noah and his children, and with Abraham, Sarah and Hagar and their children, and to all those who gather at Sinai.

L'Shanah Tovah,
David Shneyer

Introduction to the Second Edition

This "second" edition of *The New Kehila Makhzor* is actually the fourth since we started meeting twenty-five years ago in 1978. The first edition was typewritten, cut and pasted together and stitched with staples down the center. The second version was a looseleaf text that took us through the 1980s until 1992, when we published *The New Kehila Makhzor*. The first bound edition was typeset by computer and sent on floppy discs to the graphic design company. In contrast, this latest edition took full advantage of the internet and desktop publishing. We emailed transcripts and messages back and forth and ultimately downloaded 3500 years of sacred text to send off to the printer.

While publishing has become easier, life has become much more complex since 1992. We are witnessing tremendous forces at battle with each other. The social and ecological issues weigh much more heavily upon us. We have witnessed a world gone mad with horrendous acts of violence through terrorism and war. We have also seen significant steps forward in efforts seeking non-violent resolutions. In humanity's yearning for fulfillment, the forces of goodness and lovingkindness wrestle with the forces of greed and power.

It is a great tribute to our ancestors that these *Yamim HaNoraim,* these Days of Awe, still give us the opportunity to reaffirm life, to reflect on our lives and enjoy a sense of community and a oneness with each other and the Source of Life. The timeless prayers and the message of the *makhzor* have become even more engaging.

This revised edition of *The New Kehila Makhzor* has not changed significantly. We have added a complete section of Torah and Prophetic readings for the holy days. We hope the translations flow more naturally and that you enjoy the new readings and illustrations.

The first person I would like thank for making this new edition possible is Ralph Tryon. Ralph, who learned to read Hebrew through Am Kolel ten years ago, volunteered to re-typeset both the Hebrew and English texts. He also served as the production editor, guiding the entire process and gently nudging me along. I also wish to thank Kate Losman for spending many hours reading through the translations with a critical eye and loving appreciation for language. Many thanks to Hillary Goldberg and Maida Tryon for patiently proofreading the *makhzor*. Thanks also go to Rob Pearlman for his work on the cover design and medallion on the back and to Rosana Azar and members of Kehila Chadasha for our beautiful banners, one of which is found on the front of this volume. Thank you to Diane, my wife, for her loving support once again. And we thank Patsy Ames of Publication Resources for her persistence in tracking down sources and the necessary copyright permissions. Finally, a thank you to Kehila Chadasha, for providing the foundation of support for the *makhzor*. It is *beshert* that this edition arrive in the 25th anniversary year.

May it be a blessing for us, for Israel and for all of humanity.

In gratitude,

David

Contents

מַעֲרִיב

Evening Service

Head of the Year

world, they say it is your birthday,
a thousand years for each day of genesis
and we are using you up,
but they have promised
that the next one will be better.

oh end of days, with your new earth
and your eternity spread before us
like a white sabbath cloth,
and your bread shaped like a hand:
how we long to come toward you,
to take that hand in our own.

but we have discarded the white fowl
which our fathers twirled over their heads.
we hold onto our sins, our scarlet threads,
and we do not go any longer to the river
whose waters contain the fish without eyelids.

there, where our fathers cast off their sins,
we lean down to untie the knot,
we are letting go of the river.

       Myra Sklarew

Changes

Sit by my side, come as close as the air
Share in my memories of gray
And wander in my world, dream about
The pictures that I play of changes.

Green leaves of summer turn red in the fall,
To brown and to yellow they fade,
And then they have to die, trapped within
The circle time parade of changes.

Scenes of my younger years were warm
in my mind
Visions of shadows that shine.
Till one day I returned and found they were
The victims of the vines of changes.

The world spinning madly it drifts in the dark,
Swims through a hallow of haze.
A race around the stars, a journey through
the Universe ablaze with changes.

Moments of magic will glow in the night
All fears of the forest are gone.
But when the morning breaks
They're swept away by golden rays of dawn,
of changes.

       Phil Ochs

Leader:

בָּרְכוּ אֶת יהוה הַמְבֹרָךְ

Barkhu Et Adonai HaMvorakh

Life calls to us: Bless the Eternal, the Source of All Blessing

Community:

בָּרוּךְ יהוה הַמְבֹרָךְ לְעוֹלָם וָעֶד

Barukh Adonai HaMvorakh L'Olam Vaed

Blessed is the Eternal, the Source of Blessing, forever

Blessed is the Ineffable,	בָּרוּךְ אַתָּה יהוה,
the Majesty of the Universe,	אֱלֹהֵינוּ מֶלֶךְ הָעוֹלָם
bringing on the evenings,	אֲשֶׁר בִּדְבָרוֹ מַעֲרִיב עֲרָבִים.
with wisdom opening the gates of the heavens,	בְּחָכְמָה פּוֹתֵחַ שְׁעָרִים
with insight changing time and	וּבִתְבוּנָה מְשַׁנֶּה עִתִּים
varying the seasons, with will setting the stars	וּמַחֲלִיף אֶת־הַזְּמַנִּים
in their watches in the expanse,	וּמְסַדֵּר אֶת־הַכּוֹכָבִים
creating day and night,	בְּמִשְׁמְרוֹתֵיהֶם בָּרָקִיעַ כִּרְצוֹנוֹ.
rolling light away from before darkness,	בּוֹרֵא יוֹם וָלָיְלָה גּוֹלֵל אוֹר
and darkness from before light,	מִפְּנֵי חֹשֶׁךְ וְחֹשֶׁךְ מִפְּנֵי אוֹר
causing the day to pass,	וּמַעֲבִיר יוֹם וּמֵבִיא לָיְלָה
bringing night, and separating day and night.	וּמַבְדִּיל בֵּין יוֹם וּבֵין לָיְלָה,
The cosmos is revealed,	יהוה צְבָאוֹת שְׁמוֹ. אֵל חַי וְקַיָּם
a living and enduring God	תָּמִיד יִמְלוֹךְ עָלֵינוּ לְעוֹלָם וָעֶד.
forever guiding us.	

Blessed is the Ineffable, bringing on the evenings.

בָּרוּךְ אַתָּה יהוה, הַמַּעֲרִיב עֲרָבִים.

Awe is an intuition for the dignity of all things, a realization that things not only are what they are but also stand, however remotely, for something supreme.

Awe is a sense for the transcendence, for the reference everywhere to mystery beyond all things.

A.J. Heschel

Fill Our Days

Fill our days with hints of Paradise.

Let us see Adam and Eve
in everyone we meet.

Let Wednesday point to Eternity
and cloudy mornings remind us of Sinai.

You are gracious unto us:

How much do we pay
for the evening sunsets?
What is the price of the stars?

Danny Siegel

With eternal love	אַהֲבַת עוֹלָם
the people Israel has been loved.	בֵּית יִשְׂרָאֵל עַמְּךָ אָהָבְתָּ.
Stories and teachings,	תּוֹרָה וּמִצְוֹת
codes, laws and judgments	חֻקִּים וּמִשְׁפָּטִים
have been taught us.	אוֹתָנוּ לִמַּדְתָּ.
When we lie down and when we arise	עַל כֵּן יהוה אֱלֹהֵינוּ
we are called upon to discuss these codes,	בְּשָׁכְבֵּנוּ וּבְקוּמֵנוּ נָשִׂיחַ בְּחֻקֶּיךָ
to rejoice in life's teachings	וְנִשְׂמַח בְּדִבְרֵי תוֹרָתֶךָ
and to do right actions always.	וּבְמִצְוֹתֶיךָ לְעוֹלָם וָעֶד.

Ki Heym Khayenu v'Orekh Yameynu
u'Vahem Nehgeh Yomam vaLaylah.
For these lessons are the life and length of our days,
and we ought reflect on them day and night.
May the love of life and learning
never be removed from us.
Blessed is the Ancient Teacher
loving the people Israel.

כִּי הֵם חַיֵּינוּ וְאֹרֶךְ יָמֵינוּ
וּבָהֶם נֶהְגֶּה יוֹמָם וָלָיְלָה.
וְאַהֲבָתְךָ אַל תָּסִיר
מִמֶּנּוּ לְעוֹלָמִים.
בָּרוּךְ אַתָּה יהוה
אוֹהֵב עַמּוֹ יִשְׂרָאֵל.

שְׁמַע יִשְׂרָאֵל יהוה אֱלֹהֵינוּ יהוה אֶחָד

Adonai   *Adonai*

Shma Yisrael YHVH Eloheynu YHVH Ekhad

Listen Israel, The Eternal is our God, the Eternal is One

בָּרוּךְ שֵׁם כְּבוֹד מַלְכוּתוֹ לְעוֹלָם וָעֶד

Barukh Shem Kavod Malkhuto L'Olam Vaed

Blessed is the Glory of Creation forever

V'Ahavta et Adonai Elohekha	וְאָהַבְתָּ אֵת יהוה אֱלֹהֶיךָ
b'Khol l'Vavkha	בְּכָל־לְבָבְךָ
u'v'Khol Naf'sh'kha	וּבְכָל־נַפְשְׁךָ
u'v'Khol M'odekha.	וּבְכָל־מְאֹדֶךָ.
V'Hayu haD'varim haEleh	וְהָיוּ הַדְּבָרִים הָאֵלֶּה
Asher Anokhi m'Tzavkha haYom	אֲשֶׁר אָנֹכִי מְצַוְּךָ הַיּוֹם
al-l'Vavekha. V'Shinantam l'Vanekha	עַל־לְבָבֶךָ. וְשִׁנַּנְתָּם לְבָנֶיךָ
v'Dibarta Bam b'Shiv't'kha b'Veytekha	וְדִבַּרְתָּ בָּם בְּשִׁבְתְּךָ בְּבֵיתֶךָ
u'v'Lekh't'kha Vaderekh u'v'Shakh'b'kha	וּבְלֶכְתְּךָ בַדֶּרֶךְ וּבְשָׁכְבְּךָ
u'v'Kumekha.	וּבְקוּמֶךָ.
U'K'shartam l'Ot al-Yadekha	וּקְשַׁרְתָּם לְאוֹת עַל־יָדֶךָ
v'Hayu l'Totafot Beyn Eynekha.	וְהָיוּ לְטֹטָפֹת בֵּין עֵינֶיךָ.
U'Kh'tavtam al-M'zuzot Beytekha	וּכְתַבְתָּם עַל־מְזֻזוֹת בֵּיתֶךָ
u'Visharekha.	וּבִשְׁעָרֶיךָ.

And you shall love the Ineffable One, your Life giver, with all your heart, with all your soul, and with all that you have.

And these words addressed to you today shall be upon your heart, and you shall teach them well to your children, speaking of them when you sit in your house, when you travel, when you lie down and when you rise up.

And you shall bind them for a sign upon your hand, and they shall be for frontlets between your eyes. And you shall inscribe them on the doorposts of your house and upon your gates.

Deuteronomy 6:4-9

6

So you shall love what is holy
with all your courage,
with all your passion,
with all your strength.
Let the words that have come down
shine in our words and our actions.
We must teach our children to know and
understand them.
We must speak about what is good
and holy within our homes
when we are working,
when we are at play,
when we lie down
and when we get up.
Let the work of our hands
speak of goodness.
Let it run in our blood
and glow from our doors and windows.

We should love ourselves, for we are of G-d.
We should love our neighbors as ourselves.
We should love the stranger, for we
were once strangers in the land of Egypt
and have been strangers in all the
lands of the world since.
Let love fill our hearts with its
clear precious water.
Heaven and earth observe how we cherish
or spoil our world.
Heaven and earth watch whether we
choose life or choose death.
We must choose life so our
children's children may live.
Be quiet and listen to the still small
voice within that speaks in love.
Open to that voice, hear it, heed it
and work for life.
Let us remember and strive to be good.
Let us remember to find what is holy
within and without.

Marge Piercy — V'ahavta

Adonai Eloheykhem Emet
The Eternal is clothed in truth.

אֲנִי יהוה אֱלֹהֵיכֶם.
יהוה אֱלֹהֵיכֶם אֱמֶת.

It has been asked...
What is it that sustains our soul?
What helps us out of the midst of danger,
guiding us towards liberation and fulfillment?

הַשָּׁם נַפְשֵׁנוּ בַּחַיִּים
וַיּוֹצֵא אֶת עַמּוֹ יִשְׂרָאֵל
מִתּוֹכָם לְחֵרוּת עוֹלָם.

Moshe and the children of Israel sang this
song with great rejoicing, all saying:

מֹשֶׁה וּבְנֵי יִשְׂרָאֵל לְךָ עָנוּ
שִׁירָה בְּשִׂמְחָה רַבָּה, וְאָמְרוּ כֻלָּם.

Mi Khamokha baElim Adonai
Mi Kamokhah Nedar baKodesh
Norah Tehilot Osey Feleh!
"Who is like unto You among the gods?
Who is like You, unique in holiness,
revered in songs, doing wonders?"

מִי־כָמֹכָה בָּאֵלִם יהוה,
מִי כָּמֹכָה נֶאְדָּר בַּקֹּדֶשׁ,
נוֹרָא תְהִלֹת עֹשֵׂה פֶלֶא.

Your children saw the power of freedom
when the unknown sea parted before Moshe.
"This is my God," they answered and said:
"The Enduring One will rule forever."
And it is said: "... for the Eternal has set Yaakov free
and liberated us from our oppression."
Blessed are You who redeemed Israel.

מַלְכוּתְךָ רָאוּ בָנֶיךָ,
בּוֹקֵעַ יָם לִפְנֵי מֹשֶׁה,
זֶה אֵלִי עָנוּ וְאָמְרוּ:
יהוה יִמְלֹךְ לְעֹלָם וָעֶד.
וְנֶאֱמַר: כִּי פָדָה יהוה אֶת יַעֲקֹב,
וּגְאָלוֹ מִיַּד חָזָק מִמֶּנּוּ.
בָּרוּךְ אַתָּה יהוה גָּאַל יִשְׂרָאֵל.

May our lives, our goings and our comings,
be guarded for life and for peace, for now, forever.
May the shelter of peace be spread over us.
Barukh Atah. The Holy One of Being
spreads forth the shelter of peace over us,
over all the people Israel, and over Jerusalem.

וּשְׁמוֹר צֵאתֵנוּ וּבוֹאֵנוּ
לְחַיִּים וּלְשָׁלוֹם מֵעַתָּה וְעַד עוֹלָם.
וּפְרוֹשׂ עָלֵינוּ סֻכַּת שְׁלוֹמֶךָ.
בָּרוּךְ אַתָּה יהוה
הַפּוֹרֵשׂ סֻכַּת שָׁלוֹם עָלֵינוּ
וְעַל כָּל־עַמּוֹ יִשְׂרָאֵל וְעַל יְרוּשָׁלָיִם.

(On Rosh HaShanah)

Tiku Vakhodesh Shofar

Bakeseh l'Yom Khageynu

Ki Khok l'Yisrael

Hu Mishpat Lelohey Yaakov.

It is written: Blow the shofar at the time
of the new moon, at the appointed time
for our festive day. It is a statute for Israel
set forth by the God of Jacob.

Exodus 31:16-17

(On Rosh HaShanah)

תִּקְעוּ בַחֹדֶשׁ שׁוֹפָר
בַּכֶּסֶה לְיוֹם חַגֵּנוּ.
כִּי חֹק לְיִשְׂרָאֵל הוּא
מִשְׁפָּט לֵאלֹהֵי יַעֲקֹב.

(On Yom Kippur)

כִּי־בַיּוֹם הַזֶּה יְכַפֵּר עֲלֵיכֶם
לְטַהֵר אֶתְכֶם מִכֹּל חַטֹּאתֵיכֶם
לִפְנֵי יהוה תִּטְהָרוּ.

(On Yom Kippur)

Ki Vayom haZeh y'Khaper Aleykhem

l'Taher Etkhem miKol Khatoteykhem

Lifney Adonai Titharu.

For on this day atonement shall be rendered
unto you to cleanse you of all your misdeeds,
so that we become pure before the Creator.

Leviticus 16:30

8

Khatzi Kaddish

חֲצִי קַדִּישׁ

Yitgadal v'Yitkadash Shmey Rabah,
b'Alma Divra Khirutey
v'Yamlikh Malkutey
b'Khayeykhon u'v'Yomeykhon u'v'Khayey
d'Khol Beyt Yisrael baAgalah
u'viZman Kariv,
v'Imru: Ameyn.

יִתְגַּדַּל וְיִתְקַדַּשׁ שְׁמֵהּ רַבָּא.
בְּעָלְמָא דִי בְרָא כִרְעוּתֵהּ.
וְיַמְלִיךְ מַלְכוּתֵהּ
בְּחַיֵּיכוֹן וּבְיוֹמֵיכוֹן וּבְחַיֵּי
דְכָל בֵּית יִשְׂרָאֵל בַּעֲגָלָא
וּבִזְמַן קָרִיב.
וְאִמְרוּ אָמֵן.

Y'hey Shmey Rabah m'Varakh
l'Alam u'l'Almey Almaya.

יְהֵא שְׁמֵהּ רַבָּה מְבָרַךְ
לְעָלַם וּלְעָלְמֵי עָלְמַיָּא.

Yitbarakh v'Yishtabakh v'Yitpaar v'Yitromam
v'Yitnasey v'Yithadar v'Yitaleh v'Yithalal
Shmey d'Kud'sha. Brikh Hu.
L'Eyla u'l'Eyla miKol Birkhata v'Shirata
Tush'b'khata v'Nekhemata daAmiran b'Alma,
v'Imru: Ameyn.

יִתְבָּרַךְ וְיִשְׁתַּבַּח וְיִתְפָּאַר וְיִתְרוֹמַם
וְיִתְנַשֵּׂא וְיִתְהַדָּר וְיִתְעַלֶּה וְיִתְהַלָּל
שְׁמֵהּ דְּקֻדְשָׁא. בְּרִיךְ הוּא.
לְעֵלָּא (וּלְעֵלָּא) מִכָּל בִּרְכָתָא וְשִׁירָתָא
תֻּשְׁבְּחָתָא וְנֶחֱמָתָא דַּאֲמִירָן בְּעָלְמָא.
וְאִמְרוּ אָמֵן.

May the Creator's great Name grow and be sanctified in a cosmos formed according to an incomprehensible Will.

May the Unity of Creation be established in your lifetime and throughout your days, and during the lifetime of the entire House of Yisrael, soon.

So may we acknowledge, honor, celebrate, and sing to the Sacred Source, though transcendent and beyond human songs and blessing.

And join in saying, amen.

AMIDAH—THE STANDING MEDITATION

עמידה

My God open up my lips as I speak Your praise.

אֲדֹנָי שְׂפָתַי תִּפְתָּח וּפִי יַגִּיד תְּהִלָּתֶךָ.

We are grateful for Life's eternal spirit,
our Origin and the God of our ancestors,
the vision and promise to Avraham,
the aloneness of Yitzkhak,
the spiritual wrestling of Yaakov,
the surprise of Sarah,
the wisdom of Rivka,
the patience of Rakhel,
the fruitfulness of Leah.
Expansive, Powerful, Awesome, Highest God,
loving kindnesses,
owning everything,
remembering our ancestors' caring
and the promise of redemption
for their children's children,
with love.

בָּרוּךְ אַתָּה יהוה, אֱלֹהֵינוּ
וֵאלֹהֵי אֲבוֹתֵינוּ, וֵאלֹהֵי אִמּוֹתֵינוּ,
אֱלֹהֵי אַבְרָהָם, אֱלֹהֵי יִצְחָק,
וֵאלֹהֵי יַעֲקֹב,
אֱלֹהֵי שָׂרָה,
אֱלֹהֵי רִבְקָה,
אֱלֹהֵי רָחֵל,
וֵאלֹהֵי לֵאָה.
הָאֵל הַגָּדוֹל הַגִּבּוֹר וְהַנּוֹרָא,
אֵל עֶלְיוֹן,
גּוֹמֵל חֲסָדִים טוֹבִים,
וְקֹנֵה הַכֹּל,
וְזוֹכֵר חַסְדֵי אָבוֹת וְאִמָּהוֹת,
וּמֵבִיא גוֹאֵל לִבְנֵי בְנֵיהֶם
לְמַעַן שְׁמוֹ בְּאַהֲבָה.

Zakhreynu l'Khayim
Melekh Khafetz baKhayim
v'Khatveynu b'Sefer haKhayim
l'Ma'ankhah Elohim Khayim.

זָכְרֵנוּ לְחַיִּים
מֶלֶךְ חָפֵץ בַּחַיִּים
וְכָתְבֵנוּ בְּסֵפֶר הַחַיִּים
לְמַעַנְךָ אֱלֹהִים חַיִּים.

May the power that desires life
remember us unto life and
inscribe us in the Book of Life
affirming the living God.

מֶלֶךְ עוֹזֵר וּפוֹקֵד
וּמוֹשִׁיעַ וּמָגֵן.
בָּרוּךְ אַתָּה יהוה
מָגֵן אַבְרָהָם וּפוֹקֵד שָׂרָה.

Some call the Ineffable YudHeyVavHey "Ruler,"
or "Helper," or "Saving Power," or "Guardian."
Here we offer blessing to the Guardian of our
ancestors.

Maariv – The Evening Service

You are the Eternality of Time,
giving life to the dead,
renewed life to the living,
hopefulness, deliverance.

Let us know that Life is sustained through
loving kindness,
the dormant renewed with much compassion.
For the fallen there is support,
for the sick there is healing,
for the imprisoned there can be release,
and trust for those who sleep in the dust.

Who can be compared to this Renewing Power?
Who can be compared to the Compassionate Parent
recalling compassion and life-giving creativity?

We trust that the renewal of life will continue.
Blessed is Creation, renewing life.

You are sacred and Creation is holy.
All who are blessed with awareness offer praise
every day. Selah! Yes!

Blessed is the realization of the Sacred.

אַתָּה גִּבּוֹר לְעוֹלָם אֲדֹנָי,
מְחַיֵּה מֵתִים אַתָּה,
רַב לְהוֹשִׁיעַ.

מְכַלְכֵּל חַיִּים בְּחֶסֶד,
מְחַיֵּה מֵתִים בְּרַחֲמִים רַבִּים,
סוֹמֵךְ נוֹפְלִים, וְרוֹפֵא חוֹלִים,
וּמַתִּיר אֲסוּרִים,
וּמְקַיֵּם אֱמוּנָתוֹ לִישֵׁנֵי עָפָר.

מִי כָמוֹךָ בַּעַל גְּבוּרוֹת וּמִי דּוֹמֶה לָּךְ,
מֶלֶךְ מֵמִית וּמְחַיֶּה וּמַצְמִיחַ יְשׁוּעָה.
מִי כָמוֹךָ אֵל הָרַחֲמִים
זוֹכֵר יְצוּרָיו לְחַיִּים בְּרַחֲמִים?

וְנֶאֱמָן אַתָּה לְהַחֲיוֹת מֵתִים.
בָּרוּךְ אַתָּה יהוה, מְחַיֵּה הַמֵּתִים.

אַתָּה קָדוֹשׁ וְשִׁמְךָ קָדוֹשׁ,
וּקְדוֹשִׁים בְּכָל־יוֹם יְהַלְלוּךָ, סֶלָה.

בָּרוּךְ אַתָּה יהוה, הָאֵל הַקָּדוֹשׁ.

And so,
May fear and concern
be instilled in all living things,
dreadful concern for all that has been created.
All creation ought to be in awe,
all of life humbled before the Life Giver.
And may all of creation form a single bond
to do Your will wholeheartedly.
For we know that You govern alone,
that Your true strength is in justice
and Your Awesome Spirit Being
is above all that has been created.

וּבְכֵן

תֵּן פַּחְדְּךָ יהוה אֱלֹהֵינוּ
עַל כָּל מַעֲשֶׂיךָ,
וְאֵימָתְךָ עַל כָּל מַה שֶּׁבָּרָאתָ,
וְיִירָאוּךָ כָּל הַמַּעֲשִׂים
וְיִשְׁתַּחֲווּ לְפָנֶיךָ כָּל הַבְּרוּאִים,
וְיֵעָשׂוּ כֻלָּם אֲגֻדָּה אֶחָת
לַעֲשׂוֹת רְצוֹנְךָ בְּלֵבָב שָׁלֵם.
כְּמוֹ שֶׁיָּדַעְנוּ יהוה אֱלֹהֵינוּ
שֶׁהַשִּׁלְטָן לְפָנֶיךָ עֹז בְּיָדְךָ
וּגְבוּרָה בִּימִינֶךָ וְשִׁמְךָ נוֹרָא
עַל כָּל מַה שֶּׁבָּרָאתָ.

And so,
May honor be granted to Your people,
praise to those who are in awe of You,
and hope to those who seek You
and voice sincere yearnings for You.
Let there be joy throughout the Land
and joyfulness for the inhabitants of Your City.
May the light of joy and justice shine forth
in our lifetime.

וּבְכֵן

תֵּן כָּבוֹד יהוה לְעַמֶּךָ
תְּהִלָּה לִירֵאֶיךָ
וְתִקְוָה טוֹבָה לְדוֹרְשֶׁיךָ
וּפִתְחוֹן פֶּה לַמְיַחֲלִים לָךְ.
שִׂמְחָה לְאַרְצֶךָ וְשָׂשׂוֹן לְעִירֶךָ,
וּצְמִיחַת קֶרֶן לְדָוִד עַבְדֶּךָ,
וַעֲרִיכַת נֵר לְבֶן־יִשַׁי מְשִׁיחֶךָ,
בִּמְהֵרָה בְיָמֵינוּ.

And when such a day arrives,
those who struggled for justice will be the first
to rejoice, the upright will be glad,
and the faithful supporters will sing with joy,
injustice closing its mouth,
all evil vanishing like smoke,
the kingdom of falsehood passing from the earth.

וּבְכֵן

צַדִּיקִים יִרְאוּ וְיִשְׂמָחוּ וִישָׁרִים
יַעֲלֹזוּ וַחֲסִידִים בְּרִנָּה יָגִילוּ
וְעוֹלָתָה תִּקְפָּץ־פִּיהָ.
וְכָל־הָרִשְׁעָה כֻּלָּהּ כְּעָשָׁן תִּכְלֶה
כִּי תַעֲבִיר מֶמְשֶׁלֶת זָדוֹן מִן־הָאָרֶץ.

You, alone, the Sacred Oneness,
will govern all Your works,
with Mount Zion as Your honored dwelling place,
and with Your sacred city,
the City of Shalom, Jerusalem.

As it is written in those holy ancient words:
"The Life Source, the Ancient of Ancients,
the Dream of Zion, will preside for all generations.
Halleluyah."

You are sacred and Your Presence is awesome,
and there is no God beside You, as it is written:
"The Eternal, the Power of All Creation,
is elevated through justice, God's holiness sanctified
by acts of justice."

Barukh Atah. Blessed is the Ineffable One,
the Sacred Power.

You have delighted in us as a people,
loving us, desiring us,
elevating us,
and sanctifying us with Mitzvot,
drawing us near to serve You,
that Your Great Holy Presence
be known to us.

וְתִמְלֹךְ אַתָּה יהוה לְבַדֶּךָ
עַל כָּל מַעֲשֶׂיךָ
בְּהַר צִיּוֹן מִשְׁכַּן כְּבוֹדֶךָ
וּבִירוּשָׁלַיִם עִיר קָדְשֶׁךָ.

כַּכָּתוּב בְּדִבְרֵי קָדְשֶׁךָ:
יִמְלֹךְ יהוה לְעוֹלָם
אֱלֹהַיִךְ צִיּוֹן לְדֹר וָדֹר
הַלְלוּיָהּ.

קָדוֹשׁ אַתָּה וְנוֹרָא שְׁמֶךָ
וְאֵין אֱלוֹהַּ מִבַּלְעָדֶיךָ. כַּכָּתוּב:
וַיִּגְבַּהּ יהוה צְבָאוֹת
בַּמִּשְׁפָּט וְהָאֵל הַקָּדוֹשׁ
נִקְדַּשׁ בִּצְדָקָה.

בָּרוּךְ אַתָּה יהוה הַמֶּלֶךְ הַקָּדוֹשׁ.

אַתָּה בְחַרְתָּנוּ מִכָּל הָעַמִּים.
אָהַבְתָּ אוֹתָנוּ וְרָצִיתָ בָּנוּ.
וְרוֹמַמְתָּנוּ מִכָּל הַלְּשׁוֹנוֹת
וְקִדַּשְׁתָּנוּ בְּמִצְוֹתֶיךָ.
וְקֵרַבְתָּנוּ מַלְכֵּנוּ לַעֲבוֹדָתֶךָ
וְשִׁמְךָ הַגָּדוֹל וְהַקָּדוֹשׁ
עָלֵינוּ קָרָאתָ.

The gravest sin for a Jew
is to forget what being a Jew represents.
A. J. Heschel

With love we have been given

וַתִּתֶּן לָנוּ יהוה אֱלֹהֵינוּ בְּאַהֲבָה

(On Rosh HaShanah)

this Day of Remembering,
this Day of Shofar Sounds.

(On Rosh HaShanah)

אֶת יוֹם (לשבת הַשַּׁבָּת הַזֶּה וְאֶת יוֹם)
הַזִּכָּרוֹן הַזֶּה יוֹם (לשבת זִכְרוֹן) תְּרוּעָה.

(On Yom Kippur)

this Day of Atonement,
for renouncing our wrongs,
for asking for forgiveness,
for cleansing, for reconciliation.

(On Yom Kippur)

אֶת יוֹם (לשבת הַשַּׁבָּת הַזֶּה לִקְדוּשָׁה
וְלִמְנוּחָה וְאֶת יוֹם) הַכִּפּוּרִים הַזֶּה
לִמְחִילָה וְלִסְלִיחָה וְלִכַפָּרָה וְלִמְחָל־בּוֹ
אֶת־כָּל־עֲוֹנוֹתֵינוּ.

A day of holy gathering
reminding us of our liberation
from the straits of enslavement.

(לשבת בְּאַהֲבָה) מִקְרָא קֹדֶשׁ
זֵכֶר לִיצִיאַת מִצְרָיִם.

Allow our memory to ascend,
to come, to reach us.
May our memory and our reckoning,
and our ancestors memory,
and the memory of the dream of a Messianic Time,
and the memory of the vision of Jerusalem,
as a City of Peace, a Holy City,
and those memories of all Your people
the House of Israel, whether in the Land
or in the Diaspora, be before You.
On this Day may these memories,
these dreams of redemption,
inspire graciousness, lovingkindness,
and compassion in us,
for life and for peace.

אֱלֹהֵינוּ וֵאלֹהֵי אֲבוֹתֵינוּ
יַעֲלֶה וְיָבֹא וְיַגִּיעַ
וְיֵרָאֶה וְיֵרָצֶה וְיִשָּׁמַע
וְיִפָּקֵד וְיִזָּכֵר זִכְרוֹנֵנוּ
וּפִקְדוֹנֵנוּ וְזִכְרוֹן אֲבוֹתֵינוּ
וְזִכְרוֹן מָשִׁיחַ בֶּן־דָּוִד עַבְדֶּךָ
וְזִכְרוֹן יְרוּשָׁלַיִם עִיר קָדְשֶׁךָ
וְזִכְרוֹן כָּל עַמְּךָ
בֵּית יִשְׂרָאֵל לְפָנֶיךָ.
לִפְלֵיטָה לְטוֹבָה לְחֵן וּלְחֶסֶד
וּלְרַחֲמִים לְחַיִּים וּלְשָׁלוֹם
(On Rosh HaShanah)
בְּיוֹם הַזִּכָּרוֹן הַזֶּה.
(On Yom Kippur)
הַכִּפּוּרִים הַזֶּה.

Maariv – The Evening Service

As we recall our Creator we ask
that the Holy One of Being
remember us well,
and delegate blessedness,
and save us for life,
and favor us with grace and compassion.
We seek guidance,
benevolence, and mercifulness.

May this vision of redemption
guide the entire world
with respectfulness,
uplifting the earth with love,
the splendor of the Presence
resting upon all the inhabitants of this planet.
So all will know their Maker,
and all will understand their Creator.

Then everyone who has breath
flowing through their nostrils will say
"... the Ineffable, the Sacred Life Breath,
the God of Yisrael, a soul-wrestling people,
is the One we are accountable to
wherever we are."

זָכְרֵנוּ יהוה אֱלֹהֵינוּ
בּוֹ לְטוֹבָה וּפָקְדֵנוּ בוֹ לִבְרָכָה,
וְהוֹשִׁיעֵנוּ בוֹ לְחַיִּים,
וּבִדְבַר יְשׁוּעָה וְרַחֲמִים.
חוּס וְחָנֵּנוּ וְרַחֵם עָלֵינוּ
וְהוֹשִׁיעֵנוּ.
כִּי אֵלֶיךָ עֵינֵינוּ
כִּי אֵל מֶלֶךְ חַנּוּן וְרַחוּם אָתָּה.

אֱלֹהֵינוּ וֵאלֹהֵי אֲבוֹתֵינוּ,
מְלוֹךְ עַל כָּל הָעוֹלָם כֻּלּוֹ
בִּכְבוֹדֶךָ וְהִנָּשֵׂא עַל כָּל־הָאָרֶץ
בִּיקָרֶךָ וְהוֹפַע בַּהֲדַר גְּאוֹן עֻזֶּךָ
עַל כָּל יוֹשְׁבֵי תֵבֵל אַרְצֶךָ.
וְיֵדַע כָּל־פָּעוּל כִּי־אַתָּה פְּעַלְתּוֹ
וְיָבִין כָּל־יְצוּר כִּי אַתָּה יְצַרְתּוֹ.

וְיֹאמַר כֹּל אֲשֶׁר
נְשָׁמָה בְּאַפּוֹ
יהוה אֱלֹהֵי יִשְׂרָאֵל
מֶלֶךְ וּמַלְכוּתוֹ
בַּכֹּל מָשָׁלָה.

May we be sanctified by our deeds,
and share in Life's sacred teachings.
May we be satisfied by the good,
and receive joy and fulfillment.

V'Taher Libeynu l'Avdekha Beh-emet.
And may our hearts be cleansed
to serve Life truthfully
as we are called upon by the God of Truth,
whose Word is enduring truth.

Blessed is the Ineffable,
governing the earth,
sanctifying the people Yisrael
(On Rosh HaShanah)
on this Day of Remembrance.
(On Yom Kippur)
on this Day of Atonement.

We hope that the people Yisrael and their
meditations, and this sacred service,
be received with love and eternal desire.

V'Tekhezehnah Eyneynu
b'Shuvkha l'Tzion b'Rakhamim.
May our eyes behold
the return of Compassion to Zion.
Blessed is the Eternal, the Ineffable One,
Restoring the Divine Presence to Zion.

אֱלֹהֵינוּ וֵאלֹהֵי אֲבוֹתֵינוּ
(לשבת רְצֵה בִמְנוּחָתֵנוּ)
קַדְּשֵׁנוּ בְּמִצְוֹתֶיךָ וְתֵן חֶלְקֵנוּ בְּתוֹרָתֶךָ
שַׂבְּעֵנוּ מִטּוּבֶךָ וְשַׂמְּחֵנוּ בִּישׁוּעָתֶךָ.

וְטַהֵר לִבֵּנוּ לְעָבְדְּךָ בֶּאֱמֶת
כִּי אַתָּה אֱלֹהִים אֱמֶת
וּדְבָרְךָ אֱמֶת וְקַיָּם לָעַד.

בָּרוּךְ אַתָּה יהוה
מֶלֶךְ עַל כָּל־הָאָרֶץ
מְקַדֵּשׁ (לשבת הַשַּׁבָּת וְ) יִשְׂרָאֵל
(On Rosh HaShanah)
וְיוֹם הַזִּכָּרוֹן.
(On Yom Kippur)
וְיוֹם הַכִּפּוּרִים.

רְצֵה יהוה אֱלֹהֵינוּ בְּעַמְּךָ יִשְׂרָאֵל
וּבִתְפִלָּתָם. וְהָשֵׁב אֶת־הָעֲבוֹדָה
לִדְבִיר בֵּיתֶךָ וְאִשֵּׁי יִשְׂרָאֵל.
וּתְפִלָּתָם בְּאַהֲבָה תְקַבֵּל בְּרָצוֹן. וּתְהִי
לְרָצוֹן תָּמִיד עֲבוֹדַת יִשְׂרָאֵל עַמֶּךָ.

וְתֶחֱזֶינָה עֵינֵינוּ
בְּשׁוּבְךָ לְצִיּוֹן בְּרַחֲמִים.
בָּרוּךְ אַתָּה יהוה,
הַמַּחֲזִיר שְׁכִינָתוֹ לְצִיּוֹן.

Just to be is a blessing.

Just to live is holy.

A.J. Heschel

We are thankful for this awareness
of the Source of Life,
an awareness that has been passed down
from one generation to the next,
forming the foundation rock of our lives and
ensuring our fulfillment.
We are grateful
and offer psalm-songs
for our lives
that have been placed in Your hands
and for our souls
that have been entrusted to You.

And we are thankful for those miracles,
those wonders, and those welcome surprises
provided us at all times,
evening, morning, and noon.
Goodness and compassion have
never been denied us.
Mercy and caring never cease
when hope eternally exists.

And for everything
may the Holy One of Being be forever blessed
and exalted.

May all the sons and daughters of the covenant
be inscribed for a good life.

Let all the living sincerely be thankful to the Creator
for liberating and helping us. Selah!

Blessed is the Ineffable, Goodness is Your name
and we are so grateful.

מוֹדִים אֲנַחְנוּ לָךְ
שָׁאַתָּה הוּא יהוה אֱלֹהֵינוּ
וֵאלֹהֵי אֲבוֹתֵינוּ לְעוֹלָם וָעֶד,
צוּר חַיֵּינוּ, מָגֵן יִשְׁעֵנוּ
אַתָּה הוּא לְדוֹר וָדוֹר.
נוֹדֶה לְּךָ
וּנְסַפֵּר תְּהִלָּתֶךָ
עַל חַיֵּינוּ
הַמְּסוּרִים בְּיָדֶךָ,
וְעַל נִשְׁמוֹתֵינוּ הַפְּקוּדוֹת לָךְ.

וְעַל נִסֶּיךָ שֶׁבְּכָל יוֹם עִמָּנוּ,
וְעַל נִפְלְאוֹתֶיךָ וְטוֹבוֹתֶיךָ
שֶׁבְּכָל עֵת,
עֶרֶב וָבֹקֶר וְצָהֳרָיִם.
הַטּוֹב כִּי לֹא כָלוּ רַחֲמֶיךָ,
וְהַמְרַחֵם כִּי לֹא תַמּוּ חֲסָדֶיךָ
מֵעוֹלָם קִוִּינוּ לָךְ.

וְעַל כֻּלָּם
יִתְבָּרַךְ וְיִתְרוֹמַם שִׁמְךָ מַלְכֵּנוּ
תָּמִיד לְעוֹלָם וָעֶד.

וּכְתוֹב לְחַיִּים טוֹבִים
כָּל בְּנֵי בְרִיתֶךָ.

וְכֹל הַחַיִּים יוֹדוּךָ סֶּלָה,
וִיהַלְלוּ אֶת שִׁמְךָ בֶּאֱמֶת,
הָאֵל יְשׁוּעָתֵנוּ וְעֶזְרָתֵנוּ סֶלָה.

בָּרוּךְ אַתָּה יהוה,
הַטּוֹב שִׁמְךָ וּלְךָ נָאֶה לְהוֹדוֹת.

Shalom Rav Al Yisrael Amkha
Tasim l'Olam
Ki Atah Hu Melekh Adon l'Khol haShalom.
v'Tov b'Eynekha l'Varekh Et Amkha Yisrael
b'Khol Et u'v'Khol Shah-ah Bishlomekha.

שָׁלוֹם רָב עַל יִשְׂרָאֵל עַמְּךָ
תָּשִׂים לְעוֹלָם,
כִּי אַתָּה הוּא מֶלֶךְ אָדוֹן לְכָל הַשָּׁלוֹם.
וְטוֹב בְּעֵינֶיךָ לְבָרֵךְ אֶת עַמְּךָ יִשְׂרָאֵל
בְּכָל עֵת וּבְכָל שָׁעָה בִּשְׁלוֹמֶךָ.

May abundant peace be granted
Yisrael, Your people, forever.
It is good in Your soul eyes
to bless Your people Yisrael
at all times and at all hours
with Your peace.

(On Yom Kippur continue with Vidui)

B'Sefer Khayim Brakhah v'Shalom
u'Farnasah Tovah.
Nizakher v'Nikatev l'Fanekha
Anakhnu v'Khol Amkhah
Anakhnu v'Khol Amkhah Beyt Yisrael l'Khayim Tovim,
l'Khayim Tovim u'l'Shalom b'Sefer Khayim.

בְּסֵפֶר חַיִּים, בְּרָכָה וְשָׁלוֹם
וּפַרְנָסָה טוֹבָה
נִזָּכֵר וְנִכָּתֵב לְפָנֶיךָ
אֲנַחְנוּ וְכָל עַמְּךָ בֵּית יִשְׂרָאֵל
לְחַיִּים טוֹבִים וּלְשָׁלוֹם.

May we be remembered and inscribed in the
Book of Life, of Blessing, of Peace and Sustenance.
May there be good life and harmony for all of the
House of Israel.

Blessed is the Eternal creating Peace.

בָּרוּךְ אַתָּה יהוה עוֹשֶׂה הַשָּׁלוֹם.

May the words of my mouth
And the meditations of my heart be acceptable
before You.

יִהְיוּ לְרָצוֹן אִמְרֵי פִי
וְהֶגְיוֹן לִבִּי לְפָנֶיךָ.

Oseh Shalom Bimromav
Hu Yaaseh Shalom Aleynu
v'Al Kol Yisrael
v'Al Kol Yoshvey Tevel
v'Imru: Ameyn.
May the One making harmony in the
heavenly spheres realize peace here,
for all of Israel and for all humankind.
Amen.

עֹשֶׂה שָׁלוֹם בִּמְרוֹמָיו
הוּא יַעֲשֶׂה שָׁלוֹם עָלֵינוּ
וְעַל כָּל יִשְׂרָאֵל
וְעַל כָּל יוֹשְׁבֵי תֵבֵל
וְאִמְרוּ: אָמֵן.

Sometime

Sometime there will be
a great love
like the love of rain
erasing frontiers,
growing in all the ears
of corn of the Middle East.

Sometime, long before
the End of Days, we shall
beat into peace
all words of hate and war.

Yehudit Kaffri
translated by Ann Darr and Moshe Dor

KIDDUSH

קִדּוּשׁ

בָּרוּךְ אַתָּה יהוה אֱלֹהֵינוּ מֶלֶךְ הָעוֹלָם בּוֹרֵא פְּרִי הַגָּפֶן.

בָּרוּךְ אַתָּה יהוה אֱלֹהֵינוּ מֶלֶךְ הָעוֹלָם אֲשֶׁר בָּחַר בָּנוּ
מִכָּל־עָם וְרוֹמְמָנוּ מִכָּל־לָשׁוֹן וְקִדְּשָׁנוּ בְּמִצְוֹתָיו. וַתִּתֶּן
לָנוּ יהוה אֱלֹהֵינוּ בְּאַהֲבָה אֶת (לשבת יוֹם הַשַּׁבָּת הַזֶּה וְאֶת)
יוֹם הַזִּכָּרוֹן הַזֶּה, יוֹם (לשבת זִכְרוֹן) תְּרוּעָה (לשבת בְּאַהֲבָה)
מִקְרָא קֹדֶשׁ זֵכֶר לִיצִיאַת מִצְרָיִם. כִּי בָנוּ בָחַרְתָּ וְאוֹתָנוּ קִדַּשְׁתָּ
וּדְבָרְךָ אֱמֶת וְקַיָּם לָעַד.
בָּרוּךְ אַתָּה יהוה מֶלֶךְ עַל כָּל־הָאָרֶץ (לשבת מְקַדֵּשׁ הַשַּׁבָּת וְ)
יִשְׂרָאֵל וְיוֹם הַזִּכָּרוֹן.

בָּרוּךְ אַתָּה יהוה אֱלֹהֵינוּ מֶלֶךְ הָעוֹלָם
שֶׁהֶחֱיָנוּ וְקִיְּמָנוּ וְהִגִּיעָנוּ לַזְּמַן הַזֶּה.

Blessed are You, Eternal One, Guiding Power of the Universe, creating the fruit of the vine.

Blessed are You, Eternal One, Guiding Power of the Universe, who has taken delight in us and who has exalted us by sanctifying our lives with right actions, mitzvot.

With love You have given us (this Shabbat and) this Day of Remembrance, a day for the shofar sounds, a day for holy gathering and for recalling our ancient liberation from bondage.

You have taken delight in us and have hallowed us. Your word is true and endures forever.

Blessed are You, Eternal One, guiding all the earth, sanctifying (the Shabbat) the people Israel and this Day of Remembrance.

Blessed are You, Life's Source, the Guide of the Universe, for giving us life, for giving us existence, and for enabling us to reach this season.

Barukh Atah Adonai Eloheynu Melekh Ha'olam, Shehekheyanu, v'Kiy'manu, v'Higi-anu, Lazman Hazeh.

Ameyn.

ALEYNU

עָלֵינוּ

Aleynu l'Shabeyakh la'Adon haKol
Lateyt G'dulah l'Yotzer B'reyshit.

עָלֵינוּ לְשַׁבֵּחַ לַאֲדוֹן הַכֹּל
לָתֵת גְּדֻלָּה לְיוֹצֵר בְּרֵאשִׁית.

Va'Anakhnu Korim
u'Mishtakhavim u'Modim
Lifney Melekh Mal'khey haM'lakhim
HaKadosh Barukh Hu.

וַאֲנַחְנוּ כּוֹרְעִים
וּמִשְׁתַּחֲוִים וּמוֹדִים
לִפְנֵי מֶלֶךְ מַלְכֵי הַמְּלָכִים
הַקָּדוֹשׁ בָּרוּךְ הוּא.

It is our duty and privilege to acknowledge
and ascribe greatness to the Artist within Creation.
So we bend our knees, bow our heads, and give
thanks before the Holy One of Being.

We put our hope in the awareness and in the promise
that there will come a time when greed and injustice
will be gone from the earth.
We hope for a world completely repaired,
all the inhabitants of this planet turning to each other
in reconciliation, realizing that no one shall be
excluded from the security of life.

עַל כֵּן נְקַוֶּה לְךָ יהוה אֱלֹהֵינוּ
לִרְאוֹת מְהֵרָה בְּתִפְאֶרֶת עֻזֶּךָ,
לְהַעֲבִיר גִּלּוּלִים מִן הָאָרֶץ
וְהָאֱלִילִים כָּרוֹת יִכָּרֵתוּן.
לְתַקֵּן עוֹלָם בְּמַלְכוּת שַׁדַּי.

V'Ne'emar: v'Hayah Adonai,
l'Melekh Al Kol haAretz.
Bayom Hahu, Bayom Hahu, Yihyeh Adonai Ekhad
u'Shmo Ekhad.

וְנֶאֱמַר: וְהָיָה יהוה
לְמֶלֶךְ עַל כָּל הָאָרֶץ,
בַּיּוֹם הַהוּא יִהְיֶה יהוה אֶחָד
וּשְׁמוֹ אֶחָד.

It has been said: "The Eternal Source of Being
will govern over the entire earth. On that day all
peoples will realize their unity."

MOURNER'S KADDISH

קדוש יתום

Yitgadal v'Yitkadash Shmey Rabah,
b'Alma Divra Khirutey
v'Yamlikh Malkutey
b'Khayeykhon u'v'Yomeykhon u'v'Khayey
d'Khol Beyt Yisrael
baAgalah u'Vizman Kariv.
V'Imru: Ameyn.

יִתְגַּדַּל וְיִתְקַדַּשׁ שְׁמֵהּ רַבָּא.
בְּעָלְמָה דִּי בְרָא כִרְעוּתֵהּ.
וְיַמְלִיךְ מַלְכוּתֵהּ,
בְּחַיֵּיכוֹן וּבְיוֹמֵיכוֹן וּבְחַיֵּי
דְכָל בֵּית יִשְׂרָאֵל,
בַּעֲגָלָא וּבִזְמַן קָרִיב.
וְאִמְרוּ אָמֵן:

Y'Hey Shmey Rabah m'Varakh l'Alam
u'l'Almey Almaya:

יְהֵא שְׁמֵהּ רַבָּה מְבָרַךְ לְעָלַם
וּלְעָלְמֵי עָלְמַיָּא:

Yitbarakh v'Yishtabakh v'Yitpaar v'Yitromam
v'Yitnasey v'Yithadar v'Yitaleh v'Yithalal
Shmey d'Kud'sha. Brikh Hu.
L'Eyla u'l'Eyla miKol Birkhata v'Shirata
Tush-b'khata v'Nekhemata daAmiran b'Alma.
V'Imru: Ameyn.

יִתְבָּרַךְ וְיִשְׁתַּבַּח וְיִתְפָּאַר וְיִתְרוֹמַם
וְיִתְנַשֵּׂא וְיִתְהַדָּר וְיִתְעַלֶּה וְיִתְהַלָּל
שְׁמֵהּ דְּקֻדְשָׁא. בְּרִיךְ הוּא.
לְעֵלָּא (וּלְעֵלָּא) מִכָּל בִּרְכָתָא וְשִׁירָתָא
תֻּשְׁבְּחָתָא וְנֶחֱמָתָא דַּאֲמִירָן בְּעָלְמָא.
וְאִמְרוּ אָמֵן:

Y'hey Shlama Raba Min Sh'maya
v'Khayim Aleynu v'Al Kol Yisrael.
V'Imru: Ameyn.

יְהֵא שְׁלָמָא רַבָּא מִן שְׁמַיָּא
וְחַיִּים עָלֵינוּ וְעַל כָּל יִשְׂרָאֵל.
וְאִמְרוּ אָמֵן.

Oseh Shalom Bimromav Hu Ya'aseh Shalom
Aleynu v'Al Kol Yisrael.
V'Imru: Ameyn.

עֹשֶׂה שָׁלוֹם בִּמְרוֹמָיו,
הוּא יַעֲשֶׂה שָׁלוֹם עָלֵינוּ
וְעַל כָּל יִשְׂרָאֵל. וְאִמְרוּ אָמֵן.

May the Unity of Creation be recognized in your lifetime
and throughout your days, and during the lifetime
of the entire House of Yisrael, soon.

So let us acknowledge, honor, celebrate, and sing to the
Sacred Source, though transcendent and truly beyond human songs
and blessing.

May the Source of peace grant us peace, and let us say: Amen.

YIGDAL

יגדל

Yigdal Elohim Khai v'Yishtabakh
Nimtzo v'Eyn Et El M'tzi-uto.

יִגְדַּל אֱלֹהִים חַי וְיִשְׁתַּבַּח
נִמְצָא וְאֵין עֵת אֶל מְצִיאוּתוֹ.

Ekhad v'Eyn Yakhid k'Yikhudo
Nelam v'Gom Eyn Sof l'Akhduto.

אֶחָד וְאֵין יָחִיד כְּיִחוּדוֹ
נֶעְלָם וְגַם אֵין סוֹף לְאַחְדּוּתוֹ.

Eyn Lo Demut Haguf v'Eyno Guf
Lo Na'arokh Eylav Kedushato.

אֵין לוֹ דְּמוּת הַגּוּף וְאֵינוֹ גוּף
לֹא נַעֲרוֹךְ אֵלָיו קְדֻשָּׁתוֹ.

Kadmon l'Khol Davar Asher Nivra
Rishon v'Eyn Reysheet l'Reyshito.

קַדְמוֹן לְכָל־דָּבָר אֲשֶׁר נִבְרָא
רִאשׁוֹן וְאֵין רֵאשִׁית לְרֵאשִׁיתוֹ.

Hino Adon Olam v'Khol Notzar
Yorah G'dulato u'Malkhuto.

הִנּוֹ אֲדוֹן עוֹלָם לְכָל נוֹצָר
יוֹרֶה גְדֻלָּתוֹ וּמַלְכוּתוֹ.

Shefa N'vuato Netano El
Anshey S'gulato v'Tifarto.

שֶׁפַע נְבוּאָתוֹ נְתָנוֹ אֶל
אַנְשֵׁי סְגֻלָּתוֹ וְתִפְאַרְתּוֹ.

Lo Kam b'Yisrael k'Mosheh Od Navi
Umabit Et T'munato.

לֹא קָם בְּיִשְׂרָאֵל כְּמֹשֶׁה עוֹד
נָבִיא וּמַבִּיט אֶת־תְּמוּנָתוֹ.

Torat Emet Natan l'Amo Eyl
Al Yad N'vi'o Ne'eman Beyto.

תּוֹרַת אֱמֶת נָתַן לְעַמּוֹ אֵל
עַל יַד נְבִיאוֹ נֶאֱמַן בֵּיתוֹ.

Lo Yakhalif haEyl v'Lo Yamir Dato
L'Olamim l'Zulato.

לֹא יַחֲלִיף הָאֵל וְלֹא יָמִיר דָּתוֹ
לְעוֹלָמִים, לְזוּלָתוֹ.

Tzofeh v'Yodeah S'tareynu
Mabit l'Sof Davar b'Kadmato.

צוֹפֶה וְיוֹדֵעַ סְתָרֵינוּ
מַבִּיט לְסוֹף דָּבָר בְּקַדְמָתוֹ.

Gomel l'Ish Khesed k'Mifalo
Noteyn l'Rasha Ra k'Rishato

גּוֹמֵל לְאִישׁ חֶסֶד כְּמִפְעָלוֹ
נוֹתֵן לְרָשָׁע רָע כְּרִשְׁעָתוֹ.

Yishlakh l'Keytz Yamin M'shikheynu
Lifdot M'khakey Ketz Y'shuato.

יִשְׁלַח לְקֵץ יָמִין מְשִׁיחֵנוּ
לִפְדּוֹת מְחַכֵּי קֵץ יְשׁוּעָתוֹ.

Meytim Y'khayeh Eyl b'Rov Khasdo
Barukh Adey Ad Sheym Tehilato.

מֵתִים יְחַיֶּה אֵל בְּרוֹב חַסְדּוֹ
בָּרוּךְ עֲדֵי עַד שֵׁם תְּהִלָּתוֹ.

Maariv – The Evening Service

The expansive living God transcends time,
unique and incomparable, an endless mystery of Oneness.

Without physical form, God's holiness cannot be contained,
present before there was even a beginning;

The Eternal source of the universe and all creation,
is majestic and purposeful;

Prophetic teachings have flowed to a treasured and heart-centered people.
There has never been prophet in Israel of the stature of Moses.

A Torah of truth has been given to the people
for those who wish to draw near, trusting the Eternal.

These truths are changeless forever:

> Our innermost secrets are known.
> All is known from beginning to end.
> A caring person is rewarded accordingly.
> And the wicked will receive according to their wickedness.
> In the end of days messianic time will bring liberation,
> the dead will be given renewed life with abundant loving kindness.

May the Creator forever be praised.

שַׁחֲרִית

Morning Service

INTRODUCTORY SELECTIONS

Modeh / Modah Ani l'Fanekha
Ruakh Khai v'Kayam
Sheh-khezarta Bi Nishmati, b'Khemlah
Rabah Emunatekha.
I give thanks to the living God for faithfully
returning my soul to me.

מוֹדֶה\מוֹדָה אֲנִי לְפָנֶיךָ
רוּחַ חַי וְקַיָּם,
שֶׁהֶחֱזַרְתָּ בִּי נִשְׁמָתִי בְּחֶמְלָה
רַבָּה אֱמוּנָתֶךָ.

You are a Consolation To Your Creatures

You are a consolation to Your creatures,
for in moments of forgetting,
we but call to mind Your care,
and we are comforted.

When we hope no more,
a pattern in the snow
reminds us of Your lovingkindness.

Your dawns give us confidence,
and sleep is a friend.

Our sorrows dissipate
in the presence of an infant's smile,
and the wise words of the old
revive our will-to-wish.

Your hints are everywhere,
Your signals in the most remote of places.

You are here,
and we fail words to say,
"Ma Tov!"
How good our breath,
our rushing energies,
our silences of love.

Danny Siegel

... no one can sneer at the stars, mock the dawn, ridicule the outburst of spring, or scoff at the totality of being. Away from the immense, cloistered in our own concepts, we may scorn and revile everything. But standing between earth and sky, we are silenced.

A.J. Heschel

Rom'mu Adonai Eloheynu
v'Hishtakhavu l'Har Kawdsho
Ki Kadosh Adonai Eloheynu.

רוֹמְמוּ יהוה אֱלֹהֵינוּ
וְהִשְׁתַּחֲווּ לְהַר קָדְשׁוֹ
כִּי קָדוֹשׁ יהוה אֱלֹהֵינוּ.

Acclaim the Source of life,
be humbled before the peaks of holiness.
For the Eternal, the Ineffable, our God, is sacred.

Psalm 99

Hiney Ma Tov u'Mah Na'im
Shevet Akhim Gam Yakhad.

הִנֵּה מַה טוֹב וּמַה נָּעִים
שֶׁבֶת אַחִים גַּם יָחַד.

How good and how pleasing it is when brothers and
sisters, family and friends dwell together in unity.

Psalm 133:1

Shir HaKavod

שִׁיר הַכָּבוֹד

Anim Z'mirot v'Shirim Eh-erog
Ki Eylekha Nafshi Taarog
Nafshi Khamdah b'Tzeyl Yadekha
LaDaat Kol Raz Sodekha.

אַנְעִים זְמִירוֹת וְשִׁירִים אֶאֱרוֹג
כִּי אֵלֶיךָ נַפְשִׁי תַעֲרוֹג
נַפְשִׁי חָמְדָה בְּצֵל יָדֶךָ
לָדַעַת כָּל רָז סוֹדֶךָ.

Midey Dabri bi'Khvodekha
Homeh Libi El Dodekha.
Al Keyn Adaber v'Kha Nikhbadot
v'Shimkha Akhabeyd b'Shirey y'Didot.

מִדֵּי דַבְּרִי בִּכְבוֹדֶךָ
הוֹמֶה לִבִּי אֶל דּוֹדֶיךָ
עַל כֵּן אֲדַבֵּר בְּךָ נִכְבָּדוֹת
וְשִׁמְךָ אֲכַבֵּד בְּשִׁירֵי יְדִידוֹת.

Pleasant melodies will I create
For You are my soul's delight and mate.
Oh how my soul within me yearns
Your secret mysteries to know and learn.

אֲסַפְּרָה כְבוֹדְךָ וְלֹא רְאִיתִיךָ
אֲדַמְּךָ אֲכַנְּךָ וְלֹא יְדַעְתִּיךָ
בְּיַד נְבִיאֶיךָ בְּסוֹד עֲבָדֶיךָ
דִּמִּיתָ הֲדַר כְּבוֹד הוֹדֶךָ.

The measure of my speech glorifies Your Name,
My heart filled with love for You I claim.
I speak of You with wonder and honor,
With songs of love, of yearning and desire.

adapted from The Hymn of Glory

28

PSUKEY D'ZIMRAH—VERSES OF SONG

פְּסוּקֵי דְזִמְרָה

Barukh Sheh-Amar

בָּרוּךְ שֶׁאָמַר

Blessed is the One whose word
brought the world into being.
Barukh Hu

בָּרוּךְ שֶׁאָמַר וְהָיָה הָעוֹלָם,
בָּרוּךְ הוּא. בְּרוּכָה הִיא.

Blessed is the One who maintains creation.
B'rukha Hi

בָּרוּךְ עֹשֶׂה בְרֵאשִׁית,

Blessed is the One who decrees and acts.
Barukh Hu

בָּרוּךְ אוֹמֵר וְעֹשֶׂה,

Blessed is the One who has compassion on the earth.
B'rukha Hi

בָּרוּךְ גּוֹזֵר וּמְקַיֵּם,

Blessed is the One who rewards those respectful of life.
Barukh Hu

בָּרוּךְ מְרַחֵם עַל הָאָרֶץ,

Blessed is the One who is Eternal.
B'rukha Hi

בָּרוּךְ מְרַחֵם עַל הַבְּרִיּוֹת,

Blessed is the One who liberates and saves.
Barukh Hu

בָּרוּךְ מְשַׁלֵּם שָׂכָר טוֹב לִירֵאָיו,

Blessed is the Life force.

בָּרוּךְ חַי לָעַד וְקַיָּם לָנֶצַח,

Blessed is the Eternal Source of Being, adorned with
uplifting songs.

בָּרוּךְ פּוֹדֶה וּמַצִּיל,
בָּרוּךְ שְׁמוֹ.
בָּרוּךְ אַתָּה יהוה אֵל מְהֻלָּל בַּתִּשְׁבָּחוֹת.

*Hoshi'ah Et Amekha u'Varekh Et Nakhalatekha
u'Reym v'Nahseym Ad Olam.*
Help Your people and bless Your human legacy,
and sustain them forever.

from Psalm 28

הוֹשִׁיעָה אֶת עַמֶּךָ וּבָרֵךְ אֶת נַחֲלָתֶךָ
וּרְעֵם וְנַשְּׂאֵם עַד הָעוֹלָם.

Hodu LAdonai Ki Tov Ki L'Olam Khasdo.
Give thanks to the Eternal, for the creation is good
and lovingkindness endures forever.

from Psalm 136

הוֹדוּ לַיהוה כִּי טוֹב כִּי לְעוֹלָם חַסְדּוֹ.

Mi haIsh Hekhafetz Khayim Ohev Yamim Lirot Tov.
N'Tzor Lishonkha Meyrah u'Sfatekha miDaber Mirmah.
Sur Meyrah v'Asey Tov Bakeysh Shalom v'Radfeyhu.

מִי הָאִישׁ הֶחָפֵץ חַיִּים
אֹהֵב יָמִים לִרְאוֹת טוֹב.
נְצֹר לְשׁוֹנְךָ מֵרָע
וּשְׂפָתֶיךָ מִדַּבֵּר מִרְמָה.
סוּר מֵרָע וַעֲשֵׂה טוֹב
בַּקֵּשׁ שָׁלוֹם וְרָדְפֵהוּ.

Who is the person who desires life?
Who loves life and wishes to see goodness?
You who hold your tongue from speaking harmful words
and your lips from speaking what is untrue.
Avoid wrongdoing, do good, seek peace, and pursue it.

from Psalm 34

Psalm 33

The just joyfully sing to the Source of Life,
the upright are praiseworthy.

רַנְּנוּ צַדִּיקִים בַּיָי
לַיְשָׁרִים נָאוָה תְהִלָּה.

> Give thanks to the Ineffable, they say,
> with stringed instruments,
> the nevel, the kinor,
> singing songs, old ones, new ones.

הוֹדוּ לַיָי בְּכִנּוֹר בְּנֵבֶל
עָשׂוֹר זַמְּרוּ־לוֹ.
שִׁירוּ לוֹ שִׁיר חָדָשׁ
הֵיטִיבוּ נַגֵּן בִּתְרוּעָה.

Make melodious sounds!

> God's word is sincere,
> the works of creation are trustworthy.

כִּי־יָשָׁר דְּבַר־יְיָ
וְכָל־מַעֲשֵׂהוּ בֶּאֱמוּנָה.

God loves justice and righteousness,
the Eternal's lovingkindness filling the earth.

אֹהֵב צְדָקָה וּמִשְׁפָּט
חֶסֶד יְיָ מָלְאָה הָאָרֶץ.

> Imagine a wordless word calling forth the heavens.
> Imagine a mouthless mouth proclaiming nature's forces,
> moving the oceans, giving depth to the earth.

בִּדְבַר יְיָ שָׁמַיִם
נַעֲשׂוּ וּבְרוּחַ
פִּיו כָּל־צְבָאָם.
כֹּנֵס כַּנֵּד מֵי הַיָּם

As all the earth reflects the awe of creation
so shall all the inhabitants of the world.

נֹתֵן בְּאֹצָרוֹת תְּהוֹמוֹת.
יִירְאוּ מֵיְיָ כָּל־הָאָרֶץ מִמֶּנּוּ
יָגוּרוּ כָּל־יֹשְׁבֵי תֵבֵל.

> The universe endures.
> The Eternal transcends nations,
> disdaining prejudice.

כִּי הוּא אָמַר וַיֶּהִי
הוּא־צִוָּה וַיַּעֲמֹד.

The Eternal's design endures
from generation to generation.

יְיָ הֵפִיר עֲצַת גּוֹיִם
הֵנִיא מַחְשְׁבוֹת עַמִּים.

> Happy is the people whose God is
> the Ineffable Mystery of Creation.

עֲצַת יְיָ לְעוֹלָם
תַּעֲמֹד מַחְשְׁבוֹת לִבּוֹ לְדֹר וָדֹר.
אַשְׁרֵי הַגּוֹי אֲשֶׁר־יְיָ אֱלֹהָיו
הָעָם בָּחַר לְנַחֲלָה לוֹ.

30

From the heavens the Ineffable views humankind,
gazing upon all of earth's inhabitants,
fashioning their hearts,
understanding all their doings.

Coerciveness and military might do not redeem us.

The eye of the Ineffable One is upon those in awe of
life, waiting for divine lovingkindess and caring
to spare their souls from death,
and their lives from spiritual starvation.

Our soul waits for the renewing Breath of the
Creator in which we shall truly rejoice.
For we know we will be secure
within this realm of the Sacred One.

We wait and hope for Your love and care.

Ki Vo Yismakh Libeynu
Ki v'Sheym Kawdsho Vatakhnu.
Y'hi Khasdekha Adonai Aleynu
KaAsher Yikhalnu Lakh.

מִשָּׁמַיִם הִבִּיט יְיָ רָאָה אֶת־כָּל־בְּנֵי
הָאָדָם. מִמְּכוֹן־שִׁבְתּוֹ הִשְׁגִּיחַ אֶל
כָּל־יֹשְׁבֵי הָאָרֶץ.
הַיֹּצֵר יַחַד לִבָּם הַמֵּבִין
אֶל־כָּל־מַעֲשֵׂיהֶם.
אֵין הַמֶּלֶךְ נוֹשָׁע בְּרָב־חָיִל
גִּבּוֹר לֹא־יִנָּצֵל בְּרָב־כֹּחַ.
שֶׁקֶר הַסּוּס לִתְשׁוּעָה
וּבְרֹב חֵילוֹ לֹא יְמַלֵּט.
הִנֵּה עֵין יְיָ אֶל־יְרֵאָיו לַמְיַחֲלִים לְחַסְדּוֹ.
לְהַצִּיל מִמָּוֶת נַפְשָׁם וּלְחַיּוֹתָם בָּרָעָב.
נַפְשֵׁנוּ חִכְּתָה לַייָ עֶזְרֵנוּ וּמָגִנֵּנוּ הוּא.

כִּי בוֹ יִשְׂמַח לִבֵּנוּ
כִּי בְשֵׁם קָדְשׁוֹ בָטָחְנוּ.
יְהִי חַסְדְּךָ יְיָ עָלֵינוּ
כַּאֲשֶׁר יִחַלְנוּ לָךְ.

Painting A Morning Panorama

Praised be You, O God
who paints a morning panorama
on the Appalachian peaks
that moves us to say:
Let's walk in the country,
let's go to the lake.

Praised be the One
Who makes old people young
by the simple change of the weather.

Praised be the God
of early Spring
and Indian Summers
for Your magic touch
of subtle miracles
is everywhere.

Danny Siegel

31

Halleluyah

הַלְלוּיָהּ

Praise to God in Sacred Space
Praise the creation of the mighty skies,
Halleluyah for this natural might.
Halleluyah for such immense and infinite greatness.

Halleluyah! Give praise with the sound of the shofar.
Halleluyah! Express thanks with the sound of stringed instruments.

Halleluyah with drums and dance.
Halleluyah with bells and winds.

Let everything that breathes praise the Source of Life.
Let the whole soul be thankful.

Psalm 150

Halleluyah.
Hallelu Eyl b'Kawdsho
Halleluhu biRki'ah Uzo.
Halleluhu biG'vurotav
Halleluhu k'Rov Gudlo.
Halleluhu b'Teykah Shofar
Halleluhu b'Neyvel b'Kinor.
Halleluhu b'Tof u'Makhol
Halleluhu b'Minim v'Ugav.
Halleluhu b'Tzilzt'ley Shamah
Halleluhu b'Tziltz'ley T'ruah.
Kol haN'shamah t'Hahlel Yah
Kol haN'shamah t'Hahlel Yah!

הַלְלוּיָהּ.

הַלְלוּ אֵל בְּקָדְשׁוֹ

הַלְלוּהוּ בִּרְקִיעַ עֻזּוֹ.

הַלְלוּהוּ בִגְבוּרֹתָיו

הַלְלוּהוּ כְּרֹב גֻּדְלוֹ.

הַלְלוּהוּ בְּתֵקַע שׁוֹפָר

הַלְלוּהוּ בְּנֵבֶל וְכִנּוֹר.

הַלְלוּהוּ בְּתֹף וּמָחוֹל

הַלְלוּהוּ בְּמִנִּים וְעֻגָב.

הַלְלוּהוּ בְּצִלְצְלֵי שָׁמַע

הַלְלוּהוּ בְּצִלְצְלֵי תְרוּעָה.

כֹּל הַנְּשָׁמָה תְּהַלֵּל יָהּ הַלְלוּיָהּ.

כֹּל הַנְּשָׁמָה תְּהַלֵּל יָהּ הַלְלוּיָהּ.

Artwork: Ben Shahn, Guitar and Flute

Nishmat

נְשִׁמַת כָּל־חַי תְּבָרֵךְ אֶת
שִׁמְךָ יהוה אֱלֹהֵינוּ.

The soul of every living being
shall bless Your presence.

If our mouths were filled with song like the sea,
and our tongues with song like the roaring of the waves,
and our lips with praise like the breadth of the firmament,
and our eyes were radiant like the sun and the moon,
and our hands outspread like the eagles of the sky,
and our feet light as the deer ...

... we could never sufficiently be thankful.

אִלּוּ פִינוּ מָלֵא שִׁירָה כַּיָּם
וּלְשׁוֹנֵנוּ רִנָּה כַּהֲמוֹן גַּלָּיו
וְשִׂפְתוֹתֵינוּ שֶׁבַח כְּמֶרְחֲבֵי רָקִיעַ
וְעֵינֵינוּ מְאִירוֹת כַּשֶּׁמֶשׁ וְכַיָּרֵחַ
וְיָדֵינוּ פְרוּשׂוֹת כְּנִשְׁרֵי שָׁמַיִם
וְרַגְלֵינוּ קַלּוֹת כָּאַיָּלוֹת
אֵין אֲנַחְנוּ מַסְפִּיקִים לְהוֹדוֹת לְךָ
יהוה אֱלֹהֵינוּ וֵאלֹהֵי אֲבוֹתֵינוּ
וְאִמּוֹתֵינוּ וּלְבָרֵךְ אֶת שְׁמֶךָ
עַל אַחַת מֵאָלֶף אֶלֶף אַלְפֵי אֲלָפִים
וְרֻבֵּי רְבָבוֹת פְּעָמִים הַטּוֹבוֹת
שֶׁעָשִׂיתָ עִם אֲבוֹתֵינוּ
וְאִמּוֹתֵינוּ וְעִמָּנוּ.

How uncomfortable for some, perhaps embarrassing, to bless that which we cannot
see, that which is nameless, that Eternal Thou. How difficult it is to publicly
acknowledge the countless goodnesses which were given our ancestors and to us.

Who is like You? Who is like you?

The meaning of existence is experienced in moments of exaltation. We must strive for the
summit in order to survive on the ground ... our ends must surpass our needs. The security
of existence lies in the exaltation of existence.

There is hardly a person who does not submit his soul to the beauty parlor, who does not
employ the make-up of vanity in order to belie his embarrassment. It is only before God that
we all stand naked.

A.J. Heschel

In the Garden of Shechina

I

Born from the earth
Breathed by the air
Healed in the water
Kindled with prayer.
I walk through the fiery sword of truth
And listen
With all my heart.

I am the Tree of Life
In the Garden of Shechina
Singing a psalm of wonder and love
Ki hi m'kor habr'akha.

Adonai ekhad ush'mo ekhad
L'shem ul'tiferet v'lit'hila.
Adonai ekhad ush'mo ekhad
L'shem ul'tiferet v'lit'hila.

II

If Spirit is both
Woman and Man
Then Heaven and Earth
Dance hand in hand.
The balance of power
Restores inner light
As we enter
The Covenant of Peace.

We are the Tree of Life
In the Garden of Shechina
Singing a psalm of wonder and love
Ki hi m'kor hab'rakha.

Adonai ekhad ush'mo ekhad
L'shem ul 'tiferet v'lit'hila.
Adonai ekhad ush'mo ekhad
L'shem ul'tiferet v'lit'hila.

Hanna Tiferet Siegel

In no other act does a person experience so often the disparity between the desire for expression and the means of expression as in prayer. The inadequacy of the means at our disposal appears so tangible, so tragic, that one feels it a grace to be able to give oneself up to music, to a tone, to a song, to a chant. The wave of a song carries the soul to heights which utterable meaning can never reach. Such abandonment is no escape, for the world of unutterable meanings is the nursery of the soul, the cradle of all our ideas. It is not an escape but a return to one's origins.

To become aware of the ineffable is to part company with words. The essence, the tangent to the curve of human experience lies beyond the limits of language. The world of things we perceive is but a veil. Its flutter is music, its ornament science, but what it conceals is inscrutable. Its silence remains unbroken; no word can carry it away.

Sometimes we wish the world could cry and tell us about that which made it pregnant with fear-filling grandeur. Sometimes we wish our own heart would speak of that which made it heavy with wonder.

A.J. Heschel

The Majestic

sits on the most high and exalted throne.

This majesty is ever present, lofty, and sacred.
So it has been written: "The righteous enjoy the
Eternal Presence, upright persons offer praise."

God is exalted by the speech of the upright,
blessed by the words of the just,
sanctified by the tongue of the caring,
and extolled by the nearness of saintly people.

The Eternal's presence is celebrated with joyful
song in the assemblies of the people, the house
of Yisrael, for generations.

It is the duty of all those in Your Presence
to thank, extol, honor, bless, elevate and
acclaim You, to go beyond the lyrics and songs
of David.

הַמֶּלֶךְ
יוֹשֵׁב עַל כִּסֵּא רָם וְנִשָּׂא.

שׁוֹכֵן עַד מָרוֹם וְקָדוֹשׁ שְׁמוֹ.
וְכָתוּב: רַנְּנוּ צַדִּיקִים בַּיהוה
לַיְשָׁרִים נָאוָה תְהִלָּה.

בְּפִי יְשָׁרִים תִּתְרוֹמָם.

וּבְדִבְרֵי צַדִּיקִים תִּתְבָּרַךְ.

וּבִלְשׁוֹן חֲסִידִים תִּתְקַדָּשׁ

וּבְקֶרֶב קְדוֹשִׁים תִּתְהַלָּל.

וּבְמַקְהֲלוֹת רִבְבוֹת עַמְּךָ בֵּית יִשְׂרָאֵל
בְּרִנָּה יִתְפָּאַר שִׁמְךָ מַלְכֵּנוּ בְּכָל דּוֹר וָדוֹר.

שֶׁכֵּן חוֹבַת כָּל הַיְצוּרִים
לְפָנֶיךָ יהוה אֱלֹהֵינוּ
וֵאלֹהֵי אֲבוֹתֵינוּ לְהוֹדוֹת לְהַלֵּל לְשַׁבֵּחַ
לְפָאֵר לְרוֹמֵם לְהַדֵּר לְבָרֵךְ לְעַלֵּה וּלְקַלֵּס
עַל כָּל דִּבְרֵי שִׁירוֹת וְתִשְׁבְּחוֹת
דָּוִד בֶּן יִשַׁי עַבְדְּךָ מְשִׁיחֶךָ.

Praised be Your Presence forever.
You are the majesty of the universe
and the holiness in time and space.

It is pleasing to sing and praise,
celebrate and proclaim
Your strength, grandeur and steadfastness.

Barukh. Blessed is the Ancient Presence,
the life of the universe,
the majesty of nature,
worthy of celebration,
revealing wonders,
and delighting in joyful song.

יִשְׁתַּבַּח שִׁמְךָ לָעַד מַלְכֵּנוּ
הָאֵל הַמֶּלֶךְ הַגָּדוֹל וְהַקָּדוֹשׁ
בַּשָּׁמַיִם וּבָאָרֶץ.

כִּי לְךָ נָאֶה יהוה אֱלֹהֵינוּ וֵאלֹהֵי אֲבוֹתֵינוּ,
שִׁיר וּשְׁבָחָה, הַלֵּל וְזִמְרָה,
עֹז וּמֶמְשָׁלָה, נֶצַח, גְּדֻלָּה וּגְבוּרָה,
תְּהִלָּה וְתִפְאֶרֶת, קְדֻשָּׁה וּמַלְכוּת,
בְּרָכוֹת וְהוֹדָאוֹת מֵעַתָּה וְעַד עוֹלָם.

בָּרוּךְ אַתָּה יהוה,
אֵל מֶלֶךְ גָּדוֹל בַּתִּשְׁבָּחוֹת,
אֵל הַהוֹדָאוֹת, אֲדוֹן הַנִּפְלָאוֹת,
הַבּוֹחֵר בְּשִׁירֵי זִמְרָה,
מֶלֶךְ, אֵל, חֵי הָעוֹלָמִים.

Half Kaddish

May Creation be exalted and sanctified
in a cosmos formed according to an
incomprehensible Will.

May the Universe of Creation be recognized
in your lifetime and throughout your days,
and during the lifetime of the entire House of Yisrael,
soon.

So let us acknowledge, honor, celebrate,
and sing to the Sacred Source,
though transcendent and truly beyond human songs
and blessing.

And join in saying, amen.

יִתְגַּדַּל וְיִתְקַדַּשׁ שְׁמֵהּ רַבָּא.
בְּעָלְמָא דִּי־בְרָא כִרְעוּתֵהּ.
וְיַמְלִיךְ מַלְכוּתֵהּ בְּחַיֵּיכוֹן
וּבְיוֹמֵיכוֹן וּבְחַיֵּי דְכָל בֵּית
יִשְׂרָאֵל בַּעֲגָלָא וּבִזְמַן קָרִיב.
וְאִמְרוּ אָמֵן.

יְהֵא שְׁמֵהּ רַבָּא מְבָרַךְ לְעָלַם
וּלְעָלְמֵי עָלְמַיָּא.

יִתְבָּרַךְ וְיִשְׁתַּבַּח וְיִתְפָּאַר וְיִתְרֹמַם
וְיִתְנַשֵּׂא וְיִתְהַדָּר וְיִתְעַלֶּה
וְיִתְהַלָּל שְׁמֵהּ דְּקֻדְשָׁא. בְּרִיךְ הוּא.
לְעֵלָּא וּלְעֵלָּא מִכָּל בִּרְכָתָא
וְשִׁירָתָא תֻּשְׁבְּחָתָא וְנֶחֱמָתָא
דַּאֲמִירָן בְּעָלְמָא. וְאִמְרוּ אָמֵן.

Leader:

בָּרְכוּ אֶת יהוה הַמְבֹרָךְ

Barkhu Et Adonai HaMvorakh

We are called to bless the Eternal, the Source of All Blessing

Community:

בָּרוּךְ יהוה הַמְבֹרָךְ לְעוֹלָם וָעֶד

Barukh Adonai HaMvorakh L'Olam Vaed

Blessed is the Eternal, the Source of Blessing, forever

We welcome the magnificence and glory of Creation.
Blessed is the Creator of Light and Darkness,
making peace and creating all things.

בָּרוּךְ אַתָּה יהוה אֱלֹהֵינוּ מֶלֶךְ
הָעוֹלָם יוֹצֵר אוֹר וּבוֹרֵא חֹשֶׁךְ
עֹשֶׂה שָׁלוֹם וּבוֹרֵא אֶת הַכֹּל.

The light of the universe is Life's Treasure.
From out of darkness comes light …

אוֹר עוֹלָם בְּאוֹצַר חַיִּים
אוֹרוֹת מֵאֹפֶל אָמַר וַיֶּהִי.

(On Yom Kippur)

We are grateful that the gates of compassion
are open to us, providing hopefulness
for those awaiting forgiveness.

(On Yom Kippur)

הַפּוֹתֵחַ לָנוּ שַׁעֲרֵי רַחֲמִים
וּמֵאִיר עֵינֵי הַמְחַכִּים לִסְלִיחָתוֹ.

Per v'Khavod Notnim Lishmo
Tzahala v'Rinah l'Zekher Malkhuto.
Glory and honor to the Creator's name.
Exult with joy over Creation.

פְּאֵר וְכָבוֹד נוֹתְנִים לִשְׁמוֹ
צָהֲלָה וְרִנָּה לְזֵכֶר מַלְכוּתוֹ.

37

To the Blessed Infinite One
we offer pleasant melodies,
to the living and enduring God
they chant holy songs and resound with praise.

Alone the Creator works mightily,
initiating new works,
omnipotent in battles,
planting seeds of justice,
blossoming into freedom,
creating cures.

So awe inspiring is this Teacher of Wonders.

Creation is continuously renewed
with inherent goodness each day.

It is said: "Give thanks to the One who lit up the world
and imbued it with lovingkindness."

Ohr Khadash al Tziyon Tair
v'Nizkeh Khulanu m'Heyra l'Oro.
May a new light shine upon Zion,
and may we all soon be worthy
to enjoy its brightness.

Barukh. Blessed is the Creator
of the heavenly lights.

לָאֵל בָּרוּךְ נְעִימוֹת יִתֵּנוּ.
לְמֶלֶךְ אֵל חַי וְקַיָּם,
זְמִירוֹת יֹאמֵרוּ
וְתִשְׁבָּחוֹת יַשְׁמִיעוּ
כִּי הוּא לְבַדּוֹ פּוֹעֵל גְּבוּרוֹת,
עֹשֶׂה חֲדָשׁוֹת,
בַּעַל מִלְחָמוֹת,
זוֹרֵעַ צְדָקוֹת,
מַצְמִיחַ יְשׁוּעוֹת,
בּוֹרֵא רְפוּאוֹת,
נוֹרָא תְהִלּוֹת, אֲדוֹן הַנִּפְלָאוֹת.
הַמְחַדֵּשׁ בְּטוּבוֹ
בְּכָל יוֹם תָּמִיד
מַעֲשֵׂה בְרֵאשִׁית.
כָּאָמוּר:
לְעֹשֵׂה אוֹרִים גְּדֹלִים,
כִּי לְעוֹלָם חַסְדּוֹ.

אוֹר חָדָשׁ עַל צִיּוֹן תָּאִיר
וְנִזְכֶּה כֻלָּנוּ מְהֵרָה לְאוֹרוֹ.

בָּרוּךְ אַתָּה יהוה,
יוֹצֵר הַמְּאוֹרוֹת.

Throughout time we have been greatly loved.
As our ancestors trusted in the One
and were taught the laws of life,
so may we be graced and instructed as well.

אַהֲבָה רַבָּה אֲהַבְתָּנוּ, יהוה אֱלֹהֵינוּ,
חֶמְלָה גְדוֹלָה וִיתֵרָה חָמַלְתָּ עָלֵינוּ.
אָבִינוּ מַלְכֵּנוּ, בַּעֲבוּר אֲבוֹתֵינוּ
שֶׁבָּטְחוּ בְךָ וַתְּלַמְּדֵם חֻקֵּי חַיִּים,

We call upon our eternal Parent,
our compassionate and caring Guide,
to have compassion for us,
to give our hearts the ability to understand,
to be mindful, to listen, to learn, to teach, to preserve,
to practice, and to fulfill the words of Torah with
love.

כֵּן תְּחׇנֵּנוּ וּתְלַמְּדֵנוּ.
אָבִינוּ, הָאָב הָרַחֲמָן הַמְרַחֵם,
רַחֵם עָלֵינוּ, וְתֵן בְּלִבֵּנוּ
לְהָבִין וּלְהַשְׂכִּיל, לִשְׁמֹעַ, לִלְמֹד
וּלְלַמֵּד לִשְׁמֹר וְלַעֲשׂוֹת וּלְקַיֵּם
אֶת כָּל דִּבְרֵי תַלְמוּד תּוֹרָתֶךָ
בְּאַהֲבָה.

V'Haer Eyneynu b'Toratekha
v'Dabek Libeynu b'Mitzvotekha
v'Yakhed Livaveynu
l'Ahavah u'l'Yirah et Sh'mekha.
V'Lo Neyvosh l'Olam Vaed.

וְהָאֵר עֵינֵינוּ בְּתוֹרָתֶךָ,
וְדַבֵּק לִבֵּנוּ בְּמִצְוֹתֶיךָ
וְיַחֵד לְבָבֵנוּ
לְאַהֲבָה וּלְיִרְאָה אֶת שְׁמֶךָ,
וְלֹא נֵבוֹשׁ לְעוֹלָם וָעֶד.

We ask that our eyes be enlightened
by those teachings that attach our hearts
to doing mitzvot and right actions.

We ask that our hearts be whole
in expressions of love,
welcoming amazement and not shame.
By trusting in the Eternal One,
clothed in holiness, omnipotence, and awe,
we become fulfilled, able to rejoice and be glad.
We hope that our people can establish itself in peace
and with dignity in the land.

כִּי בְשֵׁם קׇדְשְׁךָ הַגָּדוֹל וְהַנּוֹרָא בָּטָחְנוּ,
נָגִילָה וְנִשְׂמְחָה בִּישׁוּעָתֶךָ.
וַהֲבִיאֵנוּ לְשָׁלוֹם
מֵאַרְבַּע כַּנְפוֹת הָאָרֶץ,
וְתוֹלִכֵנוּ קוֹמְמִיּוּת לְאַרְצֵנוּ,
כִּי אֵל פּוֹעֵל יְשׁוּעוֹת אָתָּה,
וּבָנוּ בָחַרְתָּ מִכָּל עַם וְלָשׁוֹן.

Our God desires harmony, taking delight in us and
drawing us near through truth, peacemaking,
and love.

וְקֵרַבְתָּנוּ לְשִׁמְךָ הַגָּדוֹל סֶלָה בֶּאֱמֶת,
לְהוֹדוֹת לְךָ וּלְיַחֶדְךָ בְּאַהֲבָה.

Barukh. Blessed is the Eternal Unifying Force,
delighting in the people Israel with love.

בָּרוּךְ אַתָּה יהוה,
הַבּוֹחֵר בְּעַמּוֹ יִשְׂרָאֵל בְּאַהֲבָה.

Shakharit – The Morning Service

שְׁמַע יִשְׂרָאֵל יהוה אֱלֹהֵינוּ יהוה אֶחָד

Adonai   *Adonai*

Shma Yisrael YHVH Eloheynu YHVH Ekhad

Listen Israel, The Eternal is our God, the Eternal is One

בָּרוּךְ שֵׁם כְּבוֹד מַלְכוּתוֹ לְעוֹלָם וָעֶד

Barukh Shem Kavod Malkhuto L'Olam Vaed

Blessed is the Glory of Creation forever

V'Ahavta et Adonai Elohekha	וְאָהַבְתָּ אֵת יהוה אֱלֹהֶיךָ
b'Khol l'Vavkha	בְּכָל־לְבָבְךָ
u'v'Khol Naf'sh'kha	וּבְכָל־נַפְשְׁךָ
u'v'Khol M'odekha.	וּבְכָל־מְאֹדֶךָ.
V'Hayu haD'varim haEleh	וְהָיוּ הַדְּבָרִים הָאֵלֶּה
Asher Anokhi m'Tzavkha haYom	אֲשֶׁר אָנֹכִי מְצַוְּךָ הַיּוֹם
al-l'Vavekha. V'Shinantam l'Vanekha	עַל־לְבָבֶךָ. וְשִׁנַּנְתָּם לְבָנֶיךָ
v'Dibarta Bam b'Shiv't'kha b'Veytekha	וְדִבַּרְתָּ בָּם בְּשִׁבְתְּךָ בְּבֵיתֶךָ
u'v'Lekh't'kha vaDerekh uv'Shakh'b'kha	וּבְלֶכְתְּךָ בַדֶּרֶךְ וּבְשָׁכְבְּךָ
u'v'Kumekha.	וּבְקוּמֶךָ.
U'K'shartam l'Ot al-Yadekha	וּקְשַׁרְתָּם לְאוֹת עַל־יָדֶךָ
v'Hayu l'Totafot Beyn Eynekha .	וְהָיוּ לְטֹטָפֹת בֵּין עֵינֶיךָ.
U'Kh'tavtam al-M'zuzot Beytekha	וּכְתַבְתָּם עַל־מְזֻזֹת בֵּיתֶךָ
u'Visharekha.	וּבִשְׁעָרֶיךָ.

And you shall love the Ineffable Life Giver, with all your heart, with all your soul, and with all that you have. And these words addressed to you today shall be upon your heart, and you shall teach them well to your children, speaking of them when you sit in your house, when you travel, when you lie down and when you rise up. And you shall bind them for a sign upon your hand, and they shall be for frontlets between your eyes. And you shall inscribe them on the doorposts of your house and upon your gates.

Deuteronomy 6:4-9

40

וְהָיָה אִם־שָׁמֹעַ תִּשְׁמְעוּ אֶל־מִצְוֹתַי, אֲשֶׁר אָנֹכִי מְצַוֶּה אֶתְכֶם הַיּוֹם, לְאַהֲבָה אֶת־יהוה
אֱלֹהֵיכֶם, וּלְעָבְדוֹ בְּכָל־לְבַבְכֶם וּבְכָל־נַפְשְׁכֶם. וְנָתַתִּי מְטַר־אַרְצְכֶם בְּעִתּוֹ, יוֹרֶה וּמַלְקוֹשׁ,
וְאָסַפְתָּ דְגָנֶךָ וְתִירֹשְׁךָ וְיִצְהָרֶךָ. וְנָתַתִּי עֵשֶׂב בְּשָׂדְךָ לִבְהֶמְתֶּךָ, וְאָכַלְתָּ וְשָׂבָעְתָּ. הִשָּׁמְרוּ לָכֶם
פֶּן־יִפְתֶּה לְבַבְכֶם, וְסַרְתֶּם וַעֲבַדְתֶּם אֱלֹהִים אֲחֵרִים וְהִשְׁתַּחֲוִיתֶם לָהֶם. וְחָרָה אַף־יהוה בָּכֶם,
וְעָצַר אֶת־הַשָּׁמַיִם וְלֹא־יִהְיֶה מָטָר, וְהָאֲדָמָה לֹא תִתֵּן אֶת־יְבוּלָהּ וַאֲבַדְתֶּם מְהֵרָה מֵעַל הָאָרֶץ
הַטֹּבָה אֲשֶׁר יהוה נֹתֵן לָכֶם:

It shall come to pass, if you attend to My mitzvot which I establish for you this day ... to love
Creation, to serve it with all your heart, and with all your soul ... then there will be rain upon
your land in its season, the former rain and the latter rain, so that you may gather in your corn,
and your wine, and your oil. And there will be grass in your fields for your cattle, and all shall
eat and be satisfied. Now guard yourselves that your heart not be deceived and you turn aside,
and serve other gods, and submit to them. For the displeasure of Creation will be roused against
you, and the heavens be closed, so that there be no rain, and the ground not yield its fruit; and
you perish quickly from the good land which has been given you.

Deuteronomy 11:13-17

וַיֹּאמֶר יהוה אֶל־מֹשֶׁה לֵּאמֹר: דַּבֵּר אֶל־בְּנֵי יִשְׂרָאֵל וְאָמַרְתָּ אֲלֵהֶם: וְעָשׂוּ לָהֶם צִיצִת עַל־כַּנְפֵי
בִגְדֵיהֶם לְדֹרֹתָם, וְנָתְנוּ עַל־צִיצִת הַכָּנָף פְּתִיל תְּכֵלֶת. וְהָיָה לָכֶם לְצִיצִת, וּרְאִיתֶם אֹתוֹ וּזְכַרְתֶּם
אֶת־כָּל־מִצְוֹת יהוה, וַעֲשִׂיתֶם אֹתָם, וְלֹא תָתוּרוּ אַחֲרֵי לְבַבְכֶם וְאַחֲרֵי עֵינֵיכֶם, אֲשֶׁר־אַתֶּם
זֹנִים אַחֲרֵיהֶם: לְמַעַן תִּזְכְּרוּ וַעֲשִׂיתֶם אֶת־כָּל־מִצְוֹתָי, וִהְיִיתֶם קְדֹשִׁים לֵאלֹהֵיכֶם: אֲנִי יהוה
אֱלֹהֵיכֶם, אֲשֶׁר הוֹצֵאתִי אֶתְכֶם מֵאֶרֶץ מִצְרַיִם, לִהְיוֹת לָכֶם לֵאלֹהִים, אֲנִי יהוה אֱלֹהֵיכֶם:

And the Ineffable spoke to Moshe, saying: Speak unto the children of Israel, and instruct them to
make fringes, tzitzit, on the corners of their garments throughout the generations ... that you
may remember to do all My Mitzvot, and become holy unto your God. I am the Eternal your
God who brought you out of the land of Mitzrayim to be your God; I am the Eternal your God.

Numbers 15:37-41

Adonai
YHVH Eloheykhem Emet
It is true that the Life Force is Eternal.

One who is attentive to mitzvot and torah teachings
and listens to the heart is fortunate.

לְמַעַן תִּזְכְּרוּ וַעֲשִׂיתֶם אֶת־כָּל־מִצְוֹתָי
וִהְיִיתֶם קְדֹשִׁים לֵאלֹהֵיכֶם.
אֲנִי יהוה אֱלֹהֵיכֶם. יהוה אֱלֹהֵיכֶם אֱמֶת.

אַשְׁרֵי אִישׁ שֶׁיִּשְׁמַע לְמִצְוֹתֶיךָ
וְתוֹרָתְךָ וּדְבָרְךָ יָשִׂים עַל לִבּוֹ.

We are taught to reflect on the Infinite One,
clothed in majesty and wondrous abilities,
who humbles the haughty and raises up the lowly,
who liberates the captives, and frees the powerless,
who helps the poor and responds to people when they
cry out.

לְמֶלֶךְ אֵל חַי וְקַיָּם. רָם וְנִשָּׂא
גָּדוֹל וְנוֹרָא מַשְׁפִּיל גֵּאִים וּמַגְבִּיהַּ
שְׁפָלִים מוֹצִיא אֲסִירִים וּפוֹדֶה
עֲנָוִים וְעוֹזֵר דַּלִּים וְעוֹנֶה לְעַמּוֹ
בְּעֵת שַׁוְּעָם אֵלָיו.

The ancient covenant calls upon us to be partners
with the Holy One of Being. We offer praises to the
Most High, the One to whom blessing is due.
With great joy Moses and Miriam and the children of
Israel sang a song to You. We, also, proclaim:

תְּהִלּוֹת לְאֵל עֶלְיוֹן
בָּרוּךְ הוּא וּמְבוֹרָךְ.
מֹשֶׁה וּבְנֵי יִשְׂרָאֵל לְךָ עָנוּ שִׁירָה
בְּשִׂמְחָה רַבָּה וְאָמְרוּ כֻלָּם.

Mi Khamokah baEylim Adonai
Mi Khamokha Nedar baKodesh
Norah Tehilot Osey Feleh!
Who is like You among the mighty?
Who is like You dressed in holiness, deserving
awefilled praise, who performs wonders?

מִי־כָמֹכָה בָּאֵלִם יהוה,
מִי כָּמֹכָה נֶאְדָּר בַּקֹּדֶשׁ,
נוֹרָא תְהִלֹּת עֹשֵׂה פֶלֶא.

With a new song the freed rejoiced and
honored You at the shore of the Sea of Reeds.
In unison they gave thanks saying:
Adonai Yimlokh l'Olam Vaed.
The Eternal will govern always.

שִׁירָה חֲדָשָׁה שִׁבְּחוּ גְאוּלִים
לְשִׁמְךָ עַל שְׂפַת הַיָּם,
יַחַד כֻּלָּם הוֹדוּ וְהִמְלִיכוּ וְאָמְרוּ:
יהוה יִמְלֹךְ לְעוֹלָם וָעֶד.

Tzur Yisrael Kuma b'Ezrat Yisrael
u'F'dey Khinumekha Yehuda v'Yisrael.
We call upon the Enduring Rock of the people Israel
to rise and help redeem our people today,
to help all the inhabitants of Judah and Israel
to know the source of their redemption.

צוּר יִשְׂרָאֵל, קוּמָה בְּעֶזְרַת יִשְׂרָאֵל,
וּפְדֵה כִנְאֻמֶךָ יְהוּדָה וְיִשְׂרָאֵל,
גֹּאֲלֵנוּ יהוה צְבָאוֹת שְׁמוֹ
קְדוֹשׁ יִשְׂרָאֵל.

Barukh Atah Adonay Ga'al Yisrael.
Blessed is the Eternal, redeeming Israel.

בָּרוּךְ אַתָּה יהוה גָּאַל יִשְׂרָאֵל.

AMIDAH—THE STANDING MEDITATION

עֲמִידָה

We are grateful for Life's eternal spirit,
our Origin and the God of our ancestors,
the vision and promise to Avraham,
the aloneness of Yitzkhak,
the spiritual wrestling of Yaakov,
the surprise of Sarah, the wisdom of Rivka,
the patience of Rakhel, the fruitfulness of Leah.
Expansive, Powerful, Awesome, Highest God,
loving kindnesses, owning everything,
remembering our ancestors' caring,
their concern for the future fulfillment
of their children's children,
for the sake of Creation with love.

בָּרוּךְ אַתָּה יהוה, אֱלֹהֵינוּ
וֵאלֹהֵי אֲבוֹתֵינוּ, וֵאלֹהֵי אִמּוֹתֵינוּ,
אֱלֹהֵי אַבְרָהָם, אֱלֹהֵי יִצְחָק,
וֵאלֹהֵי יַעֲקֹב,
אֱלֹהֵי שָׂרָה, אֱלֹהֵי רִבְקָה,
אֱלֹהֵי רָחֵל, וֵאלֹהֵי לֵאָה.
הָאֵל הַגָּדוֹל הַגִּבּוֹר וְהַנּוֹרָא, אֵל עֶלְיוֹן,
גּוֹמֵל חֲסָדִים טוֹבִים, וְקֹנֵה הַכֹּל,
וְזוֹכֵר חַסְדֵי אָבוֹת וְאִמָּהוֹת,
וּמֵבִיא גוֹאֵל לִבְנֵי בְנֵיהֶם
לְמַעַן שְׁמוֹ בְּאַהֲבָה.

Inspired by the sages and guided by traditions
of the ages, I open my mouth in prayer and
supplication before the Majesty of the Universe,
the Guide of All.

מְסוֹד חֲכָמִים וּנְבוֹנִים, וּמִלֶּמֶד דַּעַת
מְבִינִים, אֶפְתְּחָה פִּי בִּתְפִלָּה וּבְתַחֲנוּנִים,
לְחַלּוֹת וּלְחַנֵּן פְּנֵי מֶלֶךְ מַלְכֵי הַמְּלָכִים
וַאֲדוֹנֵי הָאֲדוֹנִים.

Bless what brought us through
the sea and the fire; we are caught
in history like whales in polar ice.
Yet you have taught us to push against the walls,

to reach out and pull each other along,
to strive to find the way through
if there is no way around, to go on.
To utter ourselves with every breath

against the constriction of fear,
to know ourselves as the body born from Abraham
and Sarah, born out of rock and desert.
We reach back through two hundred arches of hips

long dust, carrying their memories inside us
to live again in our life, Isaac and Rebecca,
Rachel, Jacob, Leah. We say words shaped
by ancient use like steps worn into rock.

Marge Piercy — Blessings

43

(On Rosh HaShanah)

I am awestruck as I begin to voice my prayer,
as I rise to plead before the presence of the
One who is wondrous and terrifying.

I am deficient in good deeds and therefore in doubt,
lacking wisdom and concerned. How can I hope?

My Creator! Give me understanding and help me to take hold
of my heritage. Strengthen me, encourage me,
help me not to be weak and fearful.

Accept my prayer and let my speech be as sweet as nectar,
upright and not hypocritical. Temper my roar so that I be not
like the lion. May my words be as cautious as the caterpillar.

Gracious One. Hear my cry as I begin, my insides on fire
as my foolish deeds are reviewed
in the face of this dreaded judgment.

My soul trembles.

If I am not released from my sin my heart will ache,
tears will rush forth as streams from my eyes.

I yearn and I hope for what is just.
Please remember the worthiness of my parents.
As I reflect my heart grows hot like a fiery coal.

I begin.

(On Rosh HaShanah)

יָרֵאתִי בִּפְצוֹתִי שִׂיחַ לְהַשְׁחִיל,
קוּמִי לְחַלּוֹת פְּנֵי נוֹרָא וְדָחִיל,
וְקָטֹנְתִּי מַעַשׂ לָכֵן אֶזְחִיל,
תְּבוּנָה חָסַרְתִּי וְאֵיךְ אוֹחִיל.
יוֹצְרִי הֲבִינֵנִי מוֹרָשָׁה לְהַנְחִיל,
אַיְּלֵנִי וְאַמְּצֵנִי מֵרִפְיוֹן וָחִיל,
לַחֲשִׁי יֵרָצֶה כְּמַנְטִיף וּמַשְׁחִיל,
בְּטוּיִי יִמְתַּק כְּצוּף נָחִיל.
רְצוּי בְּיֹשֶׁר וְלֹא כְּמַכְחִיל,
מְשַׁלְּחַי לְהַמְצִיא כֹּפֶר וּמְחִיל,
שַׁאֲגִי יֵעֲרַב וְלֹא כְּמַשְׁחִיל,
הֵעָתֵר לְנִגָּשִׁים וְנֶחֱשָׁבִים כְּזָחִיל.
חַנּוּן, כְּהַבְטִיחֶךָ לְבִנְקֶרֶת מְחִיל,
זַעֲקִי קְשׁוֹב בְּעֵת אַתְחִיל,
קְרָבַי יֵחֱמָרוּ בְּחָקְרֶךָ חֲלוֹחִיל,
וּמֵאֵימַת הַדִּין נַפְשִׁי תַבְחִיל.
אִם כִּגְמוּל הַלֵּב יָחִיל,
מְקוֹרֵי עַפְעַפַּי אַזִיל כְּמַזְחִיל,
צְדָקָה אֲקַוֶּה מִמְּךָ וְאוֹחִיל,
יֹשֶׁר הוֹרַי זָכְרָה לְהַאֲחִיל.
חַם לִבִּי בַּהֲגִיגִי יַגְחִיל,
יִסְתָּעֵר בְּקִרְבִּי בְּעֵת אַתְחִיל.

---

*Zakhreynu l'Khayim Melech Khafetz baKhayim
v'Khatveynu b'Sefer haKhayim
l'Ma'ankhah Elohim Khayim.*

May the power that desires life,
remember us unto life and
inscribe us in the book of life
affirming the living God.

זָכְרֵנוּ לְחַיִּים, מֶלֶךְ חָפֵץ בַּחַיִּים
וְכָתְבֵנוּ בְּסֵפֶר הַחַיִּים,
לְמַעַנְךָ אֱלֹהִים חַיִּים.

The Ineffable is known as "Ruler,"
"Helper," "Saving Power," or "Protector."
Here we address and bless You as the
Protecting Power of our ancestors.

מֶלֶךְ עוֹזֵר וּפוֹקֵד וּמוֹשִׁיעַ וּמָגֵן.
בָּרוּךְ אַתָּה יהוה,
מָגֵן אַבְרָהָם וּפוֹקֵד שָׂרָה.

You are the Eternality of Time,
giving life to the dead, renewed life to the living,
hopefulness, deliverance.
Let us know that Life is sustained through
lovingkindness,
the dormant renewed with much compassion.
For the fallen there is support,
for the sick there is healing,
for the imprisoned there can be release,
and only faith for those who sleep in the dust.

Who can be compared do this Renewing Power?
Who can be compared to the Compassionate Parent
mindful of Creation with compassion and
life-giving creativity?
We trust that the renewal of life will continue.
Blessed is the Eternal, renewing life.

You are our God in heaven and on earth,
omnipotent and revered, above the multitudes,
Whose word is power,
Whose command results in creation,
Who is known eternally,
Who lives forever, whose eyes are clear,
enthroned incomprehensibly,
Whose crown is harmony,
Whose clothing is justice,
Whose mantle is equity,
Whose counsel is trusted and who works for truth,
Who is righteous and sincere and near unto
all who are truthful,
uplifted and present everywhere,
suspending earth in space,
alive and wondrous, exalted and sacred.

אַתָּה גִבּוֹר לְעוֹלָם אֲדֹנָי,
מְחַיֵּה מֵתִים אַתָּה,
רַב לְהוֹשִׁיעַ.
מְכַלְכֵּל חַיִּים בְּחֶסֶד,
מְחַיֵּה מֵתִים בְּרַחֲמִים רַבִּים,
סוֹמֵךְ נוֹפְלִים, וְרוֹפֵא חוֹלִים,
וּמַתִּיר אֲסוּרִים, וּמְקַיֵּם אֱמוּנָתוֹ
לִישֵׁנֵי עָפָר.

מִי כָמוֹךָ בַּעַל גְּבוּרוֹת וּמִי דוֹמֶה לָךְ,
מֶלֶךְ מֵמִית וּמְחַיֶּה וּמַצְמִיחַ יְשׁוּעָה.
מִי כָמוֹךָ אֵל הָרַחֲמִים
זוֹכֵר יְצוּרָיו לַחַיִּים בְּרַחֲמִים?
וְנֶאֱמָן אַתָּה לְהַחֲיוֹת מֵתִים.
בָּרוּךְ אַתָּה יהוה, מְחַיֵּה הַמֵּתִים.

אַתָּה הוּא אֱלֹהֵינוּ. בַּשָּׁמַיִם וּבָאָרֶץ
גִּבּוֹר וְנַעֲרָץ. דָּגוּל מֵרְבָבָה
הוּא שָׂח וַיֶּהִי. וְצִוָּה וְנִבְרָאוּ
זִכְרוֹ לָנֶצַח. חַי עוֹלָמִים
טָהוֹר עֵינַיִם. יוֹשֵׁב סֵתֶר
כִּתְרוֹ יְשׁוּעָה. לְבוּשׁוֹ צְדָקָה
מַעֲטֵהוּ קִנְאָה. נֶאְפַּד נְקָמָה
סִתְרוֹ יֹשֶׁר. עֲצָתוֹ אֱמוּנָה
פְּעֻלָּתוֹ אֱמֶת. צַדִּיק וְיָשָׁר
קָרוֹב לְקוֹרְאָיו בֶּאֱמֶת. רָם וּמִתְנַשֵּׂא
שׁוֹכֵן שְׁחָקִים. תּוֹלֶה אֶרֶץ עַל בְּלִימָה.
חַי וְקַיָּם נוֹרָא וּמָרוֹם וְקָדוֹשׁ.

U'v'Kheyn l'Kha haKol Yakhtiru,
l'Eyl Orech Din.
The Holy One of Creation, the Inner
Spirit of Life is crowned.

On this Day of Judgment
all hearts are probed,
all that is concealed is revealed,
sincerity is expected,
our deepest thoughts are known on this
Day of Judgment.

But there is compassion,
the covenant is renewed,
we are spared.

Those who trust in the One are cleansed,
our thoughts are certainly known,
but in judgment wrath is suppressed.

In judgment the Eternal is clothed with
compassion,
wrongdoing is pardoned,
the revered Judge, forgiving,
answering those who call out,
acting with mercy,
aware of all mysteries,
welcoming those who serve the Eternal,
merciful to the people,
protecting the lovers of life,
sustaining the faithful on this
Day of Judgment.

וּבְכֵן לְךָ הַכֹּל יַכְתִּירוּ

לְאֵל עוֹרֵךְ דִּין.

לְבוֹחֵן לְבָבוֹת בְּיוֹם דִּין.

לְגוֹלֶה עֲמֻקוֹת בַּדִּין.

לְדוֹבֵר מֵישָׁרִים בְּיוֹם דִּין.

לְהוֹגֶה דֵעוֹת בַּדִּין.

לְוָתִיק וְעוֹשֶׂה חֶסֶד בְּיוֹם דִּין.

לְזוֹכֵר בְּרִיתוֹ בַּדִּין.

לְחוֹמֵל מַעֲשָׂיו בְּיוֹם דִּין.

לְטַהֵר חוֹסָיו בַּדִּין.

לְיוֹדֵעַ מַחֲשָׁבוֹת בְּיוֹם דִּין.

לְכוֹבֵשׁ כַּעֲסוֹ בַּדִּין.

לְלוֹבֵשׁ צְדָקוֹת בְּיוֹם דִּין.

לְמוֹחֵל עֲוֹנוֹת בַּדִּין.

לְנוֹרָא תְהִלּוֹת בְּיוֹם דִּין.

לְסוֹלֵחַ לַעֲמוּסָיו בַּדִּין.

לְעוֹנֶה לְקוֹרְאָיו בְּיוֹם דִּין.

לְפוֹעֵל רַחֲמָיו בַּדִּין.

לְצוֹפֶה נִסְתָּרוֹת בְּיוֹם דִּין.

לְקוֹנֶה עֲבָדָיו בַּדִּין.

לְרַחֵם עַמּוֹ בְּיוֹם דִּין.

לְשׁוֹמֵר אוֹהֲבָיו בַּדִּין.

לְתוֹמֵךְ תְּמִימָיו בְּיוֹם דִּין.

Kedusha

קְדוּשָׁה

We sanctify Your name on earth
as it is in the heavens above.
As it was written by Your prophet,
as the angels called out to one another:

נְקַדֵּשׁ אֶת שִׁמְךָ בָּעוֹלָם, כְּשֵׁם
שֶׁמַּקְדִּישִׁים אוֹתוֹ בִּשְׁמֵי מָרוֹם,
כַּכָּתוּב עַל יַד נְבִיאֶךָ, וְקָרָא זֶה
אֶל זֶה וְאָמַר:

Kadosh, Kadosh, Kadosh, Adonai Tzivaot
M'Lo Khol HaAretz K'vodo.
Holy, Holy, Holy O Ineffable Force
The whole earth is full of Your glory.

קָדוֹשׁ קָדוֹשׁ קָדוֹשׁ יהוה צְבָאוֹת,
מְלֹא כָל הָאָרֶץ כְּבוֹדוֹ.

We will sanctify You as do the angels in the highest
heavens. Blessed is the glory of the Sacred that fills
the universe.
Barukh K'vod Adonai Mimkomo.

אָז בְּקוֹל רַעַשׁ גָּדוֹל אַדִּיר וְחָזָק
מַשְׁמִיעִים קוֹל, מִתְנַשְּׂאִים לְעֻמַּת
שְׂרָפִים, לְעֻמָּתָם בָּרוּךְ יֹאמֵרוּ.
בָּרוּךְ כְּבוֹד יהוה מִמְּקוֹמוֹ.

From the heavens above, may our Protecting Power
come forth to guide us, as we wait for guidance.
When will You reign in Zion? May it happen in our
time. May the Sacred be exalted in Jerusalem
in each generation, and may our eyes see a
reign of peace, as it was said in the Psalms of David:

מִמְּקוֹמְךָ מַלְכֵּנוּ תוֹפִיעַ וְתִמְלֹךְ
עָלֵינוּ כִּי מְחַכִּים אֲנַחְנוּ לָךְ. מָתַי
תִּמְלֹךְ בְּצִיּוֹן, בְּקָרוֹב בְּיָמֵינוּ לְעוֹלָם
וָעֶד תִּשְׁכּוֹן. תִּתְגַּדַּל וְתִתְקַדַּשׁ בְּתוֹךְ
יְרוּשָׁלַיִם עִירְךָ לְדוֹר וָדוֹר וּלְנֵצַח
נְצָחִים. וְעֵינֵינוּ תִרְאֶינָה מַלְכוּתֶךָ
כַּדָּבָר הָאָמוּר בְּשִׁירֵי עֻזֶּךָ עַל
יְדֵי דָוִד מְשִׁיחַ צִדְקֶךָ.

Yimlokh Adonai L'Olam, Elohayikh Tziyon,
L'Dor VaDor, Halleluya.
The Eternal reigns forever, for every generation,
Hallelujah!

יִמְלֹךְ יהוה לְעוֹלָם. אֱלֹהַיִךְ צִיּוֹן
לְדֹר וָדֹר, הַלְלוּיָהּ.

L'Dor vaDor Nagid Gadlekha u'l'Netzakh N'tzakhim
Kedushatekha Nakdish. V'Shiv-khakha Eloheynu
miPinu Lo Yamush l'Olam Vaed.
Ki El Melekh Gadol v'Kadosh Atah.

לְדוֹר וָדוֹר נַגִּיד גָּדְלֶךָ וּלְנֵצַח נְצָחִים
קְדֻשָּׁתְךָ נַקְדִּישׁ וְשִׁבְחֲךָ אֱלֹהֵינוּ
מִפִּינוּ לֹא יָמוּשׁ לְעוֹלָם וָעֶד
כִּי אֵל מֶלֶךְ גָּדוֹל וְקָדוֹשׁ אָתָּה.

May every generation tell of Your
greatness, and eternally speak of Life's sanctity.
We will sanctify life. May words of praise never
depart from our mouths.
You are majestic and You are Kadosh.

And so,
May fear and concern for Creation,
be instilled in all living things,
dreadful concern for all that has been created.
All creation ought to be in awe,
all of life humbled before the Life Giver.
May all of creation form a single bond
with a balanced heart.
For we know that the Unknown governs alone,
that true strength is in Your hand,
and true power is in Your presence.
The Awesome Spirit Being is imprinted on
all that has been created.

וּבְכֵן

תֵּן פַּחְדְּךָ יהוה אֱלֹהֵינוּ
עַל כָּל מַעֲשֶׂיךָ, וְאֵימָתְךָ עַל כָּל מַה
שֶׁבָּרָאתָ, וְיִירָאוּךָ כָּל הַמַּעֲשִׂים
וְיִשְׁתַּחֲווּ לְפָנֶיךָ כָּל הַבְּרוּאִים.
וְיֵעָשׂוּ כֻלָּם אֲגֻדָּה אֶחָת
לַעֲשׂוֹת רְצוֹנְךָ בְּלֵבָב שָׁלֵם.
כְּמוֹ שֶׁיָּדַעְנוּ יהוה אֱלֹהֵינוּ
שֶׁהַשִּׁלְטָן לְפָנֶיךָ עֹז בְּיָדְךָ
וּגְבוּרָה בִּימִינֶךָ וְשִׁמְךָ נוֹרָא
עַל כָּל מַה שֶׁבָּרָאתָ.

And so,
May honor be granted to Your people,
praise to those who are in awe,
and hope to those who seek,
and who speak frankly and who yearn.
Let there be joy throughout the land,
It is Yours.
And let there be joyfulness for the inhabitants of
the city, for it is Your city.
May this occur soon in our lifetime.

וּבְכֵן

תֵּן כָּבוֹד, יהוה לְעַמֶּךָ, תְּהִלָּה
לִירֵאֶיךָ וְתִקְוָה לְדוֹרְשֶׁיךָ, וּפִתְחוֹן פֶּה
לַמְיַחֲלִים לָךְ.
שִׂמְחָה לְאַרְצֶךָ וְשָׂשׂוֹן לְעִירֶךָ,
וּצְמִיחַת קֶרֶן לְדָוִד עַבְדֶּךָ
וַעֲרִיכַת נֵר לְבֶן יִשַׁי
מְשִׁיחֶךָ בִּמְהֵרָה בְיָמֵינוּ.

... The world is not a vacuum.
Either we make it an altar for God
or it is invaded by demons.
There can be no neutrality.
Either we are ministers of the sacred
or slaves to evil.

A. J. Heschel

When such a day arrives
those who struggled for justice will be the first
to rejoice, the upright will be glad,
and the faithful supporters will sing with joy,
injustice closing its mouth,
all evil vanishing like smoke,
the kingdom of falsehood passing
from the earth.

וּבְכֵן
צַדִּיקִים יִרְאוּ וְיִשְׂמָחוּ
וִישָׁרִים יַעֲלֹזוּ
וַחֲסִידִים בְּרִנָּה יָגִילוּ
וְעוֹלָתָה תִּקְפָּץ־פִּיהָ.
וְכָל־הָרִשְׁעָה כֻּלָּהּ כְּעָשָׁן תִּכְלֶה
כִּי תַעֲבִיר מֶמְשֶׁלֶת זָדוֹן
מִן־הָאָרֶץ.

You, alone, will govern all Your works,
with Mount Zion as Your honored dwelling place,
and the City of Shalom,
Jerusalem, Your sacred city.

וְתִמְלוֹךְ אַתָּה יהוה לְבַדֶּךָ
עַל כָּל־מַעֲשֶׂיךָ בְּהַר צִיּוֹן מִשְׁכַּן
כְּבוֹדֶךָ וּבִירוּשָׁלַיִם עִיר קָדְשֶׁךָ.

As it is written in those holy ancient words:
The Life Source, the Dream of Zion,
will preside for all generations.
Halleluyah.

כַּכָּתוּב בְּדִבְרֵי קָדְשֶׁךָ
יִמְלֹךְ יהוה לְעוֹלָם
אֱלֹהַיִךְ צִיּוֹן לְדֹר וָדֹר
הַלְלוּיָהּ.

You are Kadosh and Awesome.
There is no other God.
As it is written:
The Unity of All is uplifted by righteousness.
The Holy One of Being is sanctified by justice and
lovingkindness.

קָדוֹשׁ אַתָּה וְנוֹרָא שְׁמֶךָ
וְאֵין אֱלוֹהַּ מִבַּלְעָדֶיךָ.
כַּכָּתוּב וַיִּגְבַּהּ יהוה צְבָאוֹת
בַּמִּשְׁפָּט וְהָאֵל הַקָּדוֹשׁ
נִקְדַּשׁ בִּצְדָקָה.

Barukh Atah Adonai HaMelekh HaKadosh.
Blessed is the Sole Sovereign and Holy Presence.

בָּרוּךְ אַתָּה יהוה הַמֶּלֶךְ הַקָּדוֹשׁ.

We must beware lest we violate the holy,
lest our dogmas overthink the mystery,
lest our psalms sing it away.

A.J. Heschel

49

You have delighted in us as a people,
loving us, desiring us, elevating us,
and sanctifying us with Mitzvot,
drawing us near to serve You,
that Your Great Holy Presence
be known to us.

אַתָּה בְחַרְתָּנוּ מִכָּל הָעַמִּים.
אָהַבְתָּ אוֹתָנוּ וְרָצִיתָ בָּנוּ.
וְרוֹמַמְתָּנוּ מִכָּל הַלְּשׁוֹנוֹת
וְקִדַּשְׁתָּנוּ בְּמִצְוֹתֶיךָ.
וְקֵרַבְתָּנוּ מַלְכֵּנוּ לַעֲבוֹדָתֶךָ
וְשִׁמְךָ הַגָּדוֹל וְהַקָּדוֹשׁ עָלֵינוּ קָרָאתָ.

With love we have been given

וַתִּתֶּן לָנוּ יהוה אֱלֹהֵינוּ בְּאַהֲבָה

(on Rosh HaShanah)
this Day of Remembering,
this Day of Shofar Sounds.

(on Rosh HaShanah)
אֶת יוֹם (לְשַׁבָּת הַשַּׁבָּת הַזֶּה וְאֶת יוֹם)
הַזִּכָּרוֹן הַזֶּה
יוֹם (לְשַׁבָּת זִכְרוֹן) תְּרוּעָה

(on Yom Kippur)
this Day of Atonement,
for renouncing our wrongs,
for asking for forgiveness,
for cleansing, for reconciliation.

(on Yom Kippur)
אֶת יוֹם (לְשַׁבָּת הַשַּׁבָּת הַזֶּה לִקְדֻשָּׁה
וְלִמְנוּחָה, וְאֶת יוֹם) הַכִּפּוּרִים הַזֶּה
לִמְחִילָה וְלִסְלִיחָה וּלְכַפָּרָה וְלִמְחָל־בּוֹ
אֶת־כָּל־עֲוֹנוֹתֵינוּ

A day of holy gathering
reminding us of our liberation
from the narrowness of Mitzrayim.

(לְשַׁבָּת בְּאַהֲבָה) מִקְרָא קֹדֶשׁ
זֵכֶר לִיצִיאַת מִצְרָיִם.

We should also pray for the wicked among the peoples of the world; we should
love them too. As long as we do not pray in this way, as long as we do not love in
this way, the Messiah will not come.

To love God truly, one must love another. And if anyone tells you that (s)he
loves God and does not love a sister or brother, you will know that (s)he is lying.

from the Midrash

Allow our memory to ascend,
to come, to reach us.
May our memory and our reckoning,
and our ancestors memory,
and the memory of the dream of a Messianic Time,
and the memory of the vision of Jerusalem,
as a City of Peace,
a Holy City,
and those memories of all Your people,
the House of Israel
whether in the Land or in the Diaspora,
be before You.

May these memories,
these dreams be redemptive
and may they inspire
graciousness, lovingkindness,
and compassion,
arousing efforts for life and peace
on this Day.

אֱלֹהֵינוּ וֵאלֹהֵי אֲבוֹתֵינוּ
יַעֲלֶה וְיָבֹא וְיַגִּיעַ
וְיֵרָאֶה וְיֵרָצֶה וְיִשָּׁמַע
וְיִפָּקֵד וְיִזָּכֵר זִכְרוֹנֵנוּ
וּפִקְדוֹנֵנוּ וְזִכְרוֹן אֲבוֹתֵינוּ
וְזִכְרוֹן מָשִׁיחַ בֶּן־דָּוִד עַבְדֶּךָ
וְזִכְרוֹן יְרוּשָׁלַיִם
עִיר קָדְשֶׁךָ
וְזִכְרוֹן כָּל עַמְּךָ
בֵּית יִשְׂרָאֵל לְפָנֶיךָ.

לִפְלֵיטָה לְטוֹבָה
לְחֵן וּלְחֶסֶד וּלְרַחֲמִים
לְחַיִּים וּלְשָׁלוֹם בְּיוֹם
(On Rosh HaShanah)
הַזִּכָּרוֹן הַזֶּה.
(On Yom Kippur)
הַכִּפּוּרִים הַזֶּה.

Let a person do good deeds,
    and then ask Torah from the Everpresent One.

Let a person do righteous and fitting deeds,
    and then ask wisdom from God.

Let a person seize humility,
    and then ask understanding from the Holy One of All.

from the Midrash

As we recall our origins we ask
that the Holy One of Being
remember us well, and delegate blessedness,
and save us for life,
and enable us to receive
graciousness and compassion.

Our eyes are open for guidance,
benevolence, and mercifulness.

זָכְרֵנוּ יהוה אֱלֹהֵינוּ
בּוֹ לְטוֹבָה וּפָקְדֵנוּ בוֹ לִבְרָכָה
וְהוֹשִׁיעֵנוּ בוֹ לְחַיִּים
וּבִדְבַר יְשׁוּעָה וְרַחֲמִים
חוּס וְחָנֵּנוּ וְרַחֵם עָלֵינוּ וְהוֹשִׁיעֵנוּ.

כִּי אֵלֶיךָ עֵינֵינוּ כִּי אֵל מֶלֶךְ חַנּוּן
וְרַחוּם אַתָּה.

May this awareness govern the entire world
with respectfulness,
uplifting the earth with love,
the splendor of the Presence
resting upon all the inhabitants of this planet.

So all will know their Maker,
and all will understand their Creator.

Then everyone who has breath flowing through their
nostrils will say:
... the Ineffable, the Sacred Life Breath,
the God of Yisrael, the God of soul wrestling people,
is the One we are accountable to wherever we are.

אֱלֹהֵינוּ וֵאלֹהֵי אֲבוֹתֵינוּ,
מְלוֹךְ עַל כָּל הָעוֹלָם כֻּלּוֹ
בִּכְבוֹדֶךָ וְהִנָּשֵׂא עַל כָּל הָאָרֶץ
בִּיקָרֶךָ וְהוֹפַע בַּהֲדַר גְּאוֹן עֻזֶּךָ
עַל כָּל יוֹשְׁבֵי תֵבֵל אַרְצֶךָ.

וְיֵדַע כָּל־פָּעוּל כִּי־אַתָּה פְּעַלְתּוֹ.
וְיָבִין כָּל־יְצוּר כִּי אַתָּה יְצַרְתּוֹ.

וְיֹאמַר כֹּל אֲשֶׁר נְשָׁמָה בְּאַפּוֹ
יהוה אֱלֹהֵי יִשְׂרָאֵל מֶלֶךְ
וּמַלְכוּתוֹ בַּכֹּל מָשָׁלָה.

Just to be is a blessing
Just to live is holy.

A.J. Heschel

May we be sanctified by our deeds,
and share in those sacred teachings.
May we be satisfied by the good,
and receive joy and fulfillment from our work.

V'Taher Libeynu l'Avdekha Beh'emet
Ki Atah Elohim Emet u'D'varkha Emet
v'Kayam La'ad.
And may our hearts be cleared to serve life truthfully,
as we are called upon by the Power of truth,
Whose word endures forever.

Blessed is the Ineffable,
governing the earth,
sanctifying the people Yisrael
(on Rosh HaShanah)
on this Day of Remembrance.
(on Yom Kippur)
on this Day of Atonement.

(לשבת אֱלֹהֵינוּ וֵאלֹהֵי
אֲבוֹתֵינוּ רְצֵה בִמְנוּחָתֵנוּ)
קַדְּשֵׁנוּ בְּמִצְוֹתֶיךָ וְתֵן חֶלְקֵנוּ בְּתוֹרָתֶךָ
שַׂבְּעֵנוּ מִטּוּבֶךָ וְשַׂמְּחֵנוּ בִּישׁוּעָתֶךָ.

וְטַהֵר לִבֵּנוּ לְעָבְדְּךָ בֶּאֱמֶת
כִּי אַתָּה אֱלֹהִים אֱמֶת וּדְבָרְךָ אֱמֶת
וְקַיָּם לָעַד.

בָּרוּךְ אַתָּה יהוה
מֶלֶךְ עַל כָּל־הָאָרֶץ
מְקַדֵּשׁ (לשבת הַשַּׁבָּת וְ) יִשְׂרָאֵל
(on Rosh HaShanah)
וְיוֹם הַזִּכָּרוֹן.
(on Yom Kippur)
וְיוֹם הַכִּפּוּרִים.

We hope that our understanding
of God, of life,
will be desirable,
that the people Yisrael
and their meditations,
and this sacred service,
be received with love and with
pleasure.
V'Tekhezehnah Eyneynu b'Shuv'kha
l'Tzion b'Rakhamim.
May our eyes behold the return
of Compassion to Zion.

Blessed is the Eternal,
restoring the Shekhinah to Zion.

רְצֵה יהוה אֱלֹהֵינוּ
בְּעַמְּךָ יִשְׂרָאֵל וּבִתְפִלָּתָם.
וְהָשֵׁב אֶת־הָעֲבוֹדָה
לִדְבִיר בֵּיתֶךָ וְאִשֵּׁי יִשְׂרָאֵל.
וּתְפִלָּתָם בְּאַהֲבָה תְקַבֵּל בְּרָצוֹן.
וּתְהִי לְרָצוֹן תָּמִיד
עֲבוֹדַת יִשְׂרָאֵל עַמֶּךָ.
וְתֶחֱזֶינָה עֵינֵינוּ בְּשׁוּבְךָ
לְצִיּוֹן בְּרַחֲמִים.

בָּרוּךְ אַתָּה יהוה
הַמַּחֲזִיר שְׁכִינָתוֹ לְצִיּוֹן.

Shakharit – The Morning Service

We are thankful that we have this understanding
concerning the Source of Life,
an awareness that has been passed down
from one generation to the next
forming the foundation of our lives and
insuring our fulfillment.
We feel appreciative
and we recount with psalm-songs
our lives which have been committed
to the hands of Eternity,
our souls entrusted to the Holy One of Being.
And we are thankful for those miracles,
those wonders,
and those welcome surprises provided us at all times,
evening, morning, or noon.
Goodness and compassion have never been denied.
Mercy and caring never cease when hope eternally
exists.
So, for everything
may this Reality be forever blessed and exalted.
May all the sons and daughters of the covenant
be inscribed for a good life.
Let all the living sincerely be thankful to God
for liberating and helping us. Selah!
Blessed is the Ineffable,
The "Good" is also Your name.
And so we are grateful.

מוֹדִים אֲנַחְנוּ לָךְ
שָׁאַתָּה הוּא יהוה אֱלֹהֵינוּ
וֵאלֹהֵי אֲבוֹתֵינוּ לְעוֹלָם וָעֶד,
צוּר חַיֵּינוּ, מָגֵן יִשְׁעֵנוּ
אַתָּה הוּא לְדוֹר וָדוֹר.
נוֹדֶה לְּךָ וּנְסַפֵּר תְּהִלָּתֶךָ
עַל חַיֵּינוּ הַמְּסוּרִים בְּיָדֶךָ,
וְעַל נִשְׁמוֹתֵינוּ הַפְּקוּדוֹת לָךְ.
וְעַל נִסֶּיךָ שֶׁבְּכָל יוֹם עִמָּנוּ,
וְעַל נִפְלְאוֹתֶיךָ וְטוֹבוֹתֶיךָ
שֶׁבְּכָל עֵת, עֶרֶב וָבֹקֶר וְצָהֳרָיִם.
הַטּוֹב כִּי לֹא כָלוּ רַחֲמֶיךָ,
וְהַמְרַחֵם כִּי לֹא תַמּוּ חֲסָדֶיךָ
מֵעוֹלָם קִוִּינוּ לָךְ.
וְעַל כֻּלָּם יִתְבָּרַךְ וְיִתְרוֹמַם
שִׁמְךָ מַלְכֵּנוּ תָּמִיד לְעוֹלָם וָעֶד.
וּכְתוֹב לְחַיִּים טוֹבִים
כָּל בְּנֵי בְרִיתֶךָ.
וְכֹל הַחַיִּים יוֹדוּךָ סֶּלָה וִיהַלְלוּ אֶת שִׁמְךָ
בֶּאֱמֶת הָאֵל יְשׁוּעָתֵנוּ וְעֶזְרָתֵנוּ סֶלָה.
בָּרוּךְ אַתָּה יהוה
הַטּוֹב שִׁמְךָ וּלְךָ נָאֶה לְהוֹדוֹת.

(On Yom Kippur continue with Vidui)

Shakharit – The Morning Service

We invite our Creator, the God of our ancestors
to bless us with the threefold blessing
written in the Torah by Moshe's hand
and spoken from the mouth of Aaron
and the holy kohanim, saying:

אֱלֹהֵינוּ וֵאלֹהֵי אֲבוֹתֵינוּ, בָּרְכֵנוּ
בַּבְּרָכָה הַמְשֻׁלֶּשֶׁת בַּתּוֹרָה הַכְּתוּבָה עַל
יְדֵי מֹשֶׁה עַבְדֶּךָ, הָאֲמוּרָה מִפִּי אַהֲרֹן
וּבָנָיו כֹּהֲנִים עַם קְדוֹשֶׁךָ, כָּאָמוּר.

Yivarekh'kha Adonai v'Yishm'rekha.
May the Eternal bless you and protect you.

יְבָרֶכְךָ יהוה וְיִשְׁמְרֶךָ.

Yaer Adonai Panav Eylekha viKhuneka.
May the Source of Being illumine you and be
gracious unto you.

יָאֵר יהוה פָּנָיו אֵלֶיךָ וִיחֻנֶּךָּ.

*Yisa Adonai Panav Eylekha v'Yasem
Lakh(a)(em) Shalom.*
May the Holy One of Being bestow the holy
countenance upon you and grant you shalom, peace.

יִשָּׂא יהוה פָּנָיו אֵלֶיךָ וְיָשֵׂם
לְךָ שָׁלוֹם.

Keyn Y'hi Ratzon.
So let it be.

כֵּן יְהִי רָצוֹן.

Sim Shalom Tovah u'Vrakha
Kheyn vaKhesed v'Rakhamim
Aleynu v'Al Kol Yisrael, v'Al Kol Yisrael Amekha.
May we be granted wholeness, goodness, and blessing,
favor, kindness and compassion.

שִׂים שָׁלוֹם טוֹבָה וּבְרָכָה,
חֵן וָחֶסֶד וְרַחֲמִים,
עָלֵינוּ וְעַל כָּל יִשְׂרָאֵל עַמֶּךָ.

Barkheynu Avinu Kulanu k'Ekhad b'Ohr Panekha.
May we be blessed with the light of Your Presence.
By this light we are given the teaching of life,
lovingkindness, justice, blessedness,
compassion, life and wholeness.
And may we, the people of Israel,
be worthy in Your sight, to be blessed at all times
and at every moment with wholeness, with Shalom.

בָּרְכֵנוּ אָבִינוּ כֻּלָנוּ כְּאֶחָד בְּאוֹר פָּנֶיךָ,
כִּי בְאוֹר פָּנֶיךָ נָתַתָּ לָנוּ, יהוה אֱלֹהֵינוּ,
תּוֹרַת חַיִּים וְאַהֲבַת חֶסֶד,
וּצְדָקָה וּבְרָכָה וְרַחֲמִים וְחַיִּים וְשָׁלוֹם.
וְטוֹב בְּעֵינֶיךָ לְבָרֵךְ אֶת עַמְּךָ יִשְׂרָאֵל
בְּכָל עֵת וּבְכָל שָׁעָה בִּשְׁלוֹמֶךָ.

B'Sefer Khayim Brakhah v'Shalom
u'Farnasah Tovah.
Nizakher v'Nikatev l'Fanekha
Anakhnu v'Khol Amkhah.
Anakhnu v'Khol Amkhah Beyt Yisrael
l'Khayim Tovim, l'Khayim Tovim u'l'Shalom
b'Sefer Khayim.
May we be remembered and inscribed
in the Book of Life, of Blessing,
of Peace and Abundant Maintenance.
May there be good life and harmony for all
of the House of Israel.

בְּסֵפֶר חַיִּים בְּרָכָה וְשָׁלוֹם
וּפַרְנָסָה טוֹבָה
נִזָּכֵר וְנִכָּתֵב לְפָנֶיךָ
אֲנַחְנוּ וְכָל עַמְּךָ בֵּית יִשְׂרָאֵל
לְחַיִּים טוֹבִים וּלְשָׁלוֹם.

Barukh Atah Adonai, Oseh haShalom.
Blessed is the Eternal, maker of the peace.

בָּרוּךְ אַתָּה יהוה עוֹשֶׂה הַשָּׁלוֹם.

Oseh Shalom Bimromav
Hu Yaaseh Shalom Aleynu
v'Al Kol Yisrael v'Al Kol Yoshvey Teyvel.
V'Imru: Ameyn.
May the One making harmony in the
heavenly spheres help us to make peace here,
for all Israel and for all humankind.
And let us say. Amen.

עוֹשֶׂה שָׁלוֹם בִּמְרוֹמָיו
הוּא יַעֲשֶׂה שָׁלוֹם עָלֵינוּ
וְעַל כָּל יִשְׂרָאֵל וְעַל כָּל יוֹשְׁבֵי תֵבֵל
וְאִמְרוּ אָמֵן.

AVINU MALKEYNU

We have strayed off the path, missed the mark.

We address the Parent of the Universe,
the Majesty of Life. There is no other.

We pray for renewal this year,
that harsh decrees be annulled,
that the plans of our enemies be thwarted,
every oppressor and adversary be gone,
that pestilence, sword, guns, famine, captivity,
and destruction be removed from our midst.

Through teshuvah,
personal and social change,
we hope for a return to the Sacred.

We ask for complete healing for the sick,
We ask that our guilt be removed,
that we be remembered,
that we be inscribed in the Book of Life,
inscribed in the Book of Liberation and Wholeness,
in the Book of Maintenance and Sustenance,
in the Book of Merits,
in the Book of Pardon and Forgiveness.

We must return, do teshuvah, for the sake of those
slaughtered for affirming Your Oneness.
We must do it for the sake of those who
went through fire and water
for the sanctification of God,
for proclaiming the Unity of Creation.

For Your sake, for their sake, if not for ours alone.

אָבִינוּ מַלְכֵּנוּ

אָבִינוּ מַלְכֵּנוּ
חָטָאנוּ לְפָנֶיךָ.

אָבִינוּ מַלְכֵּנוּ
אֵין לָנוּ מֶלֶךְ אֶלָּא אָתָּה.

אָבִינוּ מַלְכֵּנוּ
עֲשֵׂה עִמָּנוּ לְמַעַן שְׁמֶךָ.

אָבִינוּ מַלְכֵּנוּ
חַדֵּשׁ עָלֵינוּ שָׁנָה טוֹבָה.

אָבִינוּ מַלְכֵּנוּ
בַּטֵּל מֵעָלֵינוּ כָּל גְּזֵרוֹת קָשׁוֹת.

אָבִינוּ מַלְכֵּנוּ
בַּטֵּל מַחְשְׁבוֹת שׂוֹנְאֵינוּ.

אָבִינוּ מַלְכֵּנוּ
הָפֵר עֲצַת אוֹיְבֵינוּ.

אָבִינוּ מַלְכֵּנוּ
כַּלֵּה כָּל צַר וּמַשְׂטִין מֵעָלֵינוּ.

אָבִינוּ מַלְכֵּנוּ
סְתֹם פִּיוֹת מַשְׂטִינֵנוּ וּמְקַטְרִיגֵנוּ.

אָבִינוּ מַלְכֵּנוּ
כַּלֵּה דֶּבֶר וְחֶרֶב וְרָעָב וּשְׁבִי
וּמַשְׁחִית מִבְּנֵי בְרִיתֶךָ.

אָבִינוּ מַלְכֵּנוּ
הַחֲזִירֵנוּ בִּתְשׁוּבָה שְׁלֵמָה לְפָנֶיךָ.

אָבִינוּ מַלְכֵּנוּ
שְׁלַח רְפוּאָה שְׁלֵמָה לְחוֹלֵי עַמֶּךָ.

Though we have been lacking in deeds,
in steps to improve relationships, with each other,
with this planet, with our Parent,
please answer us, and help us become whole.

Avinu Malkeynu,
Khaneynu vaAneynu Ki Eyn Banu Ma'asim.
Asey Imanu Tzedakah vaKhesed, v'Hoshi-eynu.

Avinu Imeynu, Khaneynu vaAneynu
Ki Eyn Banu Ma'asim.
Na'aseh Tzedakah vaKhesed,
v'Hoshi-eynu.
(adaptation)

Number My Days This Way

O God,
Number my days this way:

Days of strength to lie,
if the truth brings torment.
Days of weakness,
if strength gives rise to suffering.
Days of noise,
if silence is the cause of loneliness.
And
Nights of disconcerting dreams
if I turn smug to the taste of hunger.

Pursue me,
discomfort me,
Destroy my own complacency
with paradox and contradiction.

Remind me I am Yours.

Danny Siegel

אָבִינוּ מַלְכֵּנוּ
קְרַע רוֹעַ גְּזַר דִּינֵנוּ.

אָבִינוּ מַלְכֵּנוּ
זָכְרֵנוּ בְּזִכְרוֹן טוֹב לְפָנֶיךָ.

אָבִינוּ מַלְכֵּנוּ
כָּתְבֵנוּ בְּסֵפֶר חַיִּים טוֹבִים

אָבִינוּ מַלְכֵּנוּ
כָּתְבֵנוּ בְּסֵפֶר גְּאֻלָּה וִישׁוּעָה.

אָבִינוּ מַלְכֵּנוּ
כָּתְבֵנוּ בְּסֵפֶר פַּרְנָסָה וְכַלְכָּלָה.

אָבִינוּ מַלְכֵּנוּ
כָּתְבֵנוּ בְּסֵפֶר זְכִיּוֹת.

אָבִינוּ מַלְכֵּנוּ
כָּתְבֵנוּ בְּסֵפֶר סְלִיחָה וּמְחִילָה.

אָבִינוּ מַלְכֵּנוּ
עֲשֵׂה לְמַעַן טְבוּחִים עַל יְחוּדֶךָ.

אָבִינוּ מַלְכֵּנוּ
עֲשֵׂה לְמַעַן בָּאֵי בָאֵשׁ וּבַמַּיִם
עַל קִדּוּשׁ שְׁמֶךָ.

אָבִינוּ מַלְכֵּנוּ
חָנֵּנוּ וַעֲנֵנוּ,
כִּי אֵין בָּנוּ מַעֲשִׂים,
עֲשֵׂה עִמָּנוּ צְדָקָה וָחֶסֶד
וְהוֹשִׁיעֵנוּ.

אָבִינוּ אִמֵּנוּ
חָנֵּנוּ וַעֲנֵנוּ,
כִּי אֵין בָּנוּ מַעֲשִׂים,
נַעֲשֶׂה צְדָקָה וָחֶסֶד
וְהוֹשִׁיעֵנוּ.

TORAH SERVICE

סדר הוצאת התורה

There is nothing comparable to Adonai,
to the works of creation.
The majesty of Existence is Eternal,
to be revered by all the generations.

אֵין כָּמוֹךָ בָאֱלֹהִים אֲדֹנָי וְאֵין כְּמַעֲשֶׂיךָ.
מַלְכוּתְךָ מַלְכוּת כָּל־עֹלָמִים
וּמֶמְשַׁלְתְּךָ בְּכָל־דֹּר וָדֹר.

May we become strong in acknowledging the
Source of All.
May we be deserving of blessing and peace.

יהוה מֶלֶךְ יהוה מָלָךְ יהוה יִמְלֹךְ
לְעֹלָם וָעֶד. יהוה עֹז לְעַמּוֹ יִתֵּן
יהוה יְבָרֵךְ אֶת־עַמּוֹ בַשָּׁלוֹם.

We ask for compassion and reconciliation for Zion,
that the vision of Yerushalayim, the City of Peace,
be restored.
We trust in the redemptive process and the most
exalted Guide of All Worlds.

אֵל הָרַחֲמִים הֵיטִיבָה בִרְצוֹנְךָ אֶת־צִיּוֹן
תִּבְנֶה חוֹמוֹת יְרוּשָׁלָיִם.
כִּי בְךָ לְבַד בָּטָחְנוּ מֶלֶךְ אֵל רָם וְנִשָּׂא
אֲדוֹן עוֹלָמִים.

(The Ark is opened)
Ki mi'Tzion Tetzey Torah,
u'D'var Adonai miYerushalayim.
For out of Zion shall go forth the Teaching
and the word of the Eternal from Jerusalem.

(The Ark is opened)

כִּי מִצִּיּוֹן תֵּצֵא תוֹרָה
וּדְבַר יהוה מִירוּשָׁלָיִם.

Barukh Shenatan Torah l'Amo Yisrael biKdushato.
Praised is the One who with holiness gave Torah to
the people Israel.

בָּרוּךְ שֶׁנָּתַן תּוֹרָה
לְעַמּוֹ יִשְׂרָאֵל בִּקְדֻשָּׁתוֹ.

(Omitted on Shabbat)
Adonai Adonai Eyl Rakhum v'Khanun
Erekh Apayim v'Rav Khesed beh'Emet,
Notzer Khesed laAlafim Nosey Avon vaFesha
v'Khatah v'Nakey.

(Omitted on Shabbat)

יהוה יהוה אֵל רַחוּם וְחַנּוּן,
אֶרֶךְ אַפַּיִם וְרַב חֶסֶד וֶאֱמֶת.
נֹצֵר חֶסֶד לָאֲלָפִים נֹשֵׂא עָוֹן וָפֶשַׁע
וְחַטָּאָה, וְנַקֵּה.

Existence, that which is Eternal, is compassionate,
patient, filled with kindness and trust,
assuring love for a thousand generations,
forgiving of wrongdoing and able to pardon.

Y'hiyu l'Ratzon Imrey Fi v'Hegyon Libi l'Fanekha,
Adonai Tzuri v'Goali.
May the words of my mouth
and the meditation of my heart
be acceptable to You, my Rock and my Redeemer.

יִהְיוּ לְרָצוֹן אִמְרֵי־פִי וְהֶגְיוֹן לִבִּי לְפָנֶיךָ,
יהוה צוּרִי וְגוֹאֲלִי.

VaAni Tefilati l'Kha Adonai Et Ratzon, Elohim
b'Rav Khasdekha Aneyni beh'Emet Yishekha.
With much lovingkindness and acceptance
in truth answer me.

וַאֲנִי תְפִלָּתִי לְךָ יהוה עֵת רָצוֹן, אֱלֹהִים
בְּרָב־חַסְדֶּךָ עֲנֵנִי בֶּאֱמֶת יִשְׁעֶךָ.

(Leader, then congregation)
Shma Yisrael Adonai Eloheynu Adonai Ekhad.
Listen Israel, the Ineffable, Our God, is One.

(Leader, then congregation)
שְׁמַע יִשְׂרָאֵל יהוה אֱלֹהֵינוּ
יהוה אֶחָד.

Ekhad Eloheynu Gadol Adoneynu Kadosh
v'Norah Shmo.
Our God is One, Our Guiding Force is Great,
and God's Presence revered.

אֶחָד אֱלֹהֵינוּ גָּדוֹל אֲדוֹנֵנוּ קָדוֹשׁ
וְנוֹרָא שְׁמוֹ.

Gadlu LAdonai Iti u-N'rom'ma Shmo Yakhdav.
Celebrate the greatness of the Source of Being with
me.

גַּדְּלוּ לַיהוה אִתִּי וּנְרוֹמְמָה שְׁמוֹ יַחְדָּו.

L'Kha Adonai haG'dula v'haG'vurah
v'haTiferet v'haNeytzakh v'haHod,
Ki Khol baShamayim u'vaAretz.
L'Kha Adonai haMam'lakha
v'haMitnasey l'Khol l'Rosh.
Yours is the greatness, the might, the honor,
the victory, and the beauty.
For everything in heaven and on earth is Yours.
Your majesty is above all.
Ro'm'mu Adonai Eloheynu
v'Histakhavu l'Har Kawdsho
Ki Kadosh Adonai Eloheynu.
Praise the Mystery of Creation,
and be humbled before the Sacred Heights,
for the Eternal, our Life Force, is Sacred.

לְךָ יהוה הַגְּדֻלָּה וְהַגְּבוּרָה
וְהַתִּפְאֶרֶת וְהַנֵּצַח וְהַהוֹד,
כִּי כֹל בַּשָּׁמַיִם וּבָאָרֶץ.
לְךָ יהוה הַמַּמְלָכָה
וְהַמִּתְנַשֵּׂא לְכֹל לְרֹאשׁ.
רוֹמְמוּ יהוה אֱלֹהֵינוּ
וְהִשְׁתַּחֲווּ לַהֲדוֹם רַגְלָיו
קָדוֹשׁ הוּא.
רוֹמְמוּ יהוה אֱלֹהֵינוּ
וְהִשְׁתַּחֲווּ לְהַר קָדְשׁוֹ
כִּי קָדוֹשׁ יהוה אֱלֹהֵינוּ.

Shakharit – The Morning Service

Blessings for those called to the Torah

Before the reading

(Reader)
Barkhu Et Adonai HaMvorakh

(All)
Barukh Adonai HaMvorakh L'Olam Vaed

(Reader)
Barukh Atah Adonai
Eloheynu Melekh haOlam (Khayei Olam)
Asher Keravtanu laAvodato.
V'Natan Lanu et Torato.
Barukh Atah Adonai, Noteyn HaTorah.

Blessed are You, Eternal Presence, Our God,
Life of the universe,
who has drawn us near to Your service
and who has given us the Torah of truth.
Blessed are You, Adonai, giving the Torah.

(Reader)
בָּרְכוּ אֶת יהוה הַמְבֹרָךְ

(All)
בָּרוּךְ יהוה הַמְבֹרָךְ לְעוֹלָם וָעֶד.

(Reader)
בָּרוּךְ אַתָּה יהוה
אֱלֹהֵינוּ מֶלֶךְ הָעוֹלָם (חַיֵּי עוֹלָם).
אֲשֶׁר קֵרְבְתָנוּ לַעֲבוֹדָתוֹ.
וְנָתַן לָנוּ אֶת תּוֹרָתוֹ.
בָּרוּךְ אַתָּה יהוה נוֹתֵן הַתּוֹרָה.

After the reading

Barukh Atah Adonai
Eloheynu Melekh (Khayei) Olam
Asher Natan Lanu Torah Emet
v'Khayei Olam Nata b'Tokheynu.
Barukh Atah Adonai, Noteyn HaTorah.

Blessed are You, the Eternal our God,
Life of the universe,
who has implanted life within us.
Blessed are You, Eternal Presence, giving the Torah.

בָּרוּךְ אַתָּה יהוה
אֱלֹהֵינוּ מֶלֶךְ (חַיֵּי) עוֹלָם
אֲשֶׁר נָתַן לָנוּ תּוֹרַת אֱמֶת
וְחַיֵּי עוֹלָם נָטַע בְּתוֹכֵנוּ.
בָּרוּךְ אַתָּה יהוה נוֹתֵן הַתּוֹרָה.

The Sounding of the Shofar

B'Khotzrot v'Kol Shofar
Hari'u Lifney haMelekh Adonai.
With trumpets and the shofar sound, call out
in the presence of the Majesty of the Eternal Presence.

Psalm 48:6

בְּחַצֹצְרוֹת וְקוֹל שׁוֹפָר
הָרִיעוּ לִפְנֵי הַמֶּלֶךְ יהוה.

Min haMeytzar Karati Yah
Anani baMerkhav Yah.
From constrainment I call to Yah
who answers me with the breath of the Spirit.

Psalm 118:5

מִן הַמֵּצַר קָרָאתִי יָהּ
עָנָנִי בַמֶּרְחָב יָהּ.

Alah Elohim biTruah
Adonai b'Kol Shofar.
God has ascended with a blast,
the Breath of Life with the shofar sound.

Psalm 47:6

עָלָה אֱלֹהִים בִּתְרוּעָה
יהוה בְּקוֹל שׁוֹפָר.

Barukh Atah Adonai Eloheynu Khayei Olam
Asher Kid'shanu b'Mitzvotav v'Tzivanu
liShmoah Kol Shofar.
Blessed are You, Source of Being, Life of the
Universe, sanctifying us through the commandments
and instructing us to hear the voice of the shofar.

בָּרוּךְ אַתָּה יהוה אֱלֹהֵינוּ חַיֵּי עוֹלָם
אֲשֶׁר קִדְּשָׁנוּ בְּמִצְוֹתָיו וְצִוָּנוּ
לִשְׁמֹעַ קוֹל שׁוֹפָר.

Barukh Atah Adonai Eloheynu Khayei Olam
Shehekhehyanu v'Kiy'manu v'Higi-anu laZman haZeh.
Blessed are You, Eternal One, Life of the Universe,
giving us life, sustaining us, and bringing us to reach
this season.

בָּרוּךְ אַתָּה יהוה אֱלֹהֵינוּ חַיֵּי עוֹלָם
שֶׁהֶחֱיָנוּ וְקִיְּמָנוּ וְהִגִּיעָנוּ לַזְּמַן הַזֶּה.

The Sounds

Tekiah Shevarim Teruah Tekiah
Tekiah Shevarim Teruah Tekiah
Tekiah Shevarim Teruah Tekiah

תְּקִיעָה שְׁבָרִים תְּרוּעָה תְּקִיעָה
תְּקִיעָה שְׁבָרִים תְּרוּעָה תְּקִיעָה
תְּקִיעָה שְׁבָרִים תְּרוּעָה תְּקִיעָה

Tekiah Shevarim Tekiah
Tekiah Shevarim Tekiah
Tekiah Shevarim Tekiah

תְּקִיעָה שְׁבָרִים תְּקִיעָה
תְּקִיעָה שְׁבָרִים תְּקִיעָה
תְּקִיעָה שְׁבָרִים תְּקִיעָה

Tekiah Teruah Tekiah
Tekiah Teruah Tekiah
Tekiah Teruah Tekiah G'Dolah

תְּקִיעָה תְּרוּעָה תְּקִיעָה
תְּקִיעָה תְּרוּעָה תְּקִיעָה
תְּקִיעָה תְּרוּעָה תְּקִיעָה גְדוֹלָה

Ashrey haAm Yodey Teruah.
Adonai b'Ohr Panekha yaHaleykhun.
The people who understand the call of the teruah are
fortunate because they walk in the light of
Your Presence.

אַשְׁרֵי הָעָם יֹדְעֵי תְרוּעָה.
יהוה בְּאוֹר פָּנֶיךָ יְהַלֵּכוּן.

Psalm 89:16

The Eternal is just in all ways,
loving the works of creation.
All who address the Eternal presence sincerely
are drawn near to the One.

צַדִּיק יהוה בְּכָל־דְּרָכָיו
וְחָסִיד בְּכָל־מַעֲשָׂיו.
קָרוֹב יהוה לְכָל־קֹרְאָיו
לְכֹל אֲשֶׁר יִקְרָאֻהוּ בֶאֱמֶת.

The will of those who are in awe of God
will be fulfilled, their cry heard.
And they will be freed.

רְצוֹן יְרֵאָיו יַעֲשֶׂה
וְאֶת שַׁוְעָתָם יִשְׁמַע וְיוֹשִׁיעֵם.

The Eternal One guards the lovers of creation
and will destroy wickedness.

שׁוֹמֵר יהוה אֶת כָּל אֹהֲבָיו,
וְאֵת כָּל הָרְשָׁעִים יַשְׁמִיד.

My mouth will utter praise to the Source of Existence,
and all creatures will bless this sacred presence
forever.

תְּהִלַּת יהוה יְדַבֶּר פִּי
וִיבָרֵךְ כָּל בָּשָׂר שֵׁם קָדְשׁוֹ
לְעוֹלָם וָעֶד.
וַאֲנַחְנוּ נְבָרֵךְ יָה מֵעַתָּה וְעַד עוֹלָם.
הַלְלוּיָהּ.

Va-Anakhnu n'Varekh Yah meyAtah v'Ad Olam.
Let us bless Yah from this time forth.
HalleluYah.

Psalm 145:17-22

Returning the Torah to the Ark

Yehal'lu Et Shem Adonai Ki Nisgav Sh'mo l'Vado.
The people will praise the Name, the Ineffable Life
Force, alone exalted.

יְהַלְלוּ אֶת־שֵׁם יהוה
כִּי־נִשְׂגָּב שְׁמוֹ לְבַדּוֹ.

Hodu Al Eretz v'Shamayim
vaYarem Keren l'Amo.
Tehilah l'Khol Khasidav
Livney Yisrael Am k'Rovo.
Halleluyah, Halleluyah.

הוֹדוֹ עַל־אֶרֶץ וְשָׁמָיִם
וַיָּרֶם קֶרֶן לְעַמּוֹ.
תְּהִלָּה לְכָל־חֲסִידָיו
לִבְנֵי יִשְׂרָאֵל עַם קְרֹבוֹ.
הַלְלוּיָהּ.

Give thanks to all of Creation, that we have been
enlightened and raised up. Praise to the people of
kindness among the children of Israel, a people drawn
near unto the Eternal One. Halleluyah!

Etz Khayim Hi laMakhazikim Bah
v'Tomkheha m'Ushar.
D'Rakheha Darkhey Noam,
v'Khol n'Tivoteha Shalom.
HaShiveynu Adonai, Eylekha v'Nashuva,
Khadesh Yameynu k'Kedem.

עֵץ חַיִּים הִיא לַמַּחֲזִיקִים בָּהּ,
וְתוֹמְכֶיהָ מְאֻשָּׁר.
דְּרָכֶיהָ דַּרְכֵי נֹעַם
וְכָל נְתִיבוֹתֶיהָ שָׁלוֹם.
הֲשִׁיבֵנוּ יהוה אֵלֶיךָ וְנָשׁוּבָה,
חַדֵּשׁ יָמֵינוּ כְּקֶדֶם.

The Torah is a tree of life to those who grasp it.
Those who support it are fortunate.
Its ways are ways of pleasantness
and all its paths lead toward peace.
May we return to the sense of the Eternal Presence.
Yes, we will return.
May our lives be renewed as in ancient times.

Khatzi Kaddish

חצי קדיש

Yitgadal v'Yitkadash Shmey Rabah,
יִתְגַּדַּל וְיִתְקַדַּשׁ שְׁמֵהּ רַבָּא.

b'Alma Divra Khirutey
בְּעָלְמָה דִי בְרָא כִרְעוּתֵהּ.

v'Yamlikh Malkutey
וְיַמְלִיךְ מַלְכוּתֵהּ

b'Khayeykhon u'v'Yomeykhon u'v'Khayey
בְּחַיֵּיכוֹן וּבְיוֹמֵיכוֹן וּבְחַיֵּי

d'Khol Beyt Yisrael baAgalah
דְּכָל בֵּית יִשְׂרָאֵל בַּעֲגָלָא

u'viZman Kariv,
וּבִזְמַן קָרִיב.

v'Imru: Ameyn.
וְאִמְרוּ אָמֵן.

Y'hey Shmey Rabah m'Varakh
יְהֵא שְׁמֵהּ רַבָּה מְבָרַךְ

l'Alam u'l'Almey Almaya.
לְעָלַם וּלְעָלְמֵי עַלְמַיָּא.

Yitbarakh v'Yishtabakh v'Yitpaar v'Yitromam
יִתְבָּרַךְ וְיִשְׁתַּבַּח וְיִתְפָּאַר וְיִתְרוֹמַם

v'Yitnasey v'Yithadar v'Yitaleh v'Yithalal
וְיִתְנַשֵּׂא וְיִתְהַדָּר וְיִתְעַלֶּה וְיִתְהַלָּל

Shmey d'Kud'sha. Brikh Hu.
שְׁמֵהּ דְּקֻדְשָׁא. בְּרִיךְ הוּא.

L'Eyla u'l'Eyla miKol Birkhata v'Shirata
לְעֵלָּא (וּלְעֵלָּא) מִכָּל בִּרְכָתָא וְשִׁירָתָא

Tush'b'khata v'Nekhemata daAmiran b'Alma,
תֻּשְׁבְּחָתָא וְנֶחֱמָתָא דַּאֲמִירָן בְּעָלְמָא.

v'Imru: Ameyn.
וְאִמְרוּ אָמֵן.

May the Creator's great Name grow and be sanctified in a cosmos formed according to an incomprehensible Will.

May the Unity of Creation be established in your lifetime and throughout your days, and during the lifetime of the entire House of Yisrael, soon.

So may we acknowledge, honor, celebrate, and sing to the Sacred Source, though transcendent and beyond human songs and blessing.

And join in saying, amen.

Artwork: Ben Shahn, Second Alphabet

מוסף
Musaf

הַנְנִי

תְּפִלָּה לִשְׁלִיחַ צִבּוּר

הִנְנִי הֶעָנִי מִמַּעַשׂ. נִרְעַשׁ וְנִפְחָד מִפַּחַד יוֹשֵׁב
תְּהִלּוֹת יִשְׂרָאֵל. בָּאתִי לַעֲמֹד וּלְהִתְחַנֵּן
לְפָנֶיךָ עַל עַמְּךָ יִשְׂרָאֵל אֲשֶׁר שְׁלָחוּנִי

Prayer said by the cantor before begining service.

MUSAF

מוּסָף

U'N'taneh Tokef K'dushah HaYom
We affirm the holiness of this awefilled
and threatening day
when the Majesty of Creation addresses us,
when we are reminded
that the foundations of Your throne
are lovingkindness and truth.
It is true that there is a judgment,
a knowing and profound awareness,
that is written, sealed, recorded
and remembered.
All is revealed in the Book of Remembrance
where the signature of humanity is reviewed.

וּנְתַנֶּה תֹּקֶף קְדֻשַּׁת הַיּוֹם
כִּי הוּא נוֹרָא וְאָיוֹם
וּבוֹ תִנָּשֵׂא מַלְכוּתֶךָ
וְיִכּוֹן בְּחֶסֶד כִּסְאֶךָ
וְתֵשֵׁב עָלָיו בֶּאֱמֶת.
אֱמֶת כִּי אַתָּה הוּא דַיָּן
וּמוֹכִיחַ וְיוֹדֵעַ וָעֵד
וְכוֹתֵב וְחוֹתֵם וְסוֹפֵר וּמוֹנֶה
וְתִזְכּוֹר כָּל הַנִּשְׁכָּחוֹת.
וְתִפְתַּח אֶת סֵפֶר הַזִּכְרוֹנוֹת
וּמֵאֵלָיו יִקָּרֵא וְחוֹתָם
יַד כָּל אָדָם בּוֹ.

The great shofar is sounded!
... a still, small voice is heard.
Even the angels,
those messengers of the spirit,
are anxious.
In fear and trembling they cry out:
"The Day of Judgment has arrived!"
Even the heavenly forces feel they are judged
and sense that they are not without fault.
On this day we pass before the Sacred,
one by one, like a flock of sheep.
As a shepherd counts sheep,
making each of them pass under the staff,
so You review every living being,
measuring the years
and decreeing the destiny of every creature.

וּבְשׁוֹפָר גָּדוֹל יִתָּקַע!
... וְקוֹל דְּמָמָה דַקָּה יִשָּׁמַע.
וּמַלְאָכִים יֵחָפֵזוּן
וְחִיל וּרְעָדָה יֹאחֵזוּן.
וְיֹאמְרוּ הִנֵּה יוֹם הַדִּין
לִפְקוֹד עַל צְבָא מָרוֹם בַּדִּין.
כִּי לֹא יִזְכּוּ בְעֵינֶיךָ בַּדִּין.
וְכָל בָּאֵי עוֹלָם תַּעֲבִיר לְפָנֶיךָ
כִּבְנֵי מָרוֹן. כְּבַקָּרַת רוֹעֶה עֶדְרוֹ
מַעֲבִיר צֹאנוֹ תַּחַת שִׁבְטוֹ,
כֵּן תַּעֲבִיר וְתִסְפּוֹר וְתִמְנֶה.
וְתִפְקוֹד נֶפֶשׁ כָּל חַי
וְתַחְתּוֹךְ קִצְבָה לְכָל בְּרִיָּה
וְתִכְתּוֹב אֶת גְּזַר דִּינָם.

B'Rosh HaShanah Yikateyvun
u'v'Yom Tzom Kippur Yekhateymun.
On Rosh HaShanah it is written
and on Yom Kippur it is sealed.

בְּרֹאשׁ הַשָּׁנָה יִכָּתֵבוּן
וּבְיוֹם צוֹם כִּפּוּר יֵחָתֵמוּן.

How many will pass away
and how many will be born,
who will live and who will die,
who will come to a timely end,
and who to an untimely end,
who will perish by fire,
who by the sword, and who by the beast,
who by hunger, and who by thirst,
who by earthquake, and who by plague,
who by strangling, and who by stoning,
who will be at rest, and who will wander aimlessly,
who will feel secure, and who will be confused,
who will be tranquil, and who will be tormented,
who will become wealthy, and who will become poor,
who will be in a low state, and who will be uplifted.

כַּמָּה יַעַבְרוּן,
וְכַמָּה יִבָּרֵאוּן.
מִי יִחְיֶה, וּמִי יָמוּת.
מִי בְקִצּוֹ, וּמִי לֹא בְקִצּוֹ.
מִי בָאֵשׁ, וּמִי בַמַּיִם.
מִי בַחֶרֶב, וּמִי בַחַיָּה.
מִי בָרָעָב, וּמִי בַצָּמָא.
מִי בָרַעַשׁ, וּמִי בַמַּגֵּפָה.
מִי בַחֲנִיקָה, וּמִי בִסְקִילָה.
מִי יָנוּחַ, וּמִי יָנוּעַ.
מִי יִשָּׁקֵט, וּמִי יִטָּרֵף.
מִי יִשָּׁלֵו, וּמִי יִתְיַסָּר.
מִי יֵעָנִי, וּמִי יֵעָשֵׁר.
מִי יִשָּׁפֵל, וּמִי יָרוּם.

How can life's severity be eased? Through

וּתְשׁוּבָה וּתְפִלָּה וּצְדָקָה
מַעֲבִירִין אֶת רוֹעַ הַגְּזֵרָה.

Teshuvah

Looking within ourselves, changing what can be changed,
repairing what can be repaired, reconciling what can be reconciled,
letting go.

Tefilah

Developing our awareness of the Source of all life by knowing the
blessings of life and sharing those blessings with each other,
asking for forgiveness, proclaiming our aspirations for wholeness,
singing when it's right to sing, crying when we need to cry,
and reflecting regularly.

Tzedakah

Doing acts of justice and lovingkindness towards others
and all of life on this planet.

Each of us originates from dust
and dust is our end.
Each of us is as a shattered urn,
grass that must wither,
a flower that will fade,
a shadow moving on, a cloud passing by,
a particle of dust
floating in the wind,
a dream
soon forgotten.
Only the Eternal is everlasting.

אָדָם יְסוֹדוֹ מֵעָפָר וְסוֹפוֹ לֶעָפָר.
בְּנַפְשׁוֹ יָבִיא לַחְמוֹ.
מָשׁוּל כְּחֶרֶס הַנִּשְׁבָּר.
כְּחָצִיר יָבֵשׁ,
וּכְצִיץ נוֹבֵל,
כְּצֵל עוֹבֵר,
וּכְעָנָן כָּלָה,
וּכְרוּחַ נוֹשָׁבֶת,
וּכְאָבָק פּוֹרֵחַ, וְכַחֲלוֹם יָעוּף.
וְאַתָּה הוּא מֶלֶךְ אֵל חַי וְקַיָּם.

I close my eyes only for a moment, and the moment's gone.
All my dreams pass before my eyes, a curiosity.

Same old song. Just a drop of water in the endless sea.
All we do crumbles to the ground though we refuse to see.

Dust in the wind. All we are is dust in the wind.

Don't hang on. Nothing lasts forever but the earth and sky.
It slips away. All your money won't another minute buy.

Dust in the wind. All we are is dust in the wind.

Kerry Livgren

Eyl Khai v'Kayam Oseh Shamayim v'Et haAretz.
Eylekha, Esah Eynai El Heharim.
Atah Mori, Eyl Khai, Eyl Khai v'Kayam.

אֵל חַי וְקַיָּם עֹשֶׂה שָׁמַיִם וְאֶת הָאָרֶץ.
אֵלֶיךָ, אֶשָּׂא עֵינַי אֶל הֶהָרִים.
אַתָּה מוֹרִי, אֵל חַי, אֵל חַי וְקַיָּם.

You are everlasting, Maker of heaven and earth.
Unto You, I lift up my eyes to the distant mountains.
You are my Teacher, an eternal and living God.

I lift my eyes beyond the dust and through the pain.
To the heart seeking life and justice without shame.

God's hand holds the measure of judgment
And all believe that God is trustworthy.

הָאוֹחֵז בְּיַד מִדַּת מִשְׁפָּט
וְכֹל מַאֲמִינִים שֶׁהוּא אֵל אֱמוּנָה.

God tests and searches the most hidden secrets
And all believe that God knows the innermost thoughts.

הַבּוֹחֵן וּבוֹדֵק גִּנְזֵי נִסְתָּרוֹת
וְכֹל מַאֲמִינִים שֶׁהוּא בּוֹחֵן כְּלָיוֹת.

God redeems from death and delivers from the grave.
And all believe that God is the Redeemer.

הַגּוֹאֵל מִמָּוֶת וּפוֹדֶה מִשַּׁחַת
וְכֹל מַאֲמִינִים שֶׁהוּא גוֹאֵל חָזָק.

God alone is the judge of all who come into the world.
And all believe that God is the true judge.

הַדָּן יְחִידִי לְבָאֵי עוֹלָם
וְכֹל מַאֲמִינִים שֶׁהוּא דַּיַּן אֱמֶת.

God is evenhanded. The great and the small are alike.
And all believe that God is the righteous judge.

הַשָּׁוֶה וּמַשְׁוֶה קָטֹן וְגָדוֹל
וְכֹל מַאֲמִינִים שֶׁהוּא שֹׁפֵט צֶדֶק.

God is simple and cares for the pure in heart.
And all believe that God's work is clear.

הַתָּם וּמִתַּמֵּם עִם תְּמִימִים
וְכֹל מַאֲמִינִים שֶׁהוּא תָּמִים פָּעֳלוֹ.

MALKHUYOT

מלכויות

The Life of Nature

I

Our ancestors acclaimed the God
Whose handiwork they read
In the mysterious heavens above
And in the varied scene of earth below,
In the orderly march of days and nights,
Of seasons and years,
And in the checkered fate of humankind.

Meanwhile have the vaulting skies
   dissolved;
Night reveals the limitless caverns of space,
Hidden by the light of day,
And unfolds horizonless vistas
Far beyond imagination's ken.
The mind is staggered,
Yet so regains its poise,
And peering through the boundless dark,
Orients itself anew
By the light of distant suns
Shrunk to glittering sparks.
The soul is faint,
Yet soon revives,
And learns to spell once more the
   name of God
Across the newly visioned firmament.

Lift your eyes, look up;
Who made these stars?
Marshalling them in order,
Summoning each one by name.
Isaiah 40:26

II

God is the oneness
That spans the fathomless depths of space
And the measureless eons of time,
Binding them together in acts,
As we do in thought.

God is the sameness
In the elemental substance of stars and
   planets,
Of this our earthly abode
And all that it holds.

God is the unity
Of all that is,
The uniformity of all that moves,
the rhythm of all things
And the nature of their interaction.

Binding up the Pleiades in a cluster
and loosening the chains of Orion;
Directing the signs of the Zodiac
and guiding the constellations of the Bear.
Based on Job 38:31-32

God is the mystery of life
Enkindling inert matter
With inner drive and purpose.

God is the creative flame
That transfigures lifeless substance,
Leaping into a higher realm of being,
Brightening into the radiant glow of feeling,
'Till it turns into the white fire of thought.

And though no sign of living things
Breaks the eternal silence of the spheres,
We cannot deem this earth,
This tiny speck in the infinitude,
Alone instinct with God.

By that token
Which unites the worlds in bonds of matter
Are all the worlds bound
In the bond of Life.

The Creator forms the mountains
and creates the wind,
and reveals the inner mind to humankind;
making the dawn and the darkness,
marching over the heights of earth;
The Eternal, the Unifying Force,
  is God's name.

Amos 4:13

God is in the faith
By which we overcome
The fear of loneliness, of helplessness,
Of failure and of death.

God is in the hope
Which, like a shaft of light,
Cleaves the dark abysms
Of sin, of suffering, and of despair.

God is in the love
Which creates, protects, forgives.
God is the spirit
Which broods upon the chaos humanity has
    wrought,
Disturbing its static wrongs,
And stirring into life the formless beginnings
Of the new and better world.

You are my portion,
Eternal One;
You are my share.
You will show me the way of life,
Fullness of joy is in Your presence;
Everlasting happiness You have provided.

Psalm 16:5,11

Mordecai Kaplan

Aleynu l'Shabeyakh laAdon haKol,
Lateyt G'dula, l'Yotzer b'Resheet,
v'Kid'shanu b'Mitzvotav
Orah u'K'dusha Natah b'Tokheynu.

עָלֵינוּ לְשַׁבֵּחַ לַאֲדוֹן הַכֹּל,
לָתֵת גְּדֻלָּה לְיוֹצֵר בְּרֵאשִׁית,
וְקִדְּשָׁנוּ בְּמִצְווֹתָיו
אוֹרָה וּקְדוּשָׁה נָטַע בְּתוֹכֵינוּ.

It is our duty to honor the Source of All Creation,
addressing us continually,
whose Light and Presence has been implanted within us.

VaAnakhnu Korim u'Mishtakhavim u'Modim
Lifney Melekh Malkhey haM'lakhim
HaKadosh Barukh Hu.

וַאֲנַחְנוּ כּוֹרְעִים וּמִשְׁתַּחֲוִים וּמוֹדִים,
לִפְנֵי מֶלֶךְ מַלְכֵי הַמְּלָכִים
הַקָּדוֹשׁ בָּרוּךְ הוּא.

So we bend the knee and bow the head, deeply, humbly,
before the Sacred, the Unity of all.

V'Taher Libeynu l'Avdekha beh'Emet.

וְטַהֵר לִבֵּנוּ לְעָבְדְּךָ בֶּאֱמֶת.

Cleanse our hearts to serve You with truth.

(the Shofar is sounded)
Tekiah Shevarim Teruah Tekiah

(the Shofar is sounded)
תְּקִיעָה שְׁבָרִים תְּרוּעָה תְּקִיעָה

Today the world was conceived.
Today all creatures everywhere stand in judgment,
some as children and some as servants. If we receive
consideration as children, grant us a parent's loving
compassion; if we receive consideration as slaves,
our eyes remain suspended, awaiting release, until
the judgment is brought forth as the light.

הַיּוֹם הֲרַת עוֹלָם.
הַיּוֹם יַעֲמִיד בַּמִּשְׁפָּט כָּל יְצוּרֵי
עוֹלָמִים, אִם כְּבָנִים אִם כַּעֲבָדִים.
אִם כְּבָנִים, רַחֲמֵנוּ כְּרַחֵם אָב עַל בָּנִים.
וְאִם כַּעֲבָדִים עֵינֵינוּ לְךָ תְלוּיוֹת,
עַד שֶׁתְּחָנֵּנוּ וְתוֹצִיא כָאוֹר מִשְׁפָּטֵנוּ,
אָיוֹם קָדוֹשׁ.

(omit on Shabbat)
Areshet s'Fateynu Ye'erav l'Fanekha
Eyl Rom v'Nisah.

May the expressions of our lips be pleasing to You,
the One most high, understanding, attentive, perceiving
and listening to the sounds of our shofar blasts,
accepting with compassion and needing our
acknowledgement of Creation.

(omit on Shabbat)
אֲרֶשֶׁת שְׂפָתֵינוּ יֶעֱרַב לְפָנֶיךָ
אֵל רָם וְנִשָּׂא.
מֵבִין וּמַאֲזִין מַבִּיט וּמַקְשִׁיב
לְקוֹל תְּקִיעָתֵנוּ.
וּתְקַבֵּל בְּרַחֲמִים וּבְרָצוֹן
סֵדֶר מַלְכֻיּוֹתֵנוּ.

Musaf

Trajectories of time propel our minds to those ancient days
when men and women with desert souls
explored the universe of faith
and charted on the map of life
a path on which to tread.

And when that path became obscure, a robed and mitred priest
encased that faith in cults and sacrifices
tying it to shrine and stone –
to anchor and to shelter it
when shifting tides eroded others' ways.

But when that anchor mired us in swamps of lethargy,
and dragged us down to crude, self-righteous pseudo piety,
the prophets blasted us into the outer space of exile –
to forge anew a way to deal with moral precepts,
long forgotten, long ignored.

And in that outer space the psalm singers sang
Comfort, anger, fear and hope, delight, despair
A dissonance so rare for us ... so rare.

And finally the Pharasaic-scholar-saints
wove all the strands of law and lore
into a fabric pre-ordained
to capture every last contingency a person might face
except the change of faith,
a veering from the path.

So back we go to where our ancestors stood,
Again with desert souls,
Exploring now the universe of faith
to chart a map of life
on which to find tomorrow.

Gustav Buchdahl

And you remember the creation and are mindful of all that has been created from the beginning.

How fortunate is the person who does not forget and the one who finds strength in You, for the one who seeks You shall not stumble nor ever be put to shame.

Thus is it written:
And God remembered Noah and all the wild animals and all the cattle with him in the ark, and God caused a wind to blow across the earth, and the waters began to subside...

Genesis 8:1

And God heard their groaning in Egyptian bondage and remembered the covenant with their ancestors...

Exodus 2:24

And thus proclaimed Your prophets: Announce it so that all Jerusalem may hear, "These are the words of the Eternal."

Jeremiah 2:2

I remember the lovingkindness of your youth, the love of your bridal days, when you followed Me in the wilderness, through an unsure land. I will remember the covenant made with you when you were young, and I will establish with you a covenant that will last forever.

Ezekiel 16:60

אַתָּה זוֹכֵר מַעֲשֵׂה עוֹלָם,
וּפוֹקֵד כָּל יְצוּרֵי קֶדֶם.

אַשְׁרֵי אִישׁ שֶׁלֹּא יִשְׁכָּחֶךָ,
וּבֶן־אָדָם יִתְאַמֶּץ־בָּךְ.
כִּי דוֹרְשֶׁיךָ לְעוֹלָם לֹא יִכָּשֵׁלוּ,
וְלֹא יִכָּלְמוּ לָנֶצַח כָּל הַחוֹסִים בָּךְ.

כַּכָּתוּב בְּתוֹרָתֶךָ.
וַיִּזְכֹּר אֱלֹהִים אֶת נֹחַ,
וְאֶת כָּל הַחַיָּה וְאֶת כָּל הַבְּהֵמָה
אֲשֶׁר אִתּוֹ בַּתֵּבָה, וַיַּעֲבֵר אֱלֹהִים
רוּחַ עַל הָאָרֶץ, וַיָּשֹׁכּוּ הַמָּיִם.

וַיִּשְׁמַע אֱלֹהִים אֶת נַאֲקָתָם,
וַיִּזְכֹּר אֱלֹהִים אֶת בְּרִיתוֹ אֶת אַבְרָהָם,
אֶת יִצְחָק וְאֶת יַעֲקֹב.

הָלוֹךְ וְקָרֵאתָ בְאָזְנֵי יְרוּשָׁלַיִם לֵאמֹר,
כֹּה אָמַר יהוה.

זָכַרְתִּי לָךְ חֶסֶד נְעוּרַיִךְ,
אַהֲבַת כְּלוּלֹתָיִךְ,
לֶכְתֵּךְ אַחֲרַי בַּמִּדְבָּר,
בְּאֶרֶץ לֹא זְרוּעָה. וְנֶאֱמַר.
וְזָכַרְתִּי אֲנִי אֶת בְּרִיתִי
אוֹתָךְ בִּימֵי נְעוּרָיִךְ,
וַהֲקִימוֹתִי לָךְ בְּרִית עוֹלָם.

HaVeyn Yakir Li Ephraim, Im Yeled Sha'ashu'im,
Ki Midey D'abri Vo Zokhor Ezk'arenu Od,
Al Keyn Hamu Meyai Lo, Rakhem Arakhamenu,
N'um Adonai.

הֲבֵן יַקִּיר לִי אֶפְרַיִם, אִם יֶלֶד שַׁעֲשׁוּעִים,
כִּי מִדֵּי דַבְּרִי בּוֹ זָכֹר אֶזְכְּרֶנּוּ עוֹד,
עַל כֵּן הָמוּ מֵעַי לוֹ, רַחֵם אֲרַחֲמֶנּוּ,
נְאֻם יהוה.

Is not Ephraim my precious son, my beloved child?
Even when I rebuke him I remember him with
tenderness, my heart yearns for him. I will surely
show him compassion, says the Eternal One.

Jeremiah 31:20

May our memories move us to strive for justice, life,
blessings, and wholeness.

(the Shofar is sounded)
Tekiah Shevarim Teruah Tekiah

(the Shofar is sounded)
תְּקִיעָה שְׁבָרִים תְּרוּעָה תְּקִיעָה

HaYom Harat Olam.
On this day, the world came into being;
on this day all of life stands in judgment
before You as children and as servants.
As children, have compassion upon us,
and as servants we depend on You,
whose light of grace judges us,
O Awesome and Holy One.

הַיּוֹם הֲרַת עוֹלָם.
הַיּוֹם יַעֲמִיד בַּמִּשְׁפָּט כָּל יְצוּרֵי עוֹלָמִים,
אִם כְּבָנִים אִם כַּעֲבָדִים.
אִם כְּבָנִים, רַחֲמֵנוּ כְּרַחֵם אָב עַל בָּנִים.
וְאִם כַּעֲבָדִים עֵינֵינוּ לְךָ תְלוּיוֹת,
עַד שֶׁתְּחָנֵּנוּ וְתוֹצִיא כָאוֹר מִשְׁפָּטֵנוּ,
אָיוֹם קָדוֹשׁ.

(omit on Shabbat)
Areshet s'Fateynu Ye'erav l'Fanekha
Eyl Rom v'Nisah.
May the expressions from our lips
be pleasing to the One who listens
to the sound of the shofar and receives
with compassion our recollections.

(omit on Shabbat)
אֲרֶשֶׁת שְׂפָתֵינוּ יֶעֱרַב לְפָנֶיךָ,
אֵל רָם וְנִשָּׂא.
מֵבִין וּמַאֲזִין, מַבִּיט וּמַקְשִׁיב
לְקוֹל תְּקִיעָתֵנוּ.
וּתְקַבֵּל בְּרַחֲמִים וּבְרָצוֹן
סֵדֶר זִכְרוֹנוֹתֵינוּ.

SHOFROT—LIBERATION AND REDEMPTION

שׁוֹפָרוֹת

You were revealed to Your people at Mount Sinai
amid clouds of glory.

אַתָּה נִגְלֵיתָ בַּעֲנַן כְּבוֹדֶךָ,
עַל עַם קָדְשֶׁךָ לְדַבֵּר עִמָּם.

On the third day, as the morning dawned,
there was thunder and a thick cloud settled
on the mountain, and the mighty sound
of the shofar was heard, and the whole
people trembled.

Exodus 19:16

וַיְהִי בַיּוֹם הַשְּׁלִישִׁי בִּהְיֹת הַבֹּקֶר
וַיְהִי קֹלֹת וּבְרָקִים וְעָנָן כָּבֵד
עַל־הָהָר וְקֹל שֹׁפָר חָזָק מְאֹד
וַיֶּחֱרַד כָּל־הָעָם אֲשֶׁר בַּמַּחֲנֶה.

All you who dwell in the world, inhabitants
of the earth, shall see when the signal of
redemption is hoisted on the mountains, and
shall hear when the shofar is sounded.

Isaiah 18:3

כָּל יֹשְׁבֵי תֵבֵל וְשֹׁכְנֵי אָרֶץ,
כִּנְשֹׂא נֵס הָרִים תִּרְאוּ,
וְכִתְקֹעַ שׁוֹפָר תִּשְׁמָעוּ.

Praise the Eternal with a shofar blast,
with stringed instruments,
with drum and with dance.

Psalm 150

הַלְלוּהוּ בִּגְבוּרֹתָיו,
הַלְלוּהוּ כְּרֹב גֻּדְלוֹ.
הַלְלוּהוּ בְּתֵקַע שׁוֹפָר,
הַלְלוּהוּ בְּנֵבֶל וְכִנּוֹר.
הַלְלוּהוּ בְּתֹף וּמָחוֹל.

T'kah B'Shofar Gadol Kheruteynu,
v'Sah Neys l'Kabetz Galuyoteynu,
v'Karev p'Zureynu miBeyn haGoyim,
u'n'Futzoteynu Kaneys m'Yark'tey Aretz.

תְּקַע בְּשׁוֹפָר גָּדוֹל לְחֵרוּתֵנוּ,
וְשָׂא נֵס לְקַבֵּץ גָּלֻיּוֹתֵינוּ,
וְקָרֵב פְּזוּרֵינוּ מִבֵּין הַגּוֹיִם,
וּנְפוּצוֹתֵינוּ כַּנֵּס מִיַּרְכְּתֵי אָרֶץ.

May the great shofar be sounded for our
freedom, uniting our scattered people.
May the shofar be sounded, awakening
all the inhabitants of the world and their
governments to the Presence and to the vision
of Shalom. May we come to Jerusalem with
song and everlasting joy.

A person cannot find redemption until that person sees the flaws of the soul and tries to efface them. Nor can a people be redeemed until it sees the flaws in its soul and tries to efface them. But whether it be an individual or a people, whoever shuts out the realization of those flaws is shutting out redemption. We can be redeemed only to the extent to which we see ourselves.

The Jew's creative forces are set aflame through striving for unity, creative action being rooted in the unity of the soul. "Only by being undivided will you have a share in the Eternal your God," says the Midrash. The creative Jews are the conquerors of duality, the yea rather than the nay, productivity rather than despair, the triumph of yearning. They are the "Let there be light" of Judaism. In their life, in their work, the people redeemed themselves.

Martin Büber

Laugh at My Dreams

Come with me. Come into my dreams.
It is I, the dreamer, who speaks.
It is a dream that in humanity I believe,
That in you I yet believe.

That still my soul for freedom yearns—
I did not barter it for the calf of gold,
That in humanity I still believe,
And in the soul, the spirit strong.

In the future, too, I believe,
Though the day may yet be far,
It will surely come—when one nation to the other
Peace will bring and blessings, too.

Sakhki Sakhki al haKhalomot
Zeh Ani haKholem Sakh.
Sakhki Ki b'Adam Ah-amin
Ki Odeni Mah-amin Bakh.

Ki Od Nafshi Dror Sho-efet
Lo M'khartiha l'Egel Paz.
Ki Od Ah-amin Gom baAdam
Gom b'Rukho Ruakh Az.

Saul Tchernikhovsky

שַׂחֲקִי שַׂחֲקִי עַל הַחֲלוֹמוֹת
זֶה אֲנִי הַחוֹלֵם שָׂח.
שַׂחֲקִי כִּי בָּאָדָם אַאֲמִין
כִּי עוֹדֶנִי מַאֲמִין בָּךְ.

כִּי עוֹד נָפְשִׁי דְּרוֹר שׁוֹאֶפֶת
לֹא מְכַרְתִּיהָ לְעֵגֶל פָּז.
כִּי עוֹד אַאֲמִין גַּם בָּאָדָם
גַּם בְּרוּחוֹ רוּחַ עָז.

Jerusalem of Gold

The olive trees that stand in silence upon the hills of time.
To hear the voices of the city as bells of evening chime.
The shofar sounding from the Temple to call the world to prayer,
The shepherd pauses in the valley and peace is everywhere.

Yerushalayim Shel Zahav
v'Shel n'Khoshet v'Shel Ohr
haLo l'Khol Shirayikh—Ani Kinor.

יְרוּשָׁלַיִם שֶׁל זָהָב
וְשֶׁל נְחֹשֶׁת וְשֶׁל אוֹר
הֲלֹא לְכָל שִׁירַיִךְ אֲנִי כִּנּוֹר.

Naomi Shemer and Norman Newell

(the Shofar is sounded)
Tekiah Shevarim Teruah Tekiah

(the Shofar is sounded)
תְּקִיעָה שְׁבָרִים תְּרוּעָה תְּקִיעָה

Today commemorates the world's conception.
Today all creatures stand in judgment,
whether as children or as servants.
If we are as children grant us love and
mercifulness.
If we are enslaved, favor us and grant us
freedom's light.
Yes, we are fearful of the Eternal as well
as awed by the Holiness of Being.

הַיּוֹם הֲרַת עוֹלָם.
הַיּוֹם יַעֲמִיד בַּמִּשְׁפָּט
כָּל יְצוּרֵי עוֹלָמִים,
אִם כְּבָנִים אִם כַּעֲבָדִים.
אִם כְּבָנִים, רַחֲמֵנוּ כְּרַחֵם אָב עַל בָּנִים.
וְאִם כַּעֲבָדִים עֵינֵינוּ לְךָ תְלוּיוֹת,
עַד שֶׁתְּחָנֵּנוּ וְתוֹצִיא כָאוֹר מִשְׁפָּטֵנוּ,
אָיוֹם קָדוֹשׁ.

(omit on Shabbat)
Areshet s'Fateynu Ye'erav l'Fanekha
Eyl Rom v'Nisah.
May our words be pleasing
to the One most high,
listening to our shofar sounds.
Please lovingly receive this call for liberation
and redemption.

(omit on Shabbat)
אֲרֶשֶׁת שְׂפָתֵינוּ יֶעֱרַב לְפָנֶיךָ,
אֵל רָם וְנִשָּׂא.
מֵבִין וּמַאֲזִין, מַבִּיט וּמַקְשִׁיב
לְקוֹל תְּקִיעָתֵנוּ.
וּתְקַבֵּל בְּרַחֲמִים וּבְרָצוֹן
סֵדֶר שׁוֹפְרוֹתֵינוּ.

Ancient Blessing of the Kohanim

Yivarekh'kha Adonai v'Yishm'rekha.
Keyn Y'hi Ratzon.

יְבָרֶכְךָ יהוה וְיִשְׁמְרֶךָ.
כֵּן יְהִי רָצוֹן.

Yaer Adonai Panav Eylekha Vikhuneka.
Keyn Y'hi Ratzon.

יָאֵר יהוה פָּנָיו אֵלֶיךָ וִיחֻנֶּךָּ.
כֵּן יְהִי רָצוֹן.

Yisa Adonai Panav Eylekha v'Yasem l'Kha Shalom.
Keyn Y'hi Ratzon.

יִשָּׂא יהוה פָּנָיו אֵלֶיךָ וְיָשֵׂם לְךָ שָׁלוֹם.
כֵּן יְהִי רָצוֹן.

May the Eternal Spirit bless you and guard you.
May you be illumined by the countenance of
Creation and be given grace.
May the Source of Being lift you and grant you
wholeness and harmony.

הַיּוֹם תְּאַמְּצֵנוּ.   אָמֵן.

הַיּוֹם תְּבָרְכֵנוּ.   אָמֵן.

הַיּוֹם תְּגַדְּלֵנוּ.   אָמֵן.

הַיּוֹם תִּדְרְשֵׁנוּ לְטוֹבָה.   אָמֵן.

הַיּוֹם תִּכְתְּבֵנוּ לְחַיִּים טוֹבִים.   אָמֵן.

הַיּוֹם תִּשְׁמַע שַׁוְעָתֵנוּ.   אָמֵן.

הַיּוֹם תְּקַבֵּל בְּרַחֲמִים וּבְרָצוֹן אֶת־תְּפִלָּתֵנוּ.   אָמֵן.

הַיּוֹם תִּתְמְכֵנוּ בִּימִין צִדְקֶךָ.   אָמֵן.

HaYom T'Amtzeynu.

HaYom T'Varkheynu.

HaYom T'Gadleynu.

HaYom TiDr'sheynu L'Tovah.

HaYom TiKht'veynu L'Khayim Tovim.

HaYom TiShma Shavateynu.

HaYom T'Kabeyl b'Rakhamim u'vRatzon et T'filateynu.

HaYom Tit'm'kheynu biMin Tzidkekha.

On this day, give us strength!   Amen.

On this day, bless us!   Amen.

On this day, help us to grow!   Amen.

On this day, wish us well!   Amen.

On this day, inscribe us for a good life!   Amen.

On this day, hear our plea!   Amen.

On this day, mercifully accept our prayer.   Amen.

On this day, support us with strength of justice!   Amen.

Oseh Shalom Bimromav   עֹשֶׂה שָׁלוֹם בִּמְרוֹמָיו

Hu Yaaseh Shalom Aleynu   הוּא יַעֲשֶׂה שָׁלוֹם עָלֵינוּ

v'Al Kol Yisrael v'Al Kol Yoshvey Tevel,   וְעַל כָּל יִשְׂרָאֵל וְעַל כָּל יוֹשְׁבֵי תֵבֵל,

v'Imru Ameyn.   וְאִמְרוּ אָמֵן.

May the One, source of peace in the heavens,

grant peace to us, to all Israel, and to all humanity.

Amen.

Eyn Keyloheynu

Eyn Keyloheynu, Eyn Kadoneynu,
Eyn k'Malkeynu, Eyn k'Moshi-eynu.

אֵין כֵּאלֹהֵינוּ, אֵין כַּאדוֹנֵינוּ,
אֵין כְּמַלְכֵּנוּ, אֵין כְּמוֹשִׁיעֵנוּ.

Mi Kheyloheynu, mi Khadoneynu,
Mi Kh'malkeynu, mi Kh'moshi-eynu.

מִי־כֵאלֹהֵינוּ, מִי־כַאדוֹנֵינוּ,
מִי־כְמַלְכֵּנוּ, מִי־כְמוֹשִׁיעֵנוּ.

Nodeh Leyloheynu, Nodeh Ladoneynu,
Nodeh l'Malkeynu, Nodeh l'Moshi-eynu.

נוֹדֶה לֵאלֹהֵינוּ, נוֹדֶה לַאדוֹנֵינוּ,
נוֹדֶה לְמַלְכֵּנוּ, נוֹדֶה לְמוֹשִׁיעֵנוּ.

Barukh Eloheynu, Barukh Adoneynu,
Barukh Malkeynu, Barukh Moshi'eynu.

בָּרוּךְ אֱלֹהֵינוּ, בָּרוּךְ אֲדוֹנֵינוּ,
בָּרוּךְ מַלְכֵּנוּ, בָּרוּךְ מוֹשִׁיעֵנוּ.

Atah Hu Eloheynu, Atah Hu Adoneynu,
Atah Hu Malkeynu, Atah Hu Moshi'eynu.

אַתָּה הוּא אֱלֹהֵינוּ, אַתָּה הוּא אֲדוֹנֵינוּ,
אַתָּה הוּא מַלְכֵּנוּ, אַתָּה הוּא מוֹשִׁיעֵנוּ.

There is none like our Creator, master of our soul,
our ruler, our liberator.

Who is like our Creator, our soul guide,
our ruler, our liberator?

Let us thank our Creator, our soul teacher,
our ruler, our liberator.

Blessed is our Creator, our soul master,
our ruler, our liberator.

You are our Creator, our soul master,
our ruler, our liberator.

L'Ma'an Akhai v'Reyai.
Adabrah Nah Shalom Bakh.
L'Ma'an Beyt Adonai Eloheynu
Avaksha Tov Lakh.

לְמַעַן אַחַי וְרֵעָי,
אֲדַבְּרָה נָּא שָׁלוֹם בָּךְ.
לְמַעַן בֵּית יהוה אֱלֹהֵינוּ,
אֲבַקְשָׁה טוֹב לָךְ.

For the sake of my brothers and friends,
for the sake of my sisters and friends,
all that I ask, all that I say, is peace unto you.
For the sake of God's House, I wish the best for you.

ALEYNU

עָלֵינוּ

Aleynu l'Shabeyakh l'Adon haKol
Lateyt G'dulah l'Yotzer B'reysheet.

עָלֵינוּ לְשַׁבֵּחַ לַאֲדוֹן הַכֹּל
לָתֵת גְּדֻלָּה לְיוֹצֵר בְּרֵאשִׁית.

VaAnakhnu Korim
u'Mishtakhavim u'Modim
Lifney Melekh Mal'khey haM'lakhim
HaKadosh Barukh Hu.

וַאֲנַחְנוּ כּוֹרְעִים
וּמִשְׁתַּחֲוִים וּמוֹדִים
לִפְנֵי מֶלֶךְ מַלְכֵי הַמְּלָכִים
הַקָּדוֹשׁ בָּרוּךְ הוּא.

It is our duty and privilege to acknowledge and ascribe
greatness to the Artist within Creation.

So we bend our knees, bow our heads, and give thanks
before the greatest of rulers, the Holy One of Being.

We put our hope in this awareness and in the promise
that there will come a time when greed and injustice
will be gone from the earth.
We hope for a world completely repaired,
all the inhabitants of this planet turning to each other,
in reconciliation, understanding
that no one shall be excluded from the security of life.

עַל כֵּן נְקַוֶּה לְךָ יהוה אֱלֹהֵינוּ
לִרְאוֹת מְהֵרָה בְּתִפְאֶרֶת עֻזֶּךָ,
לְהַעֲבִיר גִּלּוּלִים מִן הָאָרֶץ
וְהָאֱלִילִים כָּרוֹת יִכָּרֵתוּן.
לְתַקֵּן עוֹלָם בְּמַלְכוּת שַׁדַּי.

V'Ne'emar: v'Hayah Adonai,
l'Melekh Al Kol haAretz.
Bayom Hahu, Bayom Hahu, Yihyeh Adonai Ekhad
u'Shmo Ekhad.
It has been said: "The Eternal Source of Being
will govern over the entire earth. On that day all peoples
will realize their unity."

וְנֶאֱמַר: וְהָיָה יהוה
לְמֶלֶךְ עַל כָּל הָאָרֶץ,
בַּיוֹם הַהוּא יִהְיֶה יהוה אֶחָד
וּשְׁמוֹ אֶחָד.

85

MOURNER'S KADDISH

קדוש יתום

Yitgadal v'Yitkadash Shmey Rabah,
b'Alma Divra Khirutey
v'Yamlikh Malkutey
b'Khayeykhon u'v'Yomeykhon u'v'Khayey
d'Khol Beyt Yisrael
baAgalah u'Vizman Kariv.
V'Imru: Ameyn.

יִתְגַּדַּל וְיִתְקַדַּשׁ שְׁמֵהּ רַבָּא.
בְּעָלְמָה דִּי בְרָא כִרְעוּתֵהּ.
וְיַמְלִיךְ מַלְכוּתֵהּ,
בְּחַיֵּיכוֹן וּבְיוֹמֵיכוֹן וּבְחַיֵּי
דְכָל בֵּית יִשְׂרָאֵל,
בַּעֲגָלָא וּבִזְמַן קָרִיב.
וְאִמְרוּ אָמֵן:

Y'Hey Shmey Rabah m'Varakh l'Alam
u'l'Almey Almaya:

יְהֵא שְׁמֵהּ רַבָּה מְבָרַךְ לְעָלַם
וּלְעָלְמֵי עָלְמַיָּא:

Yitbarakh v'Yishtabakh v'Yitpaar v'Yitromam
v'Yitnasey v'Yithadar v'Yitaleh v'Yithalal
Shmey d'Kud'sha. Brikh Hu.
L'Eyla u'l'Eyla miKol Birkhata v'Shirata
Tush'b'khata v'Nekhemata daAmiran b'Alma.
V'Imru: Ameyn.

יִתְבָּרַךְ וְיִשְׁתַּבַּח וְיִתְפָּאַר וְיִתְרוֹמַם
וְיִתְנַשֵּׂא וְיִתְהַדַּר וְיִתְעַלֶּה וְיִתְהַלָּל
שְׁמֵהּ דְּקֻדְשָׁא. בְּרִיךְ הוּא.
לְעֵלָּא (וּלְעֵלָּא) מִכָּל בִּרְכָתָא וְשִׁירָתָא
תֻּשְׁבְּחָתָא וְנֶחֱמָתָא דַּאֲמִירָן בְּעָלְמָא.
וְאִמְרוּ אָמֵן:

Y'hey Shlama Raba Min Sh'maya
v'Khayim Aleynu v'Al Kol Yisrael.
V'Imru: Ameyn.

יְהֵא שְׁלָמָא רַבָּא מִן שְׁמַיָּא
וְחַיִּים עָלֵינוּ וְעַל כָּל יִשְׂרָאֵל.
וְאִמְרוּ אָמֵן.

Oseh Shalom Bimromav Hu Ya'aseh Shalom
Aleynu v'Al Kol Yisrael.
V'Imru: Ameyn.

עֹשֶׂה שָׁלוֹם בִּמְרוֹמָיו,
הוּא יַעֲשֶׂה שָׁלוֹם עָלֵינוּ
וְעַל כָּל יִשְׂרָאֵל. וְאִמְרוּ אָמֵן.

May the Universe of Creation be recognized in your lifetime
and throughout your days, and during the lifetime
of the entire House of Yisrael, soon.

So let us acknowledge, honor, celebrate, and sing to the
Sacred Source, though transcendent and truly beyond human songs
and blessing.

May the Source of peace grant us peace, and let us say: Amen.

ADON OLAM

אֲדוֹן עוֹלָם

Adon Olam Asher Malakh, b'Terem Kol y'Tzir Nivra,
l'Ayt Naasa b'Kheftzo Kol, Azay Melekh Shmo Nikra.

V'Akharey kiKhlot haKol l'Vado Yimlokh Norah,
v'Hu Hayah v'Hu Hoveh v'Hu Yihyeh b'Tifarah.

V'Hu Ekhad v'Eyn Sheni l'Hamshilo l'Hakhbirah,
b'Li Reshit b'Li Takhlit v'Lo haOz v'Hamisrah.

V'Hu Eli v'Khai Goali, v'Tzur Khevli b'Et Tzarah,
v'Hu Nisi u'Manos Li, m'Nat Kosi b'Yom Ekra.

B'Yado Afkid Rukhi b'Et Ishan v'a'Ira,
v'Im Rukhi G'viyati Adonai Li v'Lo Ira.

אֲדוֹן עוֹלָם אֲשֶׁר מָלַךְ
בְּטֶרֶם כָּל יְצִיר נִבְרָא.
לְעֵת נַעֲשָׂה בְחֶפְצוֹ כֹּל
אֲזַי מֶלֶךְ שְׁמוֹ נִקְרָא.

וְאַחֲרֵי כִּכְלוֹת הַכֹּל
לְבַדּוֹ יִמְלוֹךְ נוֹרָא.
וְהוּא הָיָה וְהוּא הֹוֶה
וְהוּא יִהְיֶה בְּתִפְאָרָה.

וְהוּא אֶחָד וְאֵין שֵׁנִי
לְהַמְשִׁיל לוֹ לְהַחְבִּירָה.
בְּלִי רֵאשִׁית בְּלִי תַכְלִית
וְלוֹ הָעֹז וְהַמִּשְׂרָה.

וְהוּא אֵלִי וְחַי גֹּאֲלִי
וְצוּר חֶבְלִי בְּעֵת צָרָה.
וְהוּא נִסִּי וּמָנוֹס לִי
מְנָת כּוֹסִי בְּיוֹם אֶקְרָא.

בְּיָדוֹ אַפְקִיד רוּחִי
בְּעֵת אִישָׁן וְאָעִירָה.
וְעִם רוּחִי גְּוִיָּתִי
יהוה לִי וְלֹא אִירָא.

The Ancient Teacher, the Eternal Spirit, has reigned
since before the Creation.

We recall the independence of the Eternal,
the Greatness of the One,
unique, infinite and majestic.

We are confident that this Spirit is so very near,
that each of us can call upon this One
as the sole source of life and strength.

From the infinite Source of Being,
we are given a portion in life and in death.

We are sustained in troubled times,
offered guidance and protection.
If we are able to call upon the One...
we are given the sacred hand,
whether asleep or awake,
entrusting our bodies and our spirits
to the Source of Life,
the Mystery of Creation,
with whom we ought have no fear.

היום הרת עולם

היום יעמד במשפט כל עולמים אם כבנים אם כעבדים אם כבנים רחמנו כרחם אב על בנים ואם כעבדים עינינו לך תלויות עד שתחננו ותוציא כאור משפטנו איום קדוש.

Artwork: Ben Shahn, Today is the
Birthday of the World

כל נדרי

Kol Nidre

89

Kol Nidre

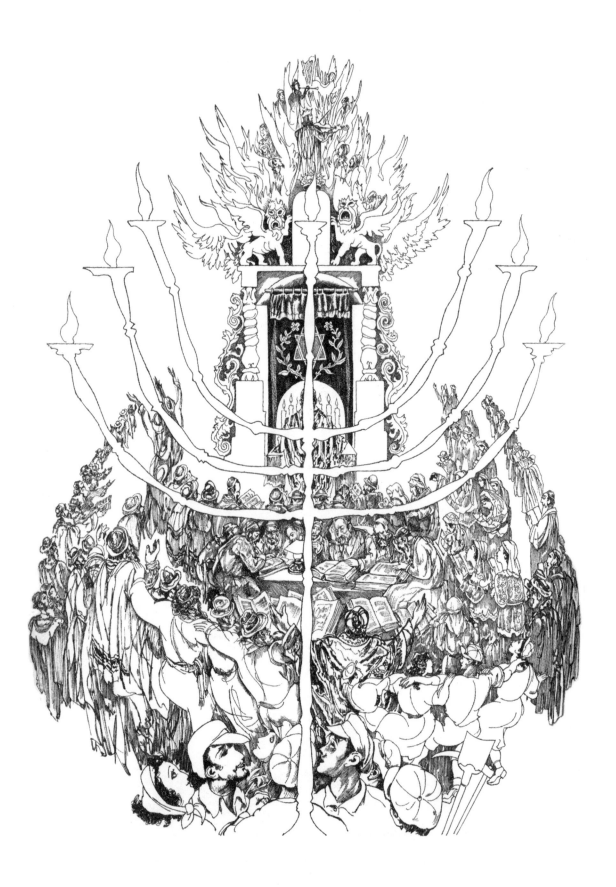

God's world is great and holy. Among the holy lands in the world is the Holy Land of Israel. In the Land of Israel the holiest city is Jerusalem. In Jerusalem the holiest place was the Temple, and in the Temple the holiest spot was the holy of holies.

There are seventy peoples in the world. Among these holy peoples is the people of Israel. The holiest of the people of Israel is the tribe of Levi. In the tribe of Levi the holiest are the priests. Among the priests, the holiest was the high priest.

There are 354* days in the year. Among these, the holidays are holy. Higher than these is the holiness of the Sabbath. Among Sabbaths the holiest is the Day of Atonement, the Sabbath of Sabbaths.

There are seventy languages in the world. Among the holy languages is the holy language of Hebrew. Holier than all else in this language is the holy Torah, and in the Torah the holiest part is the Ten Commandments. In the Ten Commandments the holiest of all words is the Name of God.

And once during the year, at a certain hour, these four supreme sanctities of the world were joined with one another. That was the Day of Atonement, when the high priest would enter the holy of holies and there utter the Name of God. And because this hour was beyond measure holy and awesome, it was the time of utmost peril not only for the high priest but for the whole of Israel. For if, in this hour, there had, God forbid, entered the mind of the high priest a false or sinful thought, the entire world would have been destroyed.

Every spot where a person raises his or her eyes to heaven is a holy of holies. Everyone, having been created by God in the Divine image and likeness, is a high priest. Every day of a person's life is a Day of Atonement, and every word that a person speaks with sincerity is the Name of the Ineffable.

*Jewish Calendar
Folk tale adapted from The Dybbuk by Saul Ansky

Eyli, Eyli

Eyli, Eyli,
Shelo Yigamer l'Olam,
haKhol v'haYam,
Rishrush Shel haMayim,
B'rak haShamayim,
T'filat haAdam.

אֵלִי, אֵלִי,
שֶׁלֹא יִגָּמֵר לְעוֹלָם,
הַחוֹל וְהַיָּם,
רִשְׁרוּשׁ שֶׁל הַמַּיִם,
בְּרַק הַשָּׁמַיִם,
תְּפִלַּת הָאָדָם.

O God, my God, I pray that these things never end:
The sand and the sea, the rush of the waters,
The crash of the heavens, the prayer of the heart.

Hannah Senesch

Kol Nidre

THE KOL NIDRE SERVICE

כל נדרי

The Ark is opened

Ohr Zaruah laTzaddik u-l'Yishrey Lev Simkhah.
Light is sown for the righteous
and for the upright in heart there is joy.

אוֹר זָרֻעַ לַצַּדִּיק וּלְיִשְׁרֵי לֵב שִׂמְחָה.

The Permission
By the authority of the heavenly court,
And by the authority of the earthly court,
With the knowledge of the ever-present God,
And with the knowledge of this congregation,
We welcome all to pray with this community and
Declare it proper to pray with others
Who have wronged either God or human beings.

בִּישִׁיבָה שֶׁל מַעֲלָה
וּבִישִׁיבָה שֶׁל מַטָּה
עַל דַּעַת הַמָּקוֹם
וְעַל דַּעַת הַקָּהָל
אָנוּ מַתִּירִין לְהִתְפַּלֵּל
עִם הָעֲבַרְיָנִים.

Kol Nidre—chant of ages,
Chant of Israel, chant of sorrow,
Measuring off the throbbing heartbeats
Of a people bowed in anguish,
Crushed by tyrants, thwarted, broken,
Wandering, often homeless, weary.
Generations set your motif
Out of trials, hopes and yearnings,
Added each its variations
To your theme and to your cadence.
Diverse lands and diverse periods
Poured their soul into your music.
When we listen with our hearts tuned,
We can see revealed before us
Heroes, martyrs, saints and scholars,
Loyal, steadfast sons and daughters of Israel
Sanctifying Life Supreme, their Source.

Kol Nidre—chant of ages
Chant of pain and chant of pathos,
Mingled with your notes of sorrow
Vibrant measures trill and quiver,
Rising to as great crescendo
With the Jews' undying spirit
As the Torah is lifted high,
Symbol of faith and vigor.
Notes of joyous exultation
Crept into your dirgeful music
As with fortitude, cherishing
all our ancestors held most sacred.
While our hearts beat to your rhythm,
Stir us with new dedication
To our ancestors' God, to serve Life Supreme
With our heart and soul and fervor.

Kol Nidre—chant of ages,
Chant of grief and chant of triumph,
Echoing, this night of memories,
In the ears and the heart of Israel,
Once again you draw together
All dispersed and those Life-affirming
To return and humbly seek the Oneness -
Supplicants for Life's grace and acceptance.
Faced by grim, appalling forces
In these days of trial and challenge,
Do we plead before God's mercy
For strength, help, and guidance.
With your plaintive chant, Kol Nidre,
Rise our prayers to heaven ascending,
For a surcease of human sorrows,
For the dawn of peace and freedom,
When all hearts are purged of hatred,
Passions, lusts that rend asunder.
Then all humankind will stand together
To acknowledge their Common Source.

Morris Silverman
High Holiday Prayer Book

כָּל נִדְרֵי וֶאֱסָרֵי וַחֲרָמֵי, וְקוֹנָמֵי וְכִנּוּיֵי, וְקִנּוּסֵי וּשְׁבוּעוֹת.
דִּנְדַרְנָא וּדְאִשְׁתַּבַּעְנָא, וּדְאַחֲרֶמְנָא וְדִאֲסַרְנָא עַל נַפְשָׁתָנָא,
מִיּוֹם כִּפֻּרִים זֶה עַד יוֹם כִּפֻּרִים הַבָּא עָלֵינוּ לְטוֹבָה.
כֻּלְּהוֹן אֲחַרַטְנָא בְהוֹן. כֻּלְּהוֹן יְהוֹן שָׁרָן.
שְׁבִיקִין שְׁבִיתִין, בְּטֵלִין וּמְבֻטָּלִין,
לָא שְׁרִירִין וְלָא קַיָּמִין.
נִדְרָנָא לָא נִדְרֵי,
וֶאֱסָרָנָא לָא אֱסָרֵי,
וּשְׁבוּעָתָנָא לָא שְׁבוּעוֹת.

Kol Nidrey veEsarey vaKharamey v'Konamey v'Khinuyey v'Kinusey u'Sh'vuot,
Dindarna u'Disht'bana u'Dakhareemna v'Di'asarna al Nafshatana,
MiYom Kippurim Zeh Ad Yom Kippurim Haba, Aleynu l'Tova.
Kul'hon Ikharatna v'Hon, Kul'hon y'Hon Sharan.
Sh'veekeen, Sh'veeteen, b'Teyleen u-m'Vutaleen,
La Sh'reereen v'La Kayameen,
Nidrana La Nidrey,
Ve'Esarana La Esarey,
U'Sh'vuatana La Sh'vuot.

All vows, bonds, devotions, promises, obligations, penalties and oaths,
wherewith we have vowed, sworn, devoted,
and bound ourselves, from this Day of Atonement to the
next Day of Atonement—may it come to us for good.
(In the event that we forget them or were coerced to break them), they shall be
absolved, released, annulled, made void and of no effect; they shall not be
binding nor shall they have any power.

Forgive the wrongdoings of this people,
and all who dwell in their midst, according
to the greatness of Your covenantal love.
For in all of us there is unwitting
transgression.

As the Source of Compassion has said:
"I have forgiven as you have asked."

*Barukh Atah Adonai Eloheynu Melekh
haOlam Shehekheyanu v'Kiyimanu
v'Higiyanu laZ'man haZeh.*

You are praised, O Eternal One, our Creator,
Sovereign of the world, giving us life, sustaining
us, and enabling us stand here this Day.

וְנִסְלַח לְכָל עֲדַת בְּנֵי יִשְׂרָאֵל
וְלַגֵּר הַגָּר בְּתוֹכָם
כִּי לְכָל הָעָם בִּשְׁגָגָה.

סְלַח נָא לַעֲוֹן הָעָם הַזֶּה כְּגֹדֶל חַסְדֶּךָ,
וְכַאֲשֶׁר נָשָׂאתָה לָעָם הַזֶּה
מִמִּצְרַיִם וְעַד הֵנָּה.
וְשָׁם נֶאֱמַר:

וַיֹּאמֶר יְהֹוָה סָלַחְתִּי כִּדְבָרֶךָ.

בָּרוּךְ אַתָּה יהוה אֱלֹהֵינוּ מֶלֶךְ
הָעוֹלָם שֶׁהֶחֱיָנוּ וְקִיְּמָנוּ
וְהִגִּיעָנוּ לַזְּמַן הַזֶּה.

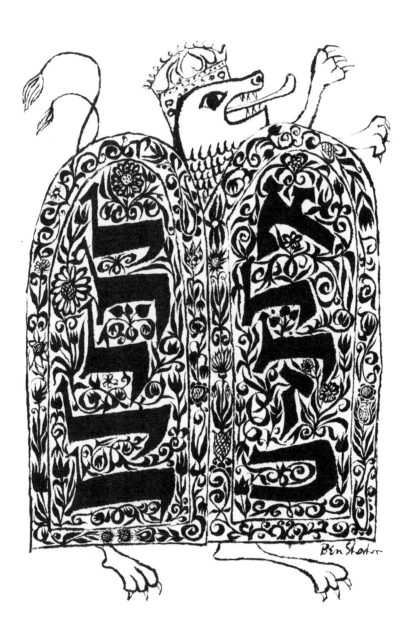

Artwork: Ben Shahn, Tablets of the Law with Lion

וידוי

Vidui

VIDUI SERVICE

Sh'ma Koleynu Adonai Eloheynu,

שְׁמַע קוֹלֵנוּ, יהוה אֱלֹהֵינוּ,

Khus v'Rakheym Aleynu,

חוּס וְרַחֵם עָלֵינוּ,

v'Kabeyl b'Rakhamim uv'Ratzon et T'filateynu.

וְקַבֵּל בְּרַחֲמִים וּבְרָצוֹן אֶת תְּפִלָּתֵנוּ.

Hashiveynu Adonai Eleykha v'Nashuvah,

הֲשִׁיבֵנוּ יהוה אֵלֶיךָ וְנָשׁוּבָה,

Khadeysh Yameynu k'Kedem.

חַדֵּשׁ יָמֵינוּ כְּקֶדֶם.

Listen to our our voices,

Have compassion on us,

Renew us as in days gone by.

Ki Anu Amekha

Ki Anu Amekha v'Atah Eloheynu,

כִּי אָנוּ עַמֶּךָ, וְאַתָּה אֱלֹהֵינוּ.

Anu Vanekha v'Atah Avinu.

אָנוּ בָנֶיךָ וְאַתָּה אָבִינוּ.

Anu Avadekha v'Atah Adoneynu,

אָנוּ עֲבָדֶיךָ, וְאַתָּה אֲדוֹנֵנוּ.

Anu k'Halekha v'Atah Khelkeynu.

אָנוּ קְהָלֶךָ, וְאַתָּה חֶלְקֵנוּ.

Anu Nakhalatekha v'Atah Goraleynu,

אָנוּ נַחֲלָתֶךָ, וְאַתָּה גוֹרָלֵנוּ.

Anu Tzonekha v'Atah Roeynu.

אָנוּ צֹאנֶךָ, וְאַתָּה רוֹעֵנוּ.

Anu Kharmekha v'Atah Notreynu,

אָנוּ כַרְמֶךָ, וְאַתָּה נוֹטְרֵנוּ.

Anu F'ulatekha v'Atah Yotzreynu.

אָנוּ פְעֻלָּתֶךָ, וְאַתָּה יוֹצְרֵנוּ.

Anu Ra'yatekha v'Atah Dodeynu,

אָנוּ רַעְיָתֶךָ, וְאַתָּה דוֹדֵנוּ.

Anu s'Gulatekha v'Atah k'Roveynu.

אָנוּ סְגֻלָּתֶךָ, וְאַתָּה קְרוֹבֵנוּ.

Anu Amekha v'Atah Malkeynu,

אָנוּ עַמֶּךָ, וְאַתָּה מַלְכֵּנוּ.

Anu Ma'amirekha v'Atah Ma'amireynu.

אָנוּ מַאֲמִירֶיךָ, וְאַתָּה מַאֲמִירֵנוּ.

We are Your people, and You are our God.

We are Your children, and You give us life.

We are Your servants, and You are our Master.

We are Your congregation, and You are our only One.

We are Your heritage, and You are our Destiny.

We are Your flock, and You are our Shepherd.

We are Your vineyard, and You are our Protector.

We are Your creatures, and You are our Creator.

We are Your companions, and You are our Beloved.

We are Your treasure, and You delight in us.

We are Your people, and You are our Sovereign.

We solely acknowledge You, and You favor us.

CONFESSIONS

Kavannah

May our prayer be worthy of ancestors' faith.
Let our prayer enter the presence of the Sacred
and not be ignored.
We are not so obstinate and stubborn as to say
"We are righteous, we have done no wrong."
Indeed, we have done wrong. We have sinned.
We have missed the mark.

אֱלֹהֵינוּ וֵאלֹהֵי אֲבוֹתֵינוּ וֵאלֹהֵי
אִמּוֹתֵינוּ תָּבֹא לְפָנֶיךָ תְּפִלָּתֵנוּ
וְאַל תִּתְעַלַּם מִתְּחִנָּתֵנוּ.
שֶׁאֵין אֲנַחְנוּ עַזֵּי פָנִים וּקְשֵׁי עֹרֶף
לוֹמַר לְפָנֶיךָ יהוה אֱלֹהֵינוּ וֵאלֹהֵי
אֲבוֹתֵינוּ צַדִּיקִים אֲנַחְנוּ וְלֹא חָטָאנוּ.
אֲבָל אֲנַחְנוּ חָטָאנוּ.

Ashamnu

Ashamnu, Bagadnu, Gazalnu, Dibarnu Dofi,
He'evinu, V'Hirshanu, Zadnu, Khamasnu,
Tafalnu Sheker, Ya'atznu Ra, Kizavnu, Latznu,
Maradnu, Ni'atznu, Sararnu, Avinu,
Pashanu, Tzararnu, Kishinu Oref, Rashanu,
Shikhatnu, Ti'avnu, Ta'inu, Ti'ta'nu.

אָשַׁמְנוּ, בָּגַדְנוּ, גָּזַלְנוּ, דִּבַּרְנוּ דֹפִי.
הֶעֱוִינוּ, וְהִרְשַׁעְנוּ, זַדְנוּ, חָמַסְנוּ,
טָפַלְנוּ שֶׁקֶר. יָעַצְנוּ רָע, כִּזַּבְנוּ, לַצְנוּ,
מָרַדְנוּ, נִאַצְנוּ, סָרַרְנוּ, עָוִינוּ,
פָּשַׁעְנוּ, צָרַרְנוּ, קִשִּׁינוּ עֹרֶף. רָשַׁעְנוּ,
שִׁחַתְנוּ, תִּעַבְנוּ, תָּעִינוּ, תִּעְתָּעְנוּ.

We have blamed, we have deceived,
We have spoiled, we have been hypocritical,
We have offended, we have been wicked,
We have been presumptuous,
We have done violence,
We have deceived, we have ill-advised,
We have lied, we have mocked,

We have rebelled,
We have been iniquitous,
We have trespassed, we have oppressed,
We have been obstinate,
We have acted wickedly,
We have been corrupt, we have wasted,
We have erred, we have led others astray.

You know the mysteries of the universe
and the best kept secrets of every living thing.
You search out the innermost rooms of our life,
with care You examine all our feelings, all our
thoughts. Not one thing is hidden from You,
nothing escapes Your gaze.
May it be Your will to forgive us all our sins, to
pardon all our iniquities, to grant us atonement
for all our transgressions.

אַתָּה יוֹדֵעַ רָזֵי עוֹלָם, וְתַעֲלוּמוֹת סִתְרֵי
כָל חָי. אַתָּה חוֹפֵשׂ כָּל חַדְרֵי בָטֶן,
וּבוֹחֵן כְּלָיוֹת וָלֵב. אֵין דָּבָר נֶעְלָם מִמֶּךָּ,
וְאֵין נִסְתָּר מִנֶּגֶד עֵינֶיךָ.
וּבְכֵן יְהִי רָצוֹן מִלְּפָנֶיךָ, שֶׁתִּסְלַח לָנוּ עַל
כָּל חַטֹּאתֵינוּ, וְתִמְחַל לָנוּ עַל כָּל
עֲוֹנוֹתֵינוּ, וּתְכַפֶּר לָנוּ עַל כָּל פְּשָׁעֵינוּ.

Vidui

Al Kheyt

Forgive us for...

The sin which we have sinned against You under
coercion or of our own free will;
And for the wrong we did by hardening our hearts.

עַל חֵטְא שֶׁחָטָאנוּ לְפָנֶיךָ בְּאֹנֶס וּבְרָצוֹן,
וְעַל חֵטְא שֶׁחָטָאנוּ לְפָנֶיךָ בְּאִמּוּץ הַלֵּב.

For the wrong we did before You unintentionally;
And for the wrong we did through misusing our words.

עַל חֵטְא שֶׁחָטָאנוּ לְפָנֶיךָ בִּבְלִי דָעַת,
וְעַל חֵטְא שֶׁחָטָאנוּ לְפָנֶיךָ בְּבִטּוּי שְׂפָתָיִם.

For the wrong we did before You by using sex
immorally;
And for the wrong we did openly and in private.

עַל חֵטְא שֶׁחָטָאנוּ לְפָנֶיךָ בְּגִלּוּי עֲרָיוֹת,
וְעַל חֵטְא שֶׁחָטָאנוּ לְפָנֶיךָ בַּגָּלוּי וּבַסָּתֶר.

For the wrong we did before You knowingly and
deceptively;
And for the wrong we did by offensive language.

עַל חֵטְא שֶׁחָטָאנוּ לְפָנֶיךָ בְּדַעַת וּבְמִרְמָה,
וְעַל חֵטְא שֶׁחָטָאנוּ לְפָנֶיךָ בְּדִבּוּר פֶּה.

For the wrong we did before You by deceiving another
person;
And for the wrong we did by malicious thoughts.

עַל חֵטְא שֶׁחָטָאנוּ לְפָנֶיךָ בְּהוֹנָאַת רֵעַ,
וְעַל חֵטְא שֶׁחָטָאנוּ לְפָנֶיךָ בְּהַרְהוֹר הַלֵּב.

For the wrong we did before You by promiscuity;
And for the wrong we did with insincere apologies,

עַל חֵטְא שֶׁחָטָאנוּ לְפָנֶיךָ בִּוְעִידַת זְנוּת,
וְעַל חֵטְא שֶׁחָטָאנוּ לְפָנֶיךָ בְּוִדּוּי פֶּה.

For the wrong we did before You by disgracing
parents and teachers;
And for the wrong we did intentionally or by mistake.

עַל חֵטְא שֶׁחָטָאנוּ לְפָנֶיךָ בְּזִלְזוּל הוֹרִים וּמוֹרִים,
וְעַל חֵטְא שֶׁחָטָאנוּ לְפָנֶיךָ בְּזָדוֹן וּבִשְׁגָגָה.

For the wrong we did before You by acts of coercion;
And for the wrong we did by desecrating creation.

עַל חֵטְא שֶׁחָטָאנוּ לְפָנֶיךָ בְּחֹזֶק יָד,
וְעַל חֵטְא שֶׁחָטָאנוּ לְפָנֶיךָ בְּחִלּוּל הַשֵּׁם.

For the wrong we did before You by foolish talk;
And for the wrong we did by inappropriate language.

עַל חֵטְא שֶׁחָטָאנוּ לְפָנֶיךָ בְּטֻמְאַת שְׂפָתַיִם,
וְעַל חֵטְא שֶׁחָטָאנוּ לְפָנֶיךָ בְּטִפְשׁוּת פֶּה.

For the wrong we did before You with the impulse to
do bad;
And for the wrong we did consciously and
unknowingly.

עַל חֵטְא שֶׁחָטָאנוּ לְפָנֶיךָ בְּיֵצֶר הָרָע,
וְעַל חֵטְא שֶׁחָטָאנוּ לְפָנֶיךָ בְּיוֹדְעִים
וּבְלֹא יוֹדְעִים.

V'Al Kulam, Eloha s'Likhot,
s'Lakh Lanu, m'Khal Lanu, Kapper Lanu.
For all our wrongs, God of forgiveness, pardon us,
forgive us, grant us atonement.

וְעַל כֻּלָּם, אֱלוֹהַּ סְלִיחוֹת,
סְלַח לָנוּ, מְחַל לָנוּ, כַּפֶּר־לָנוּ.

101

For the sin we committed before You by denial and
promises;
And for the wrong we did by accepting bribes.

עַל חֵטְא שֶׁחָטָאנוּ לְפָנֶיךָ בְּכַחַשׁ וּבְכָזָב,
וְעַל חֵטְא שֶׁחָטָאנוּ לְפָנֶיךָ בְּכַפַּת שֹׁחַד.

For the wrong we did before You by mocking others;
And for the wrong we did by speaking ill of other
people.

עַל חֵטְא שֶׁחָטָאנוּ לְפָנֶיךָ בְּלָצוֹן,
וְעַל חֵטְא שֶׁחָטָאנוּ לְפָנֶיךָ בְּלָשׁוֹן הָרָע.

For the wrong we did before You in our business
dealings;
And for the wrong we did when eating and drinking.

עַל חֵטְא שֶׁחָטָאנוּ לְפָנֶיךָ בְּמַשָּׂא וּבְמַתָּן,
וְעַל חֵטְא שֶׁחָטָאנוּ לְפָנֶיךָ בְּמַאֲכָל וּבְמִשְׁתֶּה.

For the wrong we did before You by lacking
generosity;
And for the wrong we did by arrogant pride.

עַל חֵטְא שֶׁחָטָאנוּ לְפָנֶיךָ בְּנֶשֶׁךְ וּבְמַרְבִּית,
וְעַל חֵטְא שֶׁחָטָאנוּ לְפָנֶיךָ בִּנְטִיַּת גָּרוֹן.

For the wrong we did before You by idle conversation;
And for the wrong we did by immodest glances.

עַל חֵטְא שֶׁחָטָאנוּ לְפָנֶיךָ בְּשִׂיחַ שִׂפְתוֹתֵינוּ,
וְעַל חֵטְא שֶׁחָטָאנוּ לְפָנֶיךָ בְּשִׂקּוּר עָיִן.

For the wrong we did before You by scornful eyes;
And for the wrong we did by defiance.

עַל חֵטְא שֶׁחָטָאנוּ לְפָנֶיךָ בְּעֵינַיִם רָמוֹת,
וְעַל חֵטְא שֶׁחָטָאנוּ לְפָנֶיךָ בְּעַזּוּת מֵצַח.

V'Al Kulam, Eloha s'Likhot,
s'Lakh Lanu, m'Khal Lanu, Kapper Lanu.
For all our wrongs, God of forgiveness, pardon us,
forgive us, grant us atonement.

וְעַל כֻּלָּם, אֱלוֹהַּ סְלִיחוֹת,
סְלַח לָנוּ, מְחַל לָנוּ, כַּפֶּר־לָנוּ.

For the wrong we did before You in dismissing
responsibility;
And for the wrong we did in passing harsh judgments
on others.

עַל חֵטְא שֶׁחָטָאנוּ לְפָנֶיךָ בִּפְרִיקַת עֹל,
וְעַל חֵטְא שֶׁחָטָאנוּ לְפָנֶיךָ בִּפְלִילוּת.

For the wrong we did before You by entrapment of
others;
And for the wrong we did by tormenting others.

עַל חֵטְא שֶׁחָטָאנוּ לְפָנֶיךָ בִּצְדִיַּת רֵעַ,
וְעַל חֵטְא שֶׁחָטָאנוּ לְפָנֶיךָ בְּצָרוּת עָיִן.

For the wrong we did before You by frivolity;
And for the wrong we did by being stubborn.

עַל חֵטְא שֶׁחָטָאנוּ לְפָנֶיךָ בְּקַלּוּת רֹאשׁ,
וְעַל חֵטְא שֶׁחָטָאנוּ לְפָנֶיךָ בְּקַשְׁיוּת עֹרֶף.

For the wrong we did before You by running
to do evil;
And for the wrong we did by talebearing.

עַל חֵטְא שֶׁחָטָאנוּ לְפָנֶיךָ בְּרִיצַת רַגְלַיִם לְהָרַע,
וְעַל חֵטְא שֶׁחָטָאנוּ לְפָנֶיךָ בִּרְכִילוּת.

Vidui

For the wrong we did before You by swearing falsely;
And for the wrong we did by causeless hatred.

For the wrong we did before You by betraying a trust;
And for the wrong we did by a confused heart.

עַל חֵטְא שֶׁחָטָאנוּ לְפָנֶיךָ בִּשְׁבוּעַת שָׁוְא,
וְעַל חֵטְא שֶׁחָטָאנוּ לְפָנֶיךָ בְּשִׂנְאַת חִנָּם.

עַל חֵטְא שֶׁחָטָאנוּ לְפָנֶיךָ בִּתְשׂוּמֶת־יָד,
וְעַל חֵטְא שֶׁחָטָאנוּ לְפָנֶיךָ בְּתִמְהוֹן לֵבָב.

V'Al Kulam, Eloha s'Likhot,
s'Lakh Lanu, m'Khal Lanu, Kapper Lanu.
For all of these, O God of forgiveness, pardon us,
forgive us, grant us atonement.

וְעַל כֻּלָּם, אֱלוֹהַּ סְלִיחוֹת,
סְלַח לָנוּ, מְחַל לָנוּ, כַּפֶּר־לָנוּ.

Other Important Considerations—Al Kheyt

Forgive us...

For not listening well to the concerns of others,
For not spending more time with our family,
For neglecting our health,

For worshipping money,
For ignoring the problems in our society,
For taking Israel for granted,

For not acknowledging the human rights of others,
For forgiving in Jews what we condemn in others,
For not addressing injustice,

For turning away from the plight of the hungry,
For turning away from victims of oppression,
For tolerating racism,

For tolerating discrimination towards any group,
For dismissing the disenfranchised,
For failing to protect animal life,

For polluting our earth,

For not making time for study and reflection.

Vidui

Show Us How To Fashion Holiness

O Lord—
Show us how to fashion
holiness from waste,
uncovering sparks in the broken shells
of people beaten down by circumstance
and mired in the boredom of hollowness.

Teach us to take
a neutralized reality
and create the sublime,
forming shapes of blessings with a sacred touch.

Instruct us in sympathy,
that we may learn to tear away at hopelessness
and the groan and oy of despair
by stories, jokes, and astonishing embraces.

Remove shallowness from our lives
and destroy senselessness,
that we may discover Your plan
and fulfill Your purposes.

Give us insight and vision,
and we will perform signs and wonders
in the sight of all humanity
as You Yourself once did
in the Land of Egypt and at Sinai.

Show us Life in all its glory,
and we will glorify Your name,
here and now,
everywhere and forever.

Danny Siegel

How do we find God?

God is found by good deeds and the study of the Torah.

How does the Holy One find us?

The Holy and Blessed One finds us
through love,
through brotherhood and sisterhood,
through respect, through companionship,
through truth, through peace,
through bending the knee, through humility,
through thoughtfulness,
through commerce lessened,
through respect for the learned,
through the discussion of students,
through a good heart, through decency,
through No that is really No,
through Yes that is really Yes.

from the Midrash

יזכור

Yizkor

Artwork: Ben Shahn, Trees

YIZKOR SERVICE

יזכור

What are humans that You care for them,
that You take account of them?

יהוה מָה אָדָם וַתֵּדָעֵהוּ,
בֶּן־אֱנוֹשׁ וַתְּחַשְּׁבֵהוּ.

We are like wisps of vapor,
whose days quickly pass as a shadow,
flourish and grow tall in the morn,
cut down and dried up in the evening,
humbled.

אָדָם לַהֶבֶל דָּמָה
יָמָיו כְּצֵל עוֹבֵר.
בַּבֹּקֶר יָצִיץ וְחָלָף
לָעֶרֶב יְמוֹלֵל וְיָבֵשׁ.
תָּשֵׁב אֱנוֹשׁ עַד־דַּכָּא.

You say:
"Change, people!"

וַתֹּאמֶר
שׁוּבוּ בְנֵי אָדָם.

If we were wise we would understand
what will happen to us in the end.
When we die we take nothing away,
our honors do not follow us.

לוּ חָכְמוּ יַשְׂכִּילוּ
זֹאת יָבִינוּ לְאַחֲרִיתָם.
כִּי לֹא בְמוֹתוֹ יִקַּח הַכֹּל.
לֹא־יֵרֵד אַחֲרָיו כְּבוֹדוֹ.

Observe the innocent person,
take notice of the upright,
for the end of such a person is peace.
The Eternal can be trusted to free the soul of
godly people.

שְׁמָר־תָּם וּרְאֵה יָשָׁר,
כִּי אַחֲרִית לְאִישׁ שָׁלוֹם.
פֹּדֶה יהוה נֶפֶשׁ עֲבָדָיו.
וְלֹא יֶאְשְׁמוּ כָּל־הַחֹסִים בּוֹ.

I remember the life of my beloved . . . who
has gone to *his/her* eternal home. May *his/her*
soul be bound up in the bond of life, savoring
the pleasantness of eternity.

יִזְכֹּר אֱלֹהִים נִשְׁמוֹת קְרוֹבַי שֶׁהָלְכוּ לְעוֹלָמָם.
אָנָּא תִּהְיֶינָה נַפְשׁוֹתֵיהֶם צְרוּרוֹת בִּצְרוֹר
הַחַיִּים. וּתְהִי מְנוּחָתָם כָּבוֹד. שֹׂבַע שְׂמָחוֹת
אֶת־פָּנֶיךָ. נְעִימוֹת בִּימִינְךָ נֶצַח. אָמֵן.

O Transcendent God filled with compassion, grant complete rest under Your protecting wings to the souls we are remembering today for blessing. Please may they join the company of the holy and pure who shine as bright as heaven. Bring their souls into the bonds of eternal life that they may rest in peace. Amen.

אֵל מָלֵא רַחֲמִים שׁוֹכֵן בַּמְּרוֹמִים. הַמְצֵא מְנוּחָה נְכוֹנָה תַּחַת כַּנְפֵי הַשְּׁכִינָה. בְּמַעֲלוֹת קְדוֹשִׁים וּטְהוֹרִים כְּזֹהַר הָרָקִיעַ מַזְהִירִים אֶת נִשְׁמוֹת כָּל־אֵלֶּה שֶׁהִזְכַּרְנוּ הַיּוֹם לִבְרָכָה. אָנָּא בַּעַל הָרַחֲמִים תַּסְתִּירֵם בְּסֵתֶר כְּנָפֶיךָ לְעוֹלָמִים. וְתִצְרוֹר בִּצְרוֹר הַחַיִּים אֶת נִשְׁמוֹתֵיהֶם. וְיָנוּחוּ עַל מִשְׁכְּבוֹתָם בְּשָׁלוֹם. וְנֹאמַר אָמֵן:

We Remember Them

At the rising of the sun and at its going down
we remember them.

    At the blowing of the wind and in the chill of winter
    we remember them.

At the opening of the buds and in the rebirth of spring
we remember them.

    At the blueness of the skies and in the warmth of summer
    we remember them.

At the rustling of the leaves and in the beauty of autumn
we remember them.

    At the beginning of the year and when it ends
    we remember them.

When we are weary and in need of strength
we remember them.

    When we are lost and sick at heart
    we remember them.

When we have joy we crave to share
we remember them.

    So long as we live, they too shall live,
    for they are now a part of us, as we remember them.

Sylvan Kamens and Jack Riemer
Mahzor Hadash

Vihi Noam Adonai Eloheynu Aleynu,

u'Ma'asey Yadeynu Kon'na Aleynu,

u'Ma'asey Yadeynu Kon'neyhu

וִיהִי נֹעַם אֲדֹנָי אֱלֹהֵינוּ עָלֵינוּ
וּמַעֲשֵׂה יָדֵינוּ כּוֹנְנָה עָלֵינוּ
וּמַעֲשֵׂה יָדֵינוּ כּוֹנְנֵהוּ.

Let the beauty of the Eternal Presence be with us and
may what we do have enduring worth.

Psalm 90:17

Psalm 23

The Holy One is my shepherd, I shall not want,	מִזְמוֹר לְדָוִד.
giving me repose in green meadows,	יהוה רֹעִי לֹא אֶחְסָר.
leading me beside the still waters	בִּנְאוֹת דֶּשֶׁא יַרְבִּיצֵנִי
to revive my soul,	עַל־מֵי מְנֻחוֹת יְנַהֲלֵנִי.
guiding me on the right path,	נַפְשִׁי יְשׁוֹבֵב יַנְחֵנִי
for that is God's way.	בְמַעְגְּלֵי־צֶדֶק לְמַעַן שְׁמוֹ.
Though I walk in the valley of the shadow of death,	גַּם כִּי־אֵלֵךְ בְּגֵיא צַלְמָוֶת
I fear no harm, for You are with me.	לֹא־אִירָא רָע כִּי־אַתָּה עִמָּדִי
Your rod and Your staff comfort me.	שִׁבְטְךָ וּמִשְׁעַנְתֶּךָ הֵמָּה יְנַחֲמֻנִי.
You prepare a banquet for me	תַּעֲרֹךְ לְפָנַי שֻׁלְחָן נֶגֶד צֹרְרָי
in the presence of my enemies.	
You anoint my head with oil;	דִּשַּׁנְתָּ בַשֶּׁמֶן רֹאשִׁי כּוֹסִי רְוָיָה.
my cup overflows.	
Surely goodness and lovingkindness shall be mine	אַךְ טוֹב וָחֶסֶד יִרְדְּפוּנִי
all the days of my life.	כָּל־יְמֵי חַיָּי.
And I shall dwell in the House of the Eternal forever.	וְשַׁבְתִּי בְּבֵית־יהוה לְאֹרֶךְ יָמִים.

MOURNER'S KADDISH

קדוש יתום

Yitgadal v'Yitkadash Shmey Rabah,
b'Alma Divra Khirutey
v'Yamlikh Malkutey
b'Khayeykhon u'v'Yomeykhon u'v'Khayey
d'Khol Beyt Yisrael
baAgalah u'Vizman Kariv.
V'Imru: Ameyn.

יִתְגַּדַּל וְיִתְקַדַּשׁ שְׁמֵהּ רַבָּא.
בְּעָלְמָה דִּי בְרָא כִרְעוּתֵהּ.
וְיַמְלִיךְ מַלְכוּתֵהּ,
בְּחַיֵּיכוֹן וּבְיוֹמֵיכוֹן וּבְחַיֵּי
דְכָל בֵּית יִשְׂרָאֵל,
בַּעֲגָלָא וּבִזְמַן קָרִיב.
וְאִמְרוּ אָמֵן:

Y'Hey Shmey Rabah m'Varakh l'Alam
u'l'Almey Almaya:

יְהֵא שְׁמֵהּ רַבָּה מְבָרַךְ לְעָלַם
וּלְעָלְמֵי עָלְמַיָּא:

Yitbarakh v'Yishtabakh v'Yitpaar v'Yitromam
v'Yitnasey v'Yithadar v'Yitaleh v'Yithalal
Shmey d'Kud'sha. Brikh Hu.
L'Eyla u'l'Eyla miKol Birkhata v'Shirata
Tush-b'khata v'Nekhemata daAmiran b'Alma.
V'Imru: Ameyn.

יִתְבָּרַךְ וְיִשְׁתַּבַּח וְיִתְפָּאַר וְיִתְרוֹמַם
וְיִתְנַשֵּׂא וְיִתְהַדָּר וְיִתְעַלֶּה וְיִתְהַלָּל
שְׁמֵהּ דְּקֻדְשָׁא. בְּרִיךְ הוּא.
לְעֵלָּא (וּלְעֵלָּא) מִכָּל בִּרְכָתָא וְשִׁירָתָא
תֻּשְׁבְּחָתָא וְנֶחֱמָתָא דַּאֲמִירָן בְּעָלְמָא.
וְאִמְרוּ אָמֵן:

Y'hey Shlama Raba Min Sh'maya
v'Khayim Aleynu v'Al Kol Yisrael.
V'Imru: Ameyn.

יְהֵא שְׁלָמָא רַבָּא מִן שְׁמַיָּא
וְחַיִּים עָלֵינוּ וְעַל כָּל יִשְׂרָאֵל.
וְאִמְרוּ אָמֵן.

Oseh Shalom Bimromav Hu Ya'aseh Shalom
Aleynu v'Al Kol Yisrael.
V'Imru: Ameyn.

עֹשֶׂה שָׁלוֹם בִּמְרוֹמָיו, הוּא יַעֲשֶׂה שָׁלוֹם
עָלֵנוּ וְעַל כָּל יִשְׂרָאֵל.
וְאִמְרוּ אָמֵן.

May the Universe of Creation be recognized in your lifetime
and throughout your days, and during the lifetime
of the entire House of Yisrael, soon.

So let us acknowledge, honor, celebrate, and sing to the Sacred Source,
though transcendent and truly beyond human songs and blessing.

May the Source of peace grant us peace, and let us say: Amen.

אלה אזכרה

Eyleh Ezkerah

אלה אזכרה ונפשי עלי אשפכה
כי בלעונו זרים כעונה בלי
הפוכה כי בימי השר לא
עלתה ארוכה לעשרה הרוגי מלוכה

Artwork: Ben Shahn, Warsaw 1943

EYLEH EZKERAH

אלה אזכרה

אֵלֶּה אֶזְכְּרָה וְנַפְשִׁי עָלַי אֶשְׁפְּכָה,
כִּי בְלָעוּנוּ זָרִים כְּעֻגָּה בְּלִי הֲפוּכָה,
כִּי בִימֵי הַשַּׂר לֹא עָלְתָה אֲרוּכָה,
לַעֲשָׂרָה הֲרוּגֵי מְלוּכָה.

These things do I remember;
My soul cries out to them.
Throughout time hatred has pursued me,
Ignorance has taken our martyrs in
Lengthy days of blood.

Unter Di Khurves Fun Poyln

*Unter di khurves fun Poyln
A kop mit blonde hor.
Der kop un say der khurbn
Beyde zenen vor.*

*Chorus:
Dolye, mayne dolye.*

*Iber di khurves fun Polyn
Falt un falt der shney,
Der blonder kop fun mayn meydl
Tut mir mesukn vey.*

*Der veytik zitst baym shraybtish
Un shraybt a langn briv,
Di trer in zayne oygn,
Iz emesdik un tif*

*Der groyser shive-foygl
(Mayn dershlogn gemit),
Er trogn oyf zayne fligl
Dos dozike troyer-lid.*

Under the Ruins of Poland

Under the ruins of Poland
lies a head with blond hair.
The head and the ruins are true.

Over the ruins of Poland
the snow keeps falling.
My head aches for my girl's blond head.

Pain is sitting at the desk,
writing a long letter.
The tears in her eyes
are deep and true.

A large bird of mourning
flutters its wings and
bears this song of mourning.

Itsik Manger

Lo Ira

Lo Ira Meriv'vot Am
Asher Saviv Shatu Alai.
Kuma HaShem Hoshi'eyni.

לֹא אִירָא מֵרִבְבוֹת עָם
אֲשֶׁר סָבִיב שָׁתוּ עָלָי.
קוּמָה יהוה הוֹשִׁיעֵנִי.

I will not fear the multitudes who beset me.
Arise, oh God! Save me.

Psalm 3:7-8

A Mother's Will

Judaism, my child, is the struggle to bring down God upon earth, a struggle for the sanctification of the human heart. This struggle your people wages not with the physical force but with spirit, with sincere, heartfelt prayers, and by constant striving for truth and justice.

So do you understand, my child, how we are distinct from others and wherein lies the secret of our existence on earth?

Knowing this, will your heart still be heavy, my child? Will you still say you cannot stand your fate? But you must, my child, for so were you commanded; it is your calling. This is your mission, your purpose on earth.

You must go to work alongside people of other nations...and you will teach them that they must come to a brotherhood of nations and to a union of all nations with God.

You may ask, "How does one speak to them?" This is how: "Thou shalt not murder; thou shall not steal; thou shalt not covet; love thy neighbor as thyself ..." Do these things and through their merit, my child, you will be victorious.

Published in the ghetto newspaper Warsaw-Krakow, 1940, this will was signed only "Your Mother."

Vihuda L'Olam Teshev

Vihuda l'Olam Teshev (2)
Virushalayim l'Khol Dor Vador
Virushalayim l'Dor Vador.

וִיהוּדָה לְעוֹלָם תֵּשֵׁב
וִירוּשָׁלַיִם לְכֹל דּוֹר וָדוֹר,
וִירוּשָׁלַיִם לְדוֹר וָדוֹר.

Judah shall abide forever
And Jerusalem from generation
Unto generation.

Joel 4:20

114

The Messiah Came to Europe

The Messiah came to Europe,
according to tradition,
ready to redeem humanity,
to declare everlasting peace.
He wandered the streets of villages,
looking for his people.
Mystified, puzzled, hurt, he called:
Father Most High! Your children
are nowhere to be found!
I came to proclaim, according to Thy will,
the Kingdom of Heaven, Resurrection
of Your loyal servants. No one
reawakened from dusty ashes
spread as fertilizer on European fields.

At the gates of the European cemetery
He found a survivor, who asked in anguish:
Why didn't you come when needed?
Up to the doorsteps of the gas chambers
our people sang "Ani Ma'amin—we believe."
Sadly the Messiah listened to the lonely
survivor, tears running down his white beard.
I have no answer to your crucial question;
I myself must repent and ask their forgiveness.
Until then, my redemption be suspended!

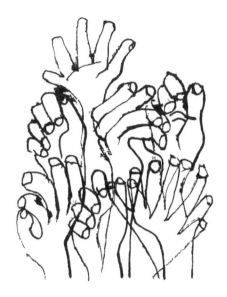

Herman Taube

Too Late

...A child of seven was reading in school the chapter which tells of the sacrifice of Isaac:

Isaac was on the way to Mount Moriah with his father; then he lay on the altar, bound, waiting to be sacrificed. My heart began to beat even faster; it actually sobbed with pity for Isaac. Behold, Abraham now lifted the knife. And now my heart froze within me with fright. Suddenly, the voice of the angel was heard: "Abraham, lay not your hand upon the lad, for now I know that you fear God." And here I broke out in tears and wept aloud. "Why are you crying?" asked the rabbi. "You know that Isaac was not killed."

And I said to him, still weeping, "But, rabbi, supposing the angel had come a second too late?"

The rabbi comforted me and calmed me by telling that an angel cannot come late.

An angel cannot be late, but man, made of flesh and blood, may be.

A.J. Heschel

Artwork: Ben Shahn, Hands (Shape of Content)

Eyleh Ezkerah

Vakht Oyf!

Vi lang, o vi lang vet ir blaybn nokh shklafn
Un trogn di shendlekhe keyt?
Vi lang vet ir glentsnde raykhtimer shafn
Far dem, vos baroybt ayer broyt?

Vi lang vet ir shteyn, ayer rukn geboygn,
Derniderikt, heymloz, farshmakht?
Es togt shoyn, vakht oyf, un tseefnt di oygn,
Derfilt ayer ayzerne makht!

Klingt umetum in di frayheyts-glokn!
Farzamlt di laydnde knekht!
Un kemft bagaystert, un kemft umdershrokn
Far ayere heylike rekht!

How long will you remain slaves
and wear degrading chains?
How long will you produce riches
for those who rob you of your bread?

How long will you stand with backs bent—
humiliated, homeless and weak?
It's daybreak, awake, open your eyes,
and see your own strength.

Ring the freedom bells everywhere,
gather together the suffering slaves,
and fight for your sacred rights!

David Edelstat

Partisanen Lied

Zog nit keinmol,
as du geist
dem letzten veg,
Ven himlen blainde
farshteln bloie teg,
Vail kumen
vet noch unzer
oisgebenkte sho,
S'vet a poik ton
unzer trot:
Mir zainen do!

זאָג ניט קיינמאָל
אַז דו גייסט דעם לעצטן וועג,
ווען הימלען בלייענדע
פארשטעלן בלויע טעג,
ווייל קומען וועט נאָך אונזער
אויסגעבענקטע שעה,
ס׳וועט א פויק טאָן
אונזער טראָט.
מיר זיינען דאָ!

Never say that you are going your last way,
Though lead-filled skies above blot out the blue of day.
The hour for which we long will certainly appear.
The earth shall thunder 'neath our tread that we are here.

Hirsch Glick

Ani Ma'Amin

Ani Ma'amin
be'Emunah Sh'leyma
b'Viyat haMashiakh.
V'Af Al Pi Sheyitmahmeah
Im Kol Zeh Akhakeh Lo,
b'Khol Yom, Sheyavo.

אֲנִי מַאֲמִין
בֶּאֱמוּנָה שְׁלֵמָה
בְּבִיאַת הַמָּשִׁיחַ
וְאַף עַל פִּי שֶׁיִּתְמַהְמֵהַּ
עִם כָּל זֶה אֲחַכֶּה לוֹ
בְּכָל יוֹם שֶׁיָבוֹא.

I believe with perfect faith
in the coming of the Messiah;
and although the Redemption may tarry,
daily I wait.

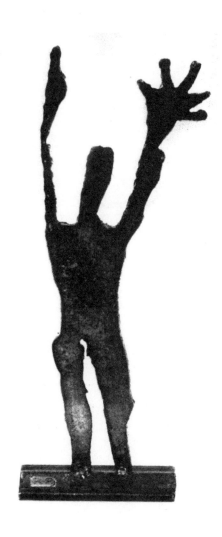

117

נעילה

Ne'ilah

NE'ILAH SERVICE

Di Zun Vet Aruntergeyn

Di zun vet aruntergeyn untern barg,
Vet kumen di libe a shtile tsu geyn
Tsum umet vos zitst oyf a goldenem shteyn
Un veynt far zikh eyner aleyn.

Di zun vet aruntergeyn untern barg,
Vet kumen di goldene pave tsu flien;
Un mitnemen vet zi undz ale ahin—
Ahin, vu di benkshaft vet tsien.

Di zun vet aruntergeyn untern barg;
Vet kumen di nakht un vet zingen lyu-lyu
Ariber di oygn vos fain shoyn tsu
Tsu shlofn in eybiker ru.

The Sun Will Set

The sun will soon set beneath the hill;
silently love will come upon the loneliness
that sits weeping upon a golden stone.

The sun will set beneath the hill;
the golden peacock will come
and take us all to the place for which we yearn.

The sun will set beneath the hill;
and night will come
and draw us all into eternal slumber.

Moshe Halpern

Pit'khu Li Sha'arei Tzedek
Avo Vam Odeh Yah.
Open the gates of justice for me so that
I may enter there. I will thank God.

Psalm 118:19

פִּתְחוּ לִי שַׁעֲרֵי צֶדֶק
אָבֹא בָם אוֹדֶה יָהּ.

Blessed is the Creator, who has given us the
teaching and truth of the Torah, and who
creates life all around us.

בָּרוּךְ (הוּא) אֱלֹהֵינוּ,
שֶׁבְּרָאָנוּ לִכְבוֹדוֹ,
וְהִבְדִּילָנוּ מִן הַתּוֹעִים,
וְנָתַן לָנוּ תּוֹרַת אֱמֶת,
וְחַיֵּי עוֹלָם נָטַע בְּתוֹכֵנוּ.

121

The name of the Eternal inspires trust
in justice and the glory of the Torah.

וְיִבְטְחוּ בְךָ יוֹדְעֵי שְׁמֶךָ,
כִּי לֹא עָזַבְתָּ דוֹרְשֶׁיךָ יהוה.
יהוה חָפֵץ לְמַעַן צִדְקוֹ,
יַגְדִּיל תּוֹרָה וְיַאְדִּיר.

May the Eternal open the gates of
wisdom and grace to those who
seek truth and justice, to those who
have followed the commandments.
M'heyra Tiftakh.

שַׁעֲרֵי אַרְמוֹן מְהֵרָה תִּפְתַּח לְבוֹאֲרֵי דַת אָמוֹן.
שַׁעֲרֵי גְנוּזִים מְהֵרָה תִּפְתַּח לְדָתְךָ אֲחוּזִים.
שַׁעֲרֵי הֵיכַל הַנֶּחֱמָדִים מְהֵרָה תִּפְתַּח לְוֹעוּדִים.
שַׁעֲרֵי זְבוּל מַחֲנַיִם מְהֵרָה תִּפְתַּח לְחַכְלִילִי עֵינָיִם.
שַׁעֲרֵי טָהֳרָה מְהֵרָה תִּפְתַּח לְיָפָה וּבָרָה.
שַׁעֲרֵי כֶתֶר הַמְיֻמָּן מְהֵרָה תִּפְתַּח לְלֹא אַלְמָן.

May we enter the gates even as they
are closing.

פְּתַח לָנוּ שַׁעַר, בְּעֵת נְעִילַת שַׁעַר,
כִּי פָנָה יוֹם.

The day is ending; the sun sets.
Let us enter the gates.

הַיּוֹם יִפְנֶה, הַשֶּׁמֶשׁ יָבֹא וְיִפְנֶה,
נָבוֹאָה שְׁעָרֶיךָ.

We ask our Creator to pardon and forgive
our errors and transgressions.
Grant us atonement.

אָנָּא אֵל נָא, שָׂא נָא, סְלַח נָא, מְחַל נָא,
חֲמָל־נָא, רַחֶם־נָא, כַּפֶּר־נָא,
כְּבוֹשׁ חֵטְא וְעָוֹן.

Piyyut: Eyl Nora Alilah

Eyl Nora Alilah
HaM'tzey Lanu M'khilah
biSh'at Han'ilah
Eyl Nora Alilah.

אֵל נוֹרָא עֲלִילָה
הַמְצֵא לָנוּ מְחִילָה
בִּשְׁעַת הַנְּעִילָה.
אֵל נוֹרָא עֲלִילָה.

O God of mighty acts,
O God of awe inspiring acts,
Pardon us.
The gates are closing.

Amidah

Adonai, Adonai Eyl Rakhum v'Khanun
Erekh Apayim v'Rav Khesed ve'Emet.
Notzer Khesed laAlafim
Nosey Avon vaFesha v'Khata'ah v'Nakey.

יהוה יהוה אֵל רַחוּם וְחַנּוּן,
אֶרֶךְ אַפַּיִם וְרַב חֶסֶד וֶאֱמֶת
נֹצֵר חֶסֶד לָאֲלָפִים
נֹשֵׂא עָוֹן וָפֶשַׁע וְחַטָּאָה, וְנַקֵּה.

Eternal Life Source, compassionate and gracious,
slow to anger, abundant in lovingkindness and truth,
preserving love for thousands of generations,
enduring wrongdoing and sinfulness,
and then granting release.

We are Your people, and You are our God.
We are Your children, and You give us life.
We are Your servants, and You are our Master.
We are Your congregation, and You are our only One.
We are Your heritage, and You are our Destiny.
We are Your flock, and You are our Shepherd.
We are Your vineyard, and You are our Protector.
We are Your creatures, and You are our Creator.
We are Your companions, and You are our Beloved.
We are Your treasure, and You delight in us.
We are Your people, and You are our Sovereign.
We solely acknowledge You, and You favor us.

כִּי אָנוּ עַמֶּךָ, וְאַתָּה אֱלֹהֵינוּ.
אָנוּ בָנֶיךָ, וְאַתָּה אָבִינוּ.
אָנוּ עֲבָדֶיךָ, וְאַתָּה אֲדוֹנֵנוּ.
אָנוּ קְהָלֶךָ, וְאַתָּה חֶלְקֵנוּ.
אָנוּ נַחֲלָתֶךָ, וְאַתָּה גוֹרָלֵנוּ.
אָנוּ צֹאנֶךָ, וְאַתָּה רוֹעֵנוּ.
אָנוּ כַרְמֶךָ, וְאַתָּה נוֹטְרֵנוּ.
אָנוּ פְעֻלָּתֶךָ, וְאַתָּה יוֹצְרֵנוּ.
אָנוּ רַעְיָתֶךָ, וְאַתָּה דוֹדֵנוּ.
אָנוּ סְגֻלָּתֶךָ, וְאַתָּה קְרוֹבֵנוּ.
אָנוּ עַמֶּךָ, וְאַתָּה מַלְכֵּנוּ.
אָנוּ מַאֲמִירֶיךָ, וְאַתָּה מַאֲמִירֵנוּ

We have transgressed, but You are compassionate.
We persist in our errors, but You are long-suffering.
We have done wrong, but You are merciful.
Our days pass like shadows, but You are Eternal.

אָנוּ עַזֵּי פָנִים, וְאַתָּה רַחוּם וְחַנּוּן.
אָנוּ קְשֵׁי עֹרֶף וְאַתָּה אֶרֶךְ אַפַּיִם.
אָנוּ מְלֵאֵי עָוֹן, וְאַתָּה מָלֵא רַחֲמִים.
אָנוּ יָמֵינוּ כְּצֵל עוֹבֵר,
וְאַתָּה הוּא וּשְׁנוֹתֶיךָ לֹא יִתָּמּוּ.

May our prayer be worthy of ancestors' faith.
Let our prayer enter the presence of the Sacred
and not be ignored.

We are not so obstinate and stubborn as to say
"We are righteous, we have done no wrong."
Indeed, we have done wrong. We have sinned.
We have missed the mark.

Ashamnu, Bagadnu, Gazalnu, Dibarnu Dofi,

He'evinu, V'Hirshanu, Zadnu, Khamasnu,

Tafalnu Sheker, Ya'atznu Ra, Kizavnu, Latznu,

Maradnu, Ni'atznu, Sararnu, Avinu,

Pashanu, Tzararnu, Kishinu Oref, Rashanu,

Shikhatnu, Ti'avnu, Ta'inu, Ti'ta'nu.

We have blamed, we have deceived, we have spoiled,
We have been hypocritical,
We have offended, we have been wicked,
We have been presumptuous, we have done violence,
We have deceived, we have ill-advised,
We have lied, we have mocked,
We have rebelled; we have been iniquitous,
We have trespassed, we have oppressed,
We have been obstinate, we have acted wickedly,
We have been corrupt, we have wasted,
We have erred, we have led others astray.

אֱלֹהֵינוּ וֵאלֹהֵי אֲבוֹתֵינוּ וֵאלֹהֵי
אִמּוֹתֵינוּ תָּבֹא לְפָנֶיךָ תְּפִלָּתֵנוּ
וְאַל תִּתְעַלַּם מִתְּחִנָּתֵנוּ.
שֶׁאֵין אֲנַחְנוּ עַזֵּי פָנִים וּקְשֵׁי עֹרֶף
לוֹמַר לְפָנֶיךָ יהוה אֱלֹהֵינוּ וֵאלֹהֵי
אֲבוֹתֵינוּ צַדִּיקִים אֲנַחְנוּ וְלֹא חָטָאנוּ.
אֲבָל אֲנַחְנוּ חָטָאנוּ.

אָשַׁמְנוּ, בָּגַדְנוּ, גָּזַלְנוּ, דִּבַּרְנוּ דֹפִי.
הֶעֱוִינוּ, וְהִרְשַׁעְנוּ, זַדְנוּ, חָמַסְנוּ,
טָפַלְנוּ שֶׁקֶר. יָעַצְנוּ רָע, כִּזַּבְנוּ, לַצְנוּ,
מָרַדְנוּ, נִאַצְנוּ, סָרַרְנוּ, עָוִינוּ,
פָּשַׁעְנוּ, צָרַרְנוּ, קִשִּׁינוּ עֹרֶף. רָשַׁעְנוּ,
שִׁחַתְנוּ, תִּעַבְנוּ, תָּעִינוּ, תִּעְתָּעְנוּ.

Ne'ilah

Ne'ilah

Wherever we stand to lift our eyes to heaven,
that place is a Holy of Holies.

S. Ansky

The sun descending settling
on the roof of the synagogue.
The cantor faces the open Ark,
His exhausted voice sounds hoarse.
My lips are dry, my mouth bitter,
My irritable tongue feels
a burning sensation, sends flash
signals to my brain, while my stomach
blows shofar. A realization:
what it is like to be hungry...
The sanctuary doors are closed,
I feel like Jonah in the whale's belly.
A thousand people pray here
and I feel lonely, uncertain.

After a day full of prayers,
a thunderstorm of psalms, poems,
an avalanche of biblical passages,
showering my God with compliments,
praise, petition, lamentations,
exhausted from memorial chants,
confession of sins never committed,
I reach the last page of the Machzor.
I close my eyes, frightened by the thought
that the liturgy I have been chanting all day
is not sincere, the words not mine.
Angels, hell, paradise, seem far away.
Now, in the last moments before
the Ark is closed, I pray:
Simple words, children, people, earth,
sunshine, health, love, peace:
God—I say—make me wise enough
to care about others who are hungry,
good enough to share my love
with the less fortunate in this world.

Herman Taube

Kol HaOlam Kulo Gesher Tzar M'od
V'HaIkar Lo l'Fakheyd Klal.

The world seems like a very narrow bridge
and the essence is not to be afraid.

Reb Nachman of Braslav

כָּל־הָעוֹלָם כֻּלּוֹ גֶּשֶׁר צַר מְאֹד
וְהָעִקָּר לֹא לְפַחֵד כְּלָל.

A Prayer

"Prayer, Man's Rational Prerogative."
Wordsworth

Bless us with the capacity
To remember and to forgive:
Bless us with the ability
To listen and understand.

Bless us with the talent
To master the vocations
We are fit for and still
Attain humility of soul.

Bless us with vision to perceive,
Conceive ideals for the future,
To be capable to persuade others
To join us in the quest for tomorrow.

Bless us with the opportunity
To serve our families, community.
So that, at the end of our days we will
Be able to say: "We have done our best."

Herman Taube

Karev Yom, Karev Yom. קָרֵב יוֹם
Asher Hu Lo Yom v'Lo Laila. אֲשֶׁר הוּא לֹא יוֹם וְלֹא לַיְלָה.
Rom Hoda, Hoda, Hoda רָם הוֹדַע
Ki l'Kha Yom Af L'Kha HaLaila. כִּי לְךָ יוֹם אַף לְךָ הַלַּיְלָה.

May the day draw near
which is neither day nor night.
May it be proclaimed
that the day and the night are Yours!

from the Haggadah

Rad HaLaila

Rad haLaila, Rav Shireynu רַד הַלַּיְלָה, רַב שִׁירֵנוּ
HaBokeyah laShamayim. הַבּוֹקֵעַ לַשָּׁמַיִם.
Shuvi Shuvi, Horateynu שׁוּבִי שׁוּבִי, הוֹרָתֵנוּ
M'Khudeshet Shivatayim. מְחֻדֶּשֶׁת שִׁבְעָתַיִם.
Shuvi Shuvi, v'Nasov, שׁוּבִי שׁוּבִי, וְנָסֹב,
Ki Darkeynu Eyn La Sof, כִּי דַּרְכֵּנוּ אֵין לָהּ סוֹף,
Ki Od Nimshekhhet כִּי עוֹד נִמְשֶׁכֶת הַשַּׁלְשֶׁלֶת,
HaShalshelet. כִּי לִבֵּנוּ לֵב אֶחָד
Ki Libeynu Lev Ekhad מִנִּי אָז וַעֲדֵי־עַד,
Mini Az va'AdeyAd כִּי עוֹד נִמְשֶׁכֶת הַשַּׁלְשֶׁלֶת.
Ki Od Nimshekhet haShalshelet. לַ לַ לַ ...
La, la, la...

Night is falling, great is our song
Piercing to the heavens.
Again, again, our hora,
Renewed sevenfold.
Again, again, and let us spin about
For our path has no end,
For the chain yet continues.
For our heart is one heart,
From now and forever,
For the chain yet continues.

Jerusalem of Gold

The olive trees that stand in silence upon the hills of time,
To hear the voices of the city as bells of evening chime.
The shofar sounding from the Temple to call the world to prayer,
The shepherd pauses in the valley and peace is everywhere.

Chorus:

Yerushalayim Shel Zahav   יְרוּשָׁלַיִם שֶׁל זָהָב
v'Shel n'Khoshet v'Shel Ohr   וְשֶׁל נְחֹשֶׁת וְשֶׁל אוֹר
haLo l'Khol Shirayikh—Ani Kinor.   הֲלֹא לְכָל שִׁירַיִךְ אֲנִי כִּנּוֹר.

The water well for those who thirsted, the ancient market square,
Your golden sun that lights the future for people everywhere.
How many songs, how many stories the stony hills recall,
Around her heart my city carries a lonely ancient wall.

Chorus

Far away beyond the desert a thousand suns will glow,
Peoples lifting one another, where light and justice flow.*
My simple voice cannot acclaim thee, too weak the words I choose,
Jerusalem, if I forget thee, may my right hand its cunning lose.

Chorus

Norman Newell, Naomi Shemer
*adaptation

Erev Ba

Shuv ha'Eder Noher,   שׁוּב הָעֵדֶר נוֹהֵר
Bimvo'ot haK'far   בִּמְבוֹאוֹת הַכְּפָר,
v'Oleh haAvak,   וְעוֹלֶה הָאָבָק
Mishvelei Afar.   מִשְׁבִילֵי עָפָר.
V'Harkhek Od Tsemed Inbalim   וְהַרְחֵק עוֹד צֶמֶד עִנְבָּלִים
m'Laveh Et Meshekh haTs'lalim.   מְלַוֶּה אֶת־מֶשֶׁךְ הַצְּלָלִים.
Erev Ba, Erev Ba.   עֶרֶב בָּא, עֶרֶב בָּא.

Again the flocks wander along the village street
And the dust rises from sandy paths
And far away the bells merge
With the gathering shadows.
Evening falls, evening falls.

Ne'ilah

Avinu Malkeynu

Avinu Malkeynu
Khaneynu vaAneynu
Ki Eyn Banu Ma'asim
Asey Imanu, Tzedakah vaKhesed,
V'Hoshi'eynu.

אָבִינוּ מַלְכֵּנוּ
חָנֵּנוּ וַעֲנֵנוּ
כִּי אֵין בָּנוּ מַעֲשִׂים
עֲשֵׂה עִמָּנוּ צְדָקָה וָחֶסֶד
וְהוֹשִׁיעֵנוּ.

We call upon the Sacred Sovereign Parent of Life.
Please answer us.
We admit our failings and lack of righteous deeds.

We ask for justice and lovingkindness;
and we ask for liberation.

Ark is closed, all remain standing

שְׁמַע יִשְׂרָאֵל יהוה אֱלֹהֵינוּ יהוה אֶחָד
Shma Yisrael Adonai Eloheynu Adonai Ekhad
Listen Israel, the Eternal our God, the Source of Being is One

three times:

בָּרוּךְ שֵׁם כְּבוֹד מַלְכוּתוֹ לְעוֹלָם וָעֶד
Barukh Shem K'vod Malkhuto l'Olam Vaed
Praised be the Glorious One whose Creation is forever

seven times:

יהוה הוּא הָאֱלֹהִים
Adonai Hu HaElohim

KADDISH SHALEM

קדוש שלם

Yitgadal v'Yitkadash Shmey Rabah,	יִתְגַּדַּל וְיִתְקַדַּשׁ שְׁמֵהּ רַבָּא.
b'Alma Divra Khirutey	בְּעָלְמָא דִּי בְרָא כִרְעוּתֵהּ.
v'Yamlikh Malkutey	וְיַמְלִיךְ מַלְכוּתֵהּ,
b'Khayeykhon u'v'Yomeykhon u'v'Khayey	בְּחַיֵּיכוֹן וּבְיוֹמֵיכוֹן וּבְחַיֵּי
d'Khol Beyt Yisrael baAgalah u'Vizman Kariv.	דְכָל בֵּית יִשְׂרָאֵל, בַּעֲגָלָא וּבִזְמַן קָרִיב.
V'Imru: Ameyn.	וְאִמְרוּ אָמֵן:

Y'Hey Shmey Rabah m'Varakh l'Alam	יְהֵא שְׁמֵהּ רַבָּה מְבָרַךְ לְעָלַם
u'l'Almey Almaya.	וּלְעָלְמֵי עָלְמַיָּא:

Yitbarakh v'Yishtabakh v'Yitpaar v'Yitromam	יִתְבָּרַךְ וְיִשְׁתַּבַּח וְיִתְפָּאַר וְיִתְרוֹמַם
v'Yitnasey v'Yithadar v'Yitaleh v'Yithalal	וְיִתְנַשֵּׂא וְיִתְהַדָּר וְיִתְעַלֶּה וְיִתְהַלָּל
Shmey d'Kud'sha. Brikh Hu.	שְׁמֵהּ דְּקֻדְשָׁא. בְּרִיךְ הוּא.
L'Eyla u'l'Eyla miKol Birkhata v'Shirata	לְעֵלָּא (וּלְעֵלָּא) מִכָּל בִּרְכָתָא וְשִׁירָתָא
Tush-b'khata v'Nekhemata daAmiran b'Alma.	תֻּשְׁבְּחָתָא וְנֶחֱמָתָא דַּאֲמִירָן בְּעָלְמָא.
V'Imru: Ameyn.	וְאִמְרוּ אָמֵן:

Titkabeyl Tz'lot'hon u'Va'ut'hon d'Khol Beyt	תִּתְקַבֵּל צְלוֹתְהוֹן וּבָעוּתְהוֹן דְּכָל (בֵּית)
Yisrael Kadam Avuhon Di vi'Sh'maya	יִשְׂרָאֵל קֳדָם אֲבוּהוֹן דִּי בִשְׁמַיָּא
V'Imru: Ameyn.	וְאִמְרוּ אָמֵן:

Y'hey Shlama Raba Min Sh'maya	יְהֵא שְׁלָמָא רַבָּא מִן שְׁמַיָּא
v'Khayim Aleynu v'Al Kol Yisrael.	וְחַיִּים עָלֵינוּ וְעַל כָּל יִשְׂרָאֵל.
V'Imru: Ameyn.	וְאִמְרוּ אָמֵן:

Oseh Shalom Bimromav	עֹשֶׂה שָׁלוֹם בִּמְרוֹמָיו,
Hu Ya'aseh Shalom Aleynu v'Al Kol Yisrael,	הוּא יַעֲשֶׂה שָׁלוֹם עָלֵינוּ וְעַל כָּל יִשְׂרָאֵל.
V'Imru: Ameyn.	וְאִמְרוּ אָמֵן:

May the Universe of Creation be recognized in your lifetime and throughout your days, and during the lifetime of the entire House of Yisrael, soon.

So let us acknowledge, honor, celebrate, and sing to the Sacred Source, though transcendent and truly beyond human songs and blessing.

May the Source of peace grant us peace, and let us say: Amen.

FINAL SOUNDING OF THE SHOFAR

תְּקִיעָה גְדוֹלָה

Tekiah G'dolah

לַשָּׁנָה הַבָּאָה בִּירוּשָׁלָיִם.

LaShana HaBa'ah biYerushalayim.

Next year in Jerusalem.

Next year in a world of truth, justice, and peace.

Artwork: Ben Shahn, Untitled

Torah and Haftarah Readings

TORAH READING FOR THE FIRST DAY OF ROSH HASHANAH

Genesis 21

ספר בראשית פרק כא

The Ineffable visited Sarah as had been promised and did for Sarah as had been spoken. Sarah conceived and gave birth to Abraham's son in his old age, at the designated time that God (Elohim) had spoken. And Abraham named the son that was born to him, to which Sarah had given birth, Isaac. And Abraham circumcised his son Isaac when he was eight days old, as God had commanded him.

Abraham was one hundred years old when his son Isaac was born. And Sarah said, "God has made me laugh. All who hear will laugh with me." And she said, "Who would have said to Abraham, that Sarah would nurse children? For I have given birth to a son in old age." And the child grew and was weaned, and Abraham hosted a great celebration on the day that Isaac was weaned.

Now Sarah saw that the son which Hagar, the Egyptian, had born unto Abraham, was teasing (Isaac). She said to Abraham, "Expel this servant woman and her son; for the son of this servant woman will not share the inheritance with my son Isaac." But the situation terribly displeased Abraham on account of his son. And Elohim said to Abraham, "Do not be troubled for the boy and for your servant woman; regarding all that Sarah tells you, listen to her, for only through Isaac your seed will be continued. Also the son of the servant woman will I make into a nation, for he is your offspring, too."

First aliyah

א וַיהֹוָה פָּקַד אֶת־שָׂרָה כַּאֲשֶׁר אָמָר וַיַּעַשׂ יְהֹוָה לְשָׂרָה כַּאֲשֶׁר דִּבֵּר: ב וַתַּהַר וַתֵּלֶד שָׂרָה לְאַבְרָהָם בֵּן לִזְקֻנָיו לַמּוֹעֵד אֲשֶׁר־דִּבֶּר אֹתוֹ אֱלֹהִים: ג וַיִּקְרָא אַבְרָהָם אֶת־שֶׁם־בְּנוֹ הַנּוֹלַד־לוֹ אֲשֶׁר־יָלְדָה־לּוֹ שָׂרָה יִצְחָק: ד וַיָּמָל אַבְרָהָם אֶת־יִצְחָק בְּנוֹ בֶּן־שְׁמֹנַת יָמִים כַּאֲשֶׁר צִוָּה אֹתוֹ אֱלֹהִים:

Second aliyah

ה וְאַבְרָהָם בֶּן־מְאַת שָׁנָה בְּהִוָּלֶד לוֹ אֵת יִצְחָק בְּנוֹ: ו וַתֹּאמֶר שָׂרָה צְחֹק עָשָׂה לִי אֱלֹהִים כָּל־הַשֹּׁמֵעַ יִצְחַק־לִי: ז וַתֹּאמֶר מִי מִלֵּל לְאַבְרָהָם הֵינִיקָה בָנִים שָׂרָה כִּי־יָלַדְתִּי בֵן לִזְקֻנָיו: ח וַיִּגְדַּל הַיֶּלֶד וַיִּגָּמַל וַיַּעַשׂ אַבְרָהָם מִשְׁתֶּה גָדוֹל בְּיוֹם הִגָּמֵל אֶת־יִצְחָק:

(On Shabbat, third aliyah)

ט וַתֵּרֶא שָׂרָה אֶת־בֶּן־הָגָר הַמִּצְרִית אֲשֶׁר־יָלְדָה לְאַבְרָהָם מְצַחֵק: י וַתֹּאמֶר לְאַבְרָהָם גָּרֵשׁ הָאָמָה הַזֹּאת וְאֶת־בְּנָהּ כִּי לֹא יִירַשׁ בֶּן־הָאָמָה הַזֹּאת עִם־בְּנִי עִם־יִצְחָק: יא וַיֵּרַע הַדָּבָר מְאֹד בְּעֵינֵי אַבְרָהָם עַל אוֹדֹת בְּנוֹ: יב וַיֹּאמֶר אֱלֹהִים אֶל־אַבְרָהָם אַל־יֵרַע בְּעֵינֶיךָ עַל־הַנַּעַר וְעַל־אֲמָתֶךָ כֹּל אֲשֶׁר תֹּאמַר אֵלֶיךָ שָׂרָה שְׁמַע בְּקֹלָהּ כִּי בְיִצְחָק יִקָּרֵא לְךָ זָרַע:

And Abraham got up early in the morning, took bread and a pouch of water, gave it to Hagar, placing it on her shoulder with the boy, and sent her away; she went and wandered in the wilderness of B'er Sheva. The water in the skin was used up, and she sent the boy under one of the bushes. She went and sat facing him, about the distance of a bowshot away, and prayed, "Let me not see the death of the boy"; and she sat facing him and wept in a loud voice. And God heard the voice of the lad, and an angel of God called to Hagar from heaven and said to her, "What is the matter, Hagar? Do not fear, for God has heard the voice of the boy where he is."

"Arise, lift up the lad, and firmly place your hand upon him, for I will make him a great nation." And God opened her eyes and she saw a well of water. She went and filled the skin with water and refreshed the lad. And Elohim was with the boy and he grew up, settling in the wilderness and becoming an archer. He settled in the wilderness of Paran, and his mother took a wife for him from the land of Egypt.

Now it was at this time that Avimelekh and Pikhol, in charge of his fighters, spoke to Abraham, saying, "God is with you in all that you do. And now, swear to me here, by God, that you will not deal falsely with me, with my son or my grandson; according to the kindness that I have done with you, do unto me and to the land in which you have lived a while." And Abraham said, "I will swear." And then Abraham reprimanded Avimelekh concerning (the conflict over) the well of water that Avimelekh's servants had seized. And Avimelekh said, "I do not know who did this,

יג וְגַם אֶת־בֶּן־הָאָמָה לְגוֹי אֲשִׂימֶנּוּ כִּי זַרְעֲךָ הוּא: יד וַיַּשְׁכֵּם אַבְרָהָם | בַּבֹּקֶר וַיִּקַּח־לֶחֶם וְחֵמַת מַיִם וַיִּתֵּן אֶל־הָגָר שָׂם עַל־שִׁכְמָהּ וְאֶת־הַיֶּלֶד וַיְשַׁלְּחֶהָ וַתֵּלֶךְ וַתֵּתַע בְּמִדְבַּר בְּאֵר שָׁבַע: טו וַיִּכְלוּ הַמַּיִם מִן־הַחֵמֶת וַתַּשְׁלֵךְ אֶת־הַיֶּלֶד תַּחַת אַחַד הַשִּׂיחִם: טז וַתֵּלֶךְ וַתֵּשֶׁב לָהּ מִנֶּגֶד הַרְחֵק כִּמְטַחֲוֵי קֶשֶׁת כִּי אָמְרָה אַל־אֶרְאֶה בְּמוֹת הַיָּלֶד וַתֵּשֶׁב מִנֶּגֶד וַתִּשָּׂא אֶת־קֹלָהּ וַתֵּבְךְּ: יז וַיִּשְׁמַע אֱלֹהִים אֶת־קוֹל הַנַּעַר וַיִּקְרָא מַלְאַךְ אֱלֹהִים | אֶל־הָגָר מִן־הַשָּׁמַיִם וַיֹּאמֶר לָהּ מַה־לָּךְ הָגָר אַל־תִּירְאִי כִּי־שָׁמַע אֱלֹהִים אֶל־קוֹל הַנַּעַר בַּאֲשֶׁר הוּא־שָׁם:

יח קוּמִי שְׂאִי אֶת־הַנַּעַר וְהַחֲזִיקִי אֶת־יָדֵךְ בּוֹ כִּי־לְגוֹי גָּדוֹל אֲשִׂימֶנּוּ: יט וַיִּפְקַח אֱלֹהִים אֶת־עֵינֶיהָ וַתֵּרֶא בְּאֵר מָיִם וַתֵּלֶךְ וַתְּמַלֵּא אֶת־הַחֵמֶת מַיִם וַתַּשְׁקְ אֶת־הַנָּעַר: כ וַיְהִי אֱלֹהִים אֶת־הַנַּעַר וַיִּגְדָּל וַיֵּשֶׁב בַּמִּדְבָּר וַיְהִי רֹבֶה קַשָּׁת: כא וַיֵּשֶׁב בְּמִדְבַּר פָּארָן וַתִּקַּח־לוֹ אִמּוֹ אִשָּׁה מֵאֶרֶץ מִצְרָיִם: פ

כב וַיְהִי בָּעֵת הַהִוא וַיֹּאמֶר אֲבִימֶלֶךְ וּפִיכֹל שַׂר־צְבָאוֹ אֶל־אַבְרָהָם לֵאמֹר אֱלֹהִים עִמְּךָ בְּכֹל אֲשֶׁר־אַתָּה עֹשֶׂה: כג וְעַתָּה הִשָּׁבְעָה לִּי בֵאלֹהִים הֵנָּה אִם־תִּשְׁקֹר לִי וּלְנִינִי וּלְנֶכְדִּי כַּחֶסֶד אֲשֶׁר־עָשִׂיתִי עִמְּךָ תַּעֲשֶׂה עִמָּדִי וְעִם־הָאָרֶץ אֲשֶׁר־גַּרְתָּה בָּהּ: כד וַיֹּאמֶר אַבְרָהָם אָנֹכִי אִשָּׁבֵעַ: כה וְהוֹכִחַ אַבְרָהָם אֶת־אֲבִימֶלֶךְ עַל־אֹדוֹת בְּאֵר הַמַּיִם אֲשֶׁר גָּזְלוּ עַבְדֵי אֲבִימֶלֶךְ: כו וַיֹּאמֶר אֲבִימֶלֶךְ לֹא יָדַעְתִּי מִי עָשָׂה אֶת־הַדָּבָר הַזֶּה וְגַם־אַתָּה לֹא־הִגַּדְתָּ לִּי וְגַם אָנֹכִי לֹא שָׁמַעְתִּי בִּלְתִּי

you did not tell me, and I also heard nothing of it until today." Then Abraham took sheep and cattle and gave them to Avimelekh, and the two of them made a covenant.

Abraham set seven ewes of the flock apart, by themselves. And Avimelekh said to Abraham, "What is the reason for these seven ewes that you have set apart?" And Abraham said, "Accept these seven from me so that it will be known that I dug this well." Therefore he called that place B'er Sheva, because there, the two of them took an oath. They made a covenant in B'er Sheva; then Avimelekh and Pikhol, his commander, arose and returned to the land of the Philistines. And Abraham planted a tamarisk tree in B'er Sheva, and there he proclaimed the Name of the Eternal (YHVH), God of the universe. And Abraham lived in the land of the Philistines a long time.

Numbers 29:1-6

In the seventh month, on the first day of the month, you shall observe a sacred assembly. You shall not work at your occupations. You shall observe it as a day of Sounding the Teruah. You shall present a pleasing offering to the Eternal, one bull of the herd, one ram, and seven yearling lambs, without blemish. The meal offering with them shall include choice flour with oil mixed in, three-tenths of a measure for a bull, two-tenths for a ram, and one-tenth for each of the seven lambs. And there shall be one goat for a sin offering, to make expiation for you. All this is in addition to the offerings for the new moon, burnt offerings of pleasing aroma to the Eternal.

הַיּֽוֹם: כז וַיִּקַּ֣ח אַבְרָהָ֗ם צֹ֣אן וּבָקָ֔ר וַיִּתֵּ֖ן לַֽאֲבִימֶ֑לֶךְ וַיִּכְרְת֥וּ שְׁנֵיהֶ֖ם בְּרִֽית:

Fifth aliyah (on Shabbat seventh aliyah)

כח וַיַּצֵּ֣ב אַבְרָהָ֔ם אֶת־שֶׁ֥בַע כִּבְשֹׂ֖ת הַצֹּ֑אן לְבַדְּהֶֽן: כט וַיֹּ֥אמֶר אֲבִימֶ֖לֶךְ אֶל־אַבְרָהָ֑ם מָ֣ה הֵ֗נָּה שֶׁ֤בַע כְּבָשֹׂת֙ הָאֵ֔לֶּה אֲשֶׁ֥ר הִצַּ֖בְתָּ לְבַדָּֽנָה: ל וַיֹּ֕אמֶר כִּ֚י אֶת־שֶׁ֣בַע כְּבָשֹׂ֔ת תִּקַּ֖ח מִיָּדִ֑י בַּֽעֲבוּר֙ תִּֽהְיֶה־לִּ֣י לְעֵדָ֔ה כִּ֥י חָפַ֖רְתִּי אֶת־הַבְּאֵ֥ר הַזֹּֽאת: לא עַל־כֵּ֗ן קָרָ֛א לַמָּק֥וֹם הַה֖וּא בְּאֵ֣ר שָׁ֑בַע כִּ֛י שָׁ֥ם נִשְׁבְּע֖וּ שְׁנֵיהֶֽם: לב וַיִּכְרְת֥וּ בְרִ֖ית בִּבְאֵ֣ר שָׁ֑בַע וַיָּ֣קָם אֲבִימֶ֗לֶךְ וּפִיכֹל֙ שַׂר־צְבָא֔וֹ וַיָּשֻׁ֖בוּ אֶל־אֶ֥רֶץ פְּלִשְׁתִּֽים: לג וַיִּטַּ֥ע אֶ֖שֶׁל בִּבְאֵ֣ר שָׁ֑בַע וַיִּ֨קְרָא־שָׁ֔ם בְּשֵׁ֥ם יְהֹוָ֖ה אֵ֥ל עוֹלָֽם: לד וַיָּ֧גָר אַבְרָהָ֛ם בְּאֶ֥רֶץ פְּלִשְׁתִּ֖ים יָמִ֥ים רַבִּֽים:

Maftir (second scroll)

ספר במדבר פרק כט

א וּבַחֹ֨דֶשׁ הַשְּׁבִיעִ֜י בְּאֶחָ֣ד לַחֹ֗דֶשׁ מִֽקְרָא־קֹ֨דֶשׁ֙ יִֽהְיֶ֣ה לָכֶ֔ם כָּל־מְלֶ֥אכֶת עֲבֹדָ֖ה לֹ֣א תַֽעֲשׂ֑וּ י֥וֹם תְּרוּעָ֖ה יִֽהְיֶ֥ה לָכֶֽם: ב וַֽעֲשִׂיתֶ֨ם עֹלָ֜ה לְרֵ֣יחַ נִיחֹ֣חַ לַֽיהֹוָ֗ה פַּ֧ר בֶּן־בָּקָ֛ר אֶחָ֖ד אַ֣יִל אֶחָ֑ד כְּבָשִׂ֧ים בְּנֵֽי־שָׁנָ֛ה שִׁבְעָ֖ה תְּמִימִֽם: ג וּמִ֨נְחָתָ֔ם סֹ֖לֶת בְּלוּלָ֣ה בַשָּׁ֑מֶן שְׁלֹשָׁ֣ה עֶשְׂרֹנִ֗ים לַפָּ֛ר שְׁנֵ֥י עֶשְׂרֹנִ֖ים לָאָֽיִל: ד וְעִשָּׂר֣וֹן אֶחָ֔ד לַכֶּ֖בֶשׂ הָאֶחָ֑ד לְשִׁבְעַ֖ת הַכְּבָשִֽׂים: ה וּשְׂעִיר־עִזִּ֥ים אֶחָ֖ד חַטָּ֑את לְכַפֵּ֖ר עֲלֵיכֶֽם: ו מִלְּבַ֞ד עֹלַ֤ת הַחֹ֨דֶשׁ֙ וּמִנְחָתָ֔הּ וְעֹלַ֥ת הַתָּמִ֖יד וּמִנְחָתָ֑הּ וְנִסְכֵּיהֶ֖ם כְּמִשְׁפָּטָ֑ם לְרֵ֣יחַ נִיחֹ֔חַ אִשֶּׁ֖ה לַֽיהֹוָֽה:

137

HAFTARAH FOR THE FIRST DAY OF ROSH HASHANAH

1 Samuel 1:1-19

And there was a certain man from Ramathaim-Zophim, the hills of Ephraim, and his name was Elkanah, the son of Yerokham, the son of Eliyhu, the son of Tokhu, the son of Tzuf the Ephratite. He had two wives, one named Hannah and the other, Peninah. Peninah had children but Hannah had no children.

Year after year this man went up from his city to worship and offer sacrifices to the Adonai Tzvaot, in Shiloh, where the two sons of Eli, Khophni and Pinkhas, were priests to Adonai. And on the day when Elkanah offered sacrifices, he gave portions to Peninah, his wife, and to all her sons and daughters. But to Hannah, he gave a double portion because he loved Hannah, though Adonai had closed up her womb. Her rival taunted her bitterly to provoke her, because God had closed up her womb. And as he did so from year to year; whenever she came up to the House of the Eternal (YHVH) she angered Hannah who wept and would not eat. And Elkanah, her husband, said to her: "Why do you weep? Why won't you eat? Why is your heart grieved? Am I not better to you than ten sons?"

Hannah arose after they had eaten and drunk in Shiloh, and Eli, the Priest, sat on the chair near the door-post of the Temple of the Eternal (YHVH). She was bitterly grieved and prayed to Adonai and wept. And she vowed a vow and said: "Adonai Tzvaot if You will look upon the despair of Your handmaid and remember me and will not forget Your handmaid and will give Your handmaid a son—then I will give him to God all the days of his life and no razor shall touch his head."

א וַיְהִי אִישׁ אֶחָד מִן־הָרָמָתַיִם צוֹפִים מֵהַר אֶפְרָיִם וּשְׁמוֹ אֶלְקָנָה בֶּן־יְרֹחָם בֶּן־אֱלִיהוּא בֶּן־תֹּחוּ בֶן־צוּף אֶפְרָתִי: ב וְלוֹ שְׁתֵּי נָשִׁים שֵׁם אַחַת חַנָּה וְשֵׁם הַשֵּׁנִית פְּנִנָּה וַיְהִי לִפְנִנָּה יְלָדִים וּלְחַנָּה אֵין יְלָדִים:

ג וְעָלָה הָאִישׁ הַהוּא מֵעִירוֹ מִיָּמִים | יָמִימָה לְהִשְׁתַּחֲוֺת וְלִזְבֹּחַ לַיהֹוָה צְבָאוֹת בְּשִׁלֹה וְשָׁם שְׁנֵי בְנֵי־עֵלִי חָפְנִי וּפִנְחָס כֹּהֲנִים לַיהֹוָה: ד וַיְהִי הַיּוֹם וַיִּזְבַּח אֶלְקָנָה וְנָתַן לִפְנִנָּה אִשְׁתּוֹ וּלְכָל־בָּנֶיהָ וּבְנוֹתֶיהָ מָנוֹת: ה וּלְחַנָּה יִתֵּן מָנָה אַחַת אַפָּיִם כִּי אֶת־חַנָּה אָהֵב וַיהֹוָה סָגַר רַחְמָהּ: ו וְכִעֲסַתָּה צָרָתָהּ גַּם־כַּעַס בַּעֲבוּר הַרְּעִמָהּ כִּי־סָגַר יְהֹוָה בְּעַד רַחְמָהּ: ז וְכֵן יַעֲשֶׂה שָׁנָה בְשָׁנָה מִדֵּי עֲלֹתָהּ בְּבֵית יְהֹוָה כֵּן תַּכְעִסֶנָּה וַתִּבְכֶּה וְלֹא תֹאכַל: ח וַיֹּאמֶר לָהּ אֶלְקָנָה אִישָׁהּ חַנָּה לָמֶה תִבְכִּי וְלָמֶה לֹא תֹאכְלִי וְלָמֶה יֵרַע לְבָבֵךְ הֲלוֹא אָנֹכִי טוֹב לָךְ מֵעֲשָׂרָה בָּנִים:

ט וַתָּקָם חַנָּה אַחֲרֵי אָכְלָה בְשִׁלֹה וְאַחֲרֵי שָׁתֹה וְעֵלִי הַכֹּהֵן יֹשֵׁב עַל־הַכִּסֵּא עַל־מְזוּזַת הֵיכַל יְהֹוָה: י וְהִיא מָרַת נָפֶשׁ וַתִּתְפַּלֵּל עַל־יְהֹוָה וּבָכֹה תִבְכֶּה: יא וַתִּדֹּר נֶדֶר וַתֹּאמַר יְהֹוָה צְבָאוֹת אִם־רָאֹה תִרְאֶה | בָּעֳנִי אֲמָתֶךָ וּזְכַרְתַּנִי וְלֹא־תִשְׁכַּח אֶת־אֲמָתֶךָ וְנָתַתָּה לַאֲמָתְךָ זֶרַע אֲנָשִׁים וּנְתַתִּיו לַיהֹוָה כָּל־יְמֵי חַיָּיו וּמוֹרָה לֹא־יַעֲלֶה עַל־רֹאשׁוֹ:

And she prayed so long to Adonai, that Eli watched her mouth. However, Hannah spoke in her heart; only her lips moved but her voice was not heard. Eli thought her to be a drunkard. He then said to her: "How long will you remain drunk? Free yourself from your need of wine!" Hannah answered and said: "No, my lord, I am a woman of grieved spirit; I have not drunk any wine or other intoxicating drinks. I have just poured out my soul in the presence of God. Do not take your handmaid for a wicked woman; it is only because of my sorrow and grief that I have spoken until now."

Then Eli answered and said: "Go in peace! And may the God of Israel grant you that which you asked." And she said: "May your servant find grace in your eyes." The woman then went on her way and she ate, no longer grieved. They arose early in the morning and prostrated themselves before Adonai and returned to their home in Ramah. And Elkanah knew Hannah, his wife, and Adonai remembered. And in a short time, Hannah conceived and bore a son and she called him Shmuel, for she had asked of him from God (YHVH).

יב וְהָיָה֙ כִּ֣י הִרְבְּתָ֔ה לְהִתְפַּלֵּ֖ל לִפְנֵ֣י יְהֹוָ֑ה וְעֵלִ֖י שֹׁמֵ֥ר אֶת־פִּֽיהָ: יג וְחַנָּ֗ה הִ֚יא מְדַבֶּ֣רֶת עַל־לִבָּ֔הּ רַ֚ק שְׂפָתֶ֣יהָ נָּע֔וֹת וְקוֹלָ֖הּ לֹ֣א יִשָּׁמֵ֑עַ וַיַּחְשְׁבֶ֥הָ עֵלִ֖י לְשִׁכֹּרָֽה: יד וַיֹּ֤אמֶר אֵלֶ֙יהָ֙ עֵלִ֔י עַד־מָתַ֖י תִּשְׁתַּכָּרִ֑ין הָסִ֥ירִי אֶת־יֵינֵ֖ךְ מֵעָלָֽיִךְ: טו וַתַּ֨עַן חַנָּ֤ה וַתֹּ֙אמֶר֙ לֹ֣א אֲדֹנִ֔י אִשָּׁ֤ה קְשַׁת־ר֙וּחַ֙ אָנֹ֔כִי וְיַ֥יִן וְשֵׁכָ֖ר לֹ֣א שָׁתִ֑יתִי וָאֶשְׁפֹּ֥ךְ אֶת־נַפְשִׁ֖י לִפְנֵ֥י יְהֹוָֽה: טז אַל־תִּתֵּן֙ אֶת־אֲמָ֣תְךָ֔ לִפְנֵ֖י בַּת־בְּלִיָּ֑עַל כִּ֥י מֵרֹ֥ב שִׂיחִ֛י וְכַעְסִ֖י דִּבַּ֥רְתִּי עַד־הֵֽנָּה:

יז וַיַּ֨עַן עֵלִ֜י וַיֹּ֗אמֶר לְכִ֣י לְשָׁל֑וֹם וֵֽאלֹהֵ֣י יִשְׂרָאֵ֗ל יִתֵּן֙ אֶת־שֵׁ֣לָתֵ֔ךְ אֲשֶׁ֥ר שָׁאַ֖לְתְּ מֵעִמּֽוֹ: יח וַתֹּ֕אמֶר תִּמְצָ֧א שִׁפְחָתְךָ֛ חֵ֖ן בְּעֵינֶ֑יךָ וַתֵּ֨לֶךְ הָאִשָּׁ֤ה לְדַרְכָּהּ֙ וַתֹּאכַ֔ל וּפָנֶ֥יהָ לֹא־הָֽיוּ־לָ֖הּ עֽוֹד: יט וַיַּשְׁכִּ֣מוּ בַבֹּ֗קֶר וַיִּשְׁתַּֽחֲווּ֙ לִפְנֵ֣י יְהֹוָ֔ה וַיָּשֻׁ֛בוּ וַיָּבֹ֥אוּ אֶל־בֵּיתָ֖ם הָרָמָ֑תָה וַיֵּ֤דַע אֶלְקָנָה֙ אֶת־חַנָּ֣ה אִשְׁתּ֔וֹ וַיִּזְכְּרֶ֖הָ יְהֹוָֽה:

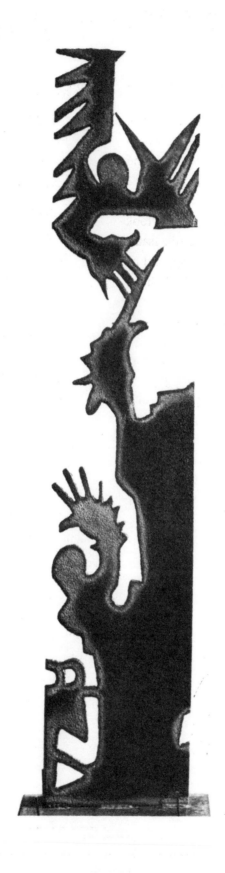

TORAH READING FOR THE SECOND DAY OF ROSH HASHANAH

Genesis 22: The Akedah

ספר בראשית פרק כב

Some time afterward, the God (HaElohim) tested Abraham, addressing him, "Abraham," and he answered, "Here I am." And God said, "Take your son, your favored one, Isaac, whom you love, and go to the land of Moriah, and offer him there as a burnt offering on one of the mountains that I designate." So early next morning, Abraham saddled his ass and took with him two of his servants and his son Isaac. He split the wood for the burnt offering, and he set out for the place of which God had told him.

On the third day, Abraham looked up and saw the place from afar. Then Abraham said to his servants, "You stay here with the ass. The boy and I will go up there; we will worship and we will return to you." Abraham took the wood for the burnt offering and put it on his son Isaac. He himself took the firestone and the knife; and the two walked off together. Then Isaac said to his father Abraham, "Father!" And he answered, "Yes, my son." And he said, "Here are the firestone and the wood; but where is the sheep for the burnt offering?" And Abraham said, "God will see to the sheep for the burnt offering, my son." And the two of them continued on together.

They arrived at the place of which God had told him. Abraham built an altar there, laid out the wood, bound his son Isaac, and laid him on the altar, on top of the wood. Abraham then picked up the knife to slay his son. Then a messenger-angel of the Eternal (YHVH) called to him from heaven: "Abraham! Abraham!"

First aliyah

א וַיְהִ֗י אַחַר֙ הַדְּבָרִ֣ים הָאֵ֔לֶּה וְהָ֣אֱלֹהִ֔ים נִסָּ֖ה אֶת־אַבְרָהָ֑ם וַיֹּ֣אמֶר אֵלָ֔יו אַבְרָהָ֖ם וַיֹּ֥אמֶר הִנֵּֽנִי: ב וַיֹּ֡אמֶר קַח־נָ֠א אֶת־בִּנְךָ֨ אֶת־יְחִֽידְךָ֤ אֲשֶׁר־אָהַ֨בְתָּ֙ אֶת־יִצְחָ֔ק וְלֶ֨ךְ־לְךָ֔ אֶל־אֶ֖רֶץ הַמֹּֽרִיָּ֑ה וְהַֽעֲלֵ֤הוּ שָׁם֙ לְעֹלָ֔ה עַ֚ל אַחַ֣ד הֶֽהָרִ֔ים אֲשֶׁ֖ר אֹמַ֥ר אֵלֶֽיךָ: ג וַיַּשְׁכֵּ֨ם אַבְרָהָ֜ם בַּבֹּ֗קֶר וַֽיַּחֲבֹשׁ֙ אֶת־חֲמֹר֔וֹ וַיִּקַּ֞ח אֶת־שְׁנֵ֤י נְעָרָיו֙ אִתּ֔וֹ וְאֵ֖ת יִצְחָ֣ק בְּנ֑וֹ וַיְבַקַּע֙ עֲצֵ֣י עֹלָ֔ה וַיָּ֣קָם וַיֵּ֔לֶךְ אֶל־הַמָּק֖וֹם אֲשֶׁר־אָֽמַר־ל֥וֹ הָֽאֱלֹהִֽים:

Second aliyah

ד בַּיּ֣וֹם הַשְּׁלִישִׁ֗י וַיִּשָּׂ֨א אַבְרָהָ֧ם אֶת־עֵינָ֛יו וַיַּ֥רְא אֶת־הַמָּק֖וֹם מֵֽרָחֹֽק: ה וַיֹּ֨אמֶר אַבְרָהָ֜ם אֶל־נְעָרָ֗יו שְׁבֽוּ־לָכֶ֥ם פֹּה֙ עִֽם־הַֽחֲמ֔וֹר וַֽאֲנִ֣י וְהַנַּ֔עַר נֵֽלְכָ֖ה עַד־כֹּ֑ה וְנִֽשְׁתַּֽחֲוֶ֖ה וְנָשׁ֥וּבָה אֲלֵיכֶֽם: ו וַיִּקַּ֨ח אַבְרָהָ֜ם אֶת־עֲצֵ֣י הָֽעֹלָ֗ה וַיָּ֨שֶׂם֙ עַל־יִצְחָ֣ק בְּנ֔וֹ וַיִּקַּ֣ח בְּיָד֔וֹ אֶת־הָאֵ֖שׁ וְאֶת־הַֽמַּֽאֲכֶ֑לֶת וַיֵּֽלְכ֥וּ שְׁנֵיהֶ֖ם יַחְדָּֽו: ז וַיֹּ֨אמֶר יִצְחָ֜ק אֶל־אַבְרָהָ֤ם אָבִיו֙ וַיֹּ֣אמֶר אָבִ֔י וַיֹּ֖אמֶר הִנֶּ֣נִּֽי בְנִ֑י וַיֹּ֗אמֶר הִנֵּ֤ה הָאֵשׁ֙ וְהָ֣עֵצִ֔ים וְאַיֵּ֥ה הַשֶּׂ֖ה לְעֹלָֽה: ח וַיֹּ֨אמֶר֙ אַבְרָהָ֔ם אֱלֹהִ֞ים יִרְאֶה־לּ֥וֹ הַשֶּׂ֛ה לְעֹלָ֖ה בְּנִ֑י וַיֵּֽלְכ֥וּ שְׁנֵיהֶ֖ם יַחְדָּֽו:

Third aliyah

ט וַיָּבֹ֗אוּ אֶֽל־הַמָּקוֹם֘ אֲשֶׁ֣ר אָֽמַר־ל֣וֹ הָֽאֱלֹהִים֒ וַיִּ֨בֶן שָׁ֤ם אַבְרָהָם֙ אֶת־הַמִּזְבֵּ֔חַ וַיַּֽעֲרֹ֖ךְ אֶת־הָֽעֵצִ֑ים וַֽיַּעֲקֹד֙ אֶת־יִצְחָ֣ק בְּנ֔וֹ וַיָּ֤שֶׂם אֹתוֹ֙ עַל־הַמִּזְבֵּ֔חַ מִמַּ֖עַל לָֽעֵצִֽים: י וַיִּשְׁלַ֤ח אַבְרָהָם֙ אֶת־יָד֔וֹ וַיִּקַּ֖ח אֶת־הַֽמַּֽאֲכֶ֑לֶת לִשְׁחֹ֖ט אֶת־בְּנֽוֹ: יא וַיִּקְרָ֨א אֵלָ֜יו מַלְאַ֤ךְ יְהֹוָה֙ מִן־הַשָּׁמַ֔יִם

141

And he answered, "Here I am." And he said, "Do not touch your hand to the lad, or do anything to him. For now I know that you are in awe of God, since you have not kept your son, your favored one, from (knowing) Me." Then Abraham looked up and saw a ram caught in the thicket by its horns. So Abraham went and took the ram and offered it up as a burnt offering in place of his son. And Abraham named that site Adonai-yireh, whence the present saying, "On the mount of the Eternal (YHVH) one can see."

The angel-messenger of the Eternal (YHVH) called to Abraham a second time from heaven and said, "By Myself I swear, the Eternal (YHVH) proclaims: Because you have done this and have not kept your son, your favored one, I will bestow My blessing upon you and make your descendants as numerous as the stars of heaven and the sands on the seashore; and your descendants shall seize the gates of their enemies. All the nations of the earth shall bless themselves by your descendants because you have heard My voice." Abraham then returned to his servants, and they departed together for B'er Sheva. Abraham then remained in B'er Sheva.

Some time later, Abraham was told, "Milcah too has borne children to your brother Nahor: Uz the first-born, and Buz his brother, and Kemuel the father of Aram; and Kesed, Hazo, Pildash, Jidlaph, and Bethuel"—Bethuel being the father of Rebekah. These eight Milcah bore to Nahor, Abraham's brother. And his concubine, whose name was Reumah, also bore children: Tebah, Gaham, Tahash, and Maacah.

וַיֹּאמֶר אַבְרָהָם | אַבְרָהָם וַיֹּאמֶר הִנֵּנִי: יב וַיֹּאמֶר אַל־תִּשְׁלַח יָדְךָ אֶל־הַנַּעַר וְאַל־תַּעַשׂ לוֹ מְאוּמָה כִּי | עַתָּה יָדַעְתִּי כִּי־יְרֵא אֱלֹהִים אַתָּה וְלֹא חָשַׂכְתָּ אֶת־בִּנְךָ אֶת־יְחִידְךָ מִמֶּנִּי: יג וַיִּשָּׂא אַבְרָהָם אֶת־עֵינָיו וַיַּרְא וְהִנֵּה־אַיִל אַחַר נֶאֱחַז בַּסְּבַךְ בְּקַרְנָיו וַיֵּלֶךְ אַבְרָהָם וַיִּקַּח אֶת־הָאַיִל וַיַּעֲלֵהוּ לְעֹלָה תַּחַת בְּנוֹ: יד וַיִּקְרָא אַבְרָהָם שֵׁם־הַמָּקוֹם הַהוּא יְהֹוָה | יִרְאֶה אֲשֶׁר יֵאָמֵר הַיּוֹם בְּהַר יְהֹוָה יֵרָאֶה:

Fourth aliyah

טו וַיִּקְרָא מַלְאַךְ יְהֹוָה אֶל־אַבְרָהָם שֵׁנִית מִן־הַשָּׁמָיִם: טז וַיֹּאמֶר בִּי נִשְׁבַּעְתִּי נְאֻם־יְהֹוָה כִּי יַעַן אֲשֶׁר עָשִׂיתָ אֶת־הַדָּבָר הַזֶּה וְלֹא חָשַׂכְתָּ אֶת־בִּנְךָ אֶת־יְחִידֶךָ: יז כִּי־בָרֵךְ אֲבָרֶכְךָ וְהַרְבָּה אַרְבֶּה אֶת־זַרְעֲךָ כְּכוֹכְבֵי הַשָּׁמַיִם וְכַחוֹל אֲשֶׁר עַל־שְׂפַת הַיָּם וְיִרַשׁ זַרְעֲךָ אֵת שַׁעַר אֹיְבָיו: יח וְהִתְבָּרְכוּ בְזַרְעֲךָ כֹּל גּוֹיֵי הָאָרֶץ עֵקֶב אֲשֶׁר שָׁמַעְתָּ בְּקֹלִי: יט וַיָּשָׁב אַבְרָהָם אֶל־נְעָרָיו וַיָּקֻמוּ וַיֵּלְכוּ יַחְדָּו אֶל־בְּאֵר שָׁבַע וַיֵּשֶׁב אַבְרָהָם בִּבְאֵר שָׁבַע: פ

Fifth aliyah

כ וַיְהִי אַחֲרֵי הַדְּבָרִים הָאֵלֶּה וַיֻּגַּד לְאַבְרָהָם לֵאמֹר הִנֵּה יָלְדָה מִלְכָּה גַם־הִוא בָּנִים לְנָחוֹר אָחִיךָ: כא אֶת־עוּץ בְּכֹרוֹ וְאֶת־בּוּז אָחִיו וְאֶת־קְמוּאֵל אֲבִי אֲרָם: כב וְאֶת־כֶּשֶׂד וְאֶת־חֲזוֹ וְאֶת־פִּלְדָּשׁ וְאֶת־יִדְלָף וְאֵת בְּתוּאֵל: כג וּבְתוּאֵל יָלַד אֶת־רִבְקָה שְׁמֹנָה אֵלֶּה יָלְדָה מִלְכָּה לְנָחוֹר אֲחִי אַבְרָהָם: כד וּפִילַגְשׁוֹ וּשְׁמָהּ רְאוּמָה וַתֵּלֶד גַּם־הִוא אֶת־טֶבַח וְאֶת־גַּחַם וְאֶת־תַּחַשׁ וְאֶת־מַעֲכָה: פ פ פ

Repeat maftir from first day.

HAFTARAH FOR THE SECOND DAY OF ROSH HASHANAH

Jeremiah 31:1-19

ספר ירמיה פרק לא

Thus said the Eternal:
The people escaped from the sword
and found favor in the wilderness;
When Israel was marching homeward,
the Eternal, from afar, was revealed to me.
Eternal love I conceived for you then,
therefore, I continue My love for you.

א כֹּה אָמַר יְהֹוָה מָצָא חֵן בַּמִּדְבָּר
עַם שְׂרִידֵי חָרֶב הָלוֹךְ לְהַרְגִּיעוֹ
יִשְׂרָאֵל: ב מֵרָחוֹק יְהֹוָה נִרְאָה לִי
וְאַהֲבַת עוֹלָם אֲהַבְתִּיךְ עַל־כֵּן
מְשַׁכְתִּיךְ חָסֶד:

Again, I will restore you, O maiden of Israel!
Again you shall take up your timbrels
and go forth to the rhythm of the dancers;
Again you shall plant vineyards on the hills of Samaria.
The planters shall plant and live to enjoy them
for the day is coming when lookouts
Shall proclaim on the heights of Ephraim:
Come, let us go up to Zion, to the Eternal our God!

ג עוֹד אֶבְנֵךְ וְנִבְנֵית בְּתוּלַת
יִשְׂרָאֵל עוֹד תַּעְדִּי תֻפַּיִךְ וְיָצָאת
בִּמְחוֹל מְשַׂחֲקִים: ד עוֹד תִּטְּעִי
כְרָמִים בְּהָרֵי שֹׁמְרוֹן נָטְעוּ נֹטְעִים
וְחִלֵּלוּ: ה כִּי יֶשׁ־יוֹם קָרְאוּ נֹצְרִים
בְּהַר אֶפְרָיִם קוּמוּ וְנַעֲלֶה צִיּוֹן
אֶל־יְהֹוָה אֱלֹהֵינוּ:

For thus said the Eternal:
Cry out in joy for Jacob,
shout at the crossroads of the nations!
Sing aloud in praise, and say: Save, O Eternal, Your people,
The remnant of Israel.
I will bring them in from the northland,
gather them from the ends of the earth—
The blind and the lame among them,
those with child and those in labor—
In a vast throng they shall return here.
They shall come with weeping,
and with compassion will I guide them.
I will lead them to streams of water,
by a level road where they will not stumble.
For I am ever a Father to Israel,
Ephraim is My first-born.

ו כִּי־כֹה | אָמַר יְהֹוָה רָנּוּ לְיַעֲקֹב
שִׂמְחָה וְצַהֲלוּ בְּרֹאשׁ הַגּוֹיִם
הַשְׁמִיעוּ הַלְלוּ וְאִמְרוּ הוֹשַׁע
יְהֹוָה אֶת־עַמְּךָ אֵת שְׁאֵרִית
יִשְׂרָאֵל: ז הִנְנִי מֵבִיא אוֹתָם
מֵאֶרֶץ צָפוֹן וְקִבַּצְתִּים מִיַּרְכְּתֵי־
אָרֶץ בָּם עִוֵּר וּפִסֵּחַ הָרָה וְיֹלֶדֶת
יַחְדָּו קָהָל גָּדוֹל יָשׁוּבוּ הֵנָּה:
ח בִּבְכִי יָבֹאוּ וּבְתַחֲנוּנִים אוֹבִילֵם
אוֹלִיכֵם אֶל־נַחֲלֵי מַיִם בְּדֶרֶךְ יָשָׁר
לֹא יִכָּשְׁלוּ בָּהּ כִּי־הָיִיתִי לְיִשְׂרָאֵל
לְאָב וְאֶפְרַיִם בְּכֹרִי הוּא:

143

Hear the word of the Eternal, O nations,

and tell it in the isles afar.

Say: He who scattered Israel will gather them,

And will guard them as a shepherd his flock.

For the Eternal will ransom Jacob,

redeem him from one too strong for him.

They shall come and shout on the heights of Zion,

radiant over the bounty of the Eternal—

Over new grain and wine and oil, and over sheep and cattle.

They shall fare like a watered garden,

and not languish again.

Then shall maidens dance joyfully,

young men and old alike.

I will turn their mourning to gladness,

I will comfort them and cheer them in their grief.

I will give the priests their fill of fatness,

And My people shall enjoy My full bounty

—declares the Eternal.

Thus said the Eternal:

A cry is heard in Ramah—

Wailing, bitter weeping—

Rachel weeping for her children.

She refuses to be comforted

For her children, who are gone.

Thus said the Eternal:

Restrain your voice from weeping,

Your eyes from shedding tears;

For there is a reward for your labor

—declares the Eternal.

They shall return from the enemy's land.

And there is hope for your future

Your children shall return to their country.

—declares the Eternal.

ט שִׁמְעוּ דְבַר־יְהֹוָה גּוֹיִם וְהַגִּידוּ בָאִיִּים מִמֶּרְחָק וְאִמְרוּ מְזָרֵה יִשְׂרָאֵל יְקַבְּצֶנּוּ וּשְׁמָרוֹ כְּרֹעֶה עֶדְרוֹ: י כִּי־פָדָה יְהֹוָה אֶת־יַעֲקֹב וּגְאָלוֹ מִיַּד חָזָק מִמֶּנּוּ: יא וּבָאוּ וְרִנְּנוּ בִמְרוֹם־צִיּוֹן וְנָהֲרוּ אֶל־טוּב יְהֹוָה עַל־דָּגָן וְעַל־תִּירֹשׁ וְעַל־יִצְהָר וְעַל־בְּנֵי־צֹאן וּבָקָר וְהָיְתָה נַפְשָׁם כְּגַן רָוֶה וְלֹא־יוֹסִיפוּ לְדַאֲבָה עוֹד:

יב אָז תִּשְׂמַח בְּתוּלָה בְּמָחוֹל וּבַחֻרִים וּזְקֵנִים יַחְדָּו וְהָפַכְתִּי אֶבְלָם לְשָׂשׂוֹן וְנִחַמְתִּים וְשִׂמַּחְתִּים מִיגוֹנָם: יג וְרִוֵּיתִי נֶפֶשׁ הַכֹּהֲנִים דָּשֶׁן וְעַמִּי אֶת־טוּבִי יִשְׂבָּעוּ נְאֻם־יְהֹוָה:

יד כֹּה | אָמַר יְהֹוָה קוֹל בְּרָמָה נִשְׁמָע נְהִי בְּכִי תַמְרוּרִים רָחֵל מְבַכָּה עַל־בָּנֶיהָ מֵאֲנָה לְהִנָּחֵם עַל־בָּנֶיהָ כִּי אֵינֶנּוּ: טו כֹּה | אָמַר יְהֹוָה מִנְעִי קוֹלֵךְ מִבֶּכִי וְעֵינַיִךְ מִדִּמְעָה כִּי יֵשׁ שָׂכָר לִפְעֻלָּתֵךְ נְאֻם־יְהֹוָה וְשָׁבוּ מֵאֶרֶץ אוֹיֵב:

טז וְיֵשׁ־תִּקְוָה לְאַחֲרִיתֵךְ נְאֻם־יְהֹוָה וְשָׁבוּ בָנִים לִגְבוּלָם:

I can hear Ephraim lamenting:
You have chastised me, and I am chastised
like a calf that has not been broken.
Receive me back, let me return, for You, O Eternal,
are my God.
Now that I have turned back, I am filled with remorse;
Now that I am made aware, I stroke my thigh.
I am ashamed and humiliated for I bear the disgrace
of my youth.

Truly, Ephraim is a dear son to Me, a darling child!
Even when I have turned against him,
My thoughts would remember him affectionately.
That is why My heart yearns for him;
I will receive him back in love and compassion.
       —declares the Eternal.

יז שָׁמוֹעַ שָׁמַעְתִּי אֶפְרַיִם מִתְנוֹדֵד יִסַּרְתַּנִי וָאִוָּסֵר כְּעֵגֶל לֹא לֻמָּד הֲשִׁיבֵנִי וְאָשׁוּבָה כִּי אַתָּה יְהֹוָה אֱלֹהָי: יח כִּי־אַחֲרֵי שׁוּבִי נִחַמְתִּי וְאַחֲרֵי הִוָּדְעִי סָפַקְתִּי עַל־יָרֵךְ בֹּשְׁתִּי וְגַם־נִכְלַמְתִּי כִּי נָשָׂאתִי חֶרְפַּת נְעוּרָי:

יט הֲבֵן יַקִּיר לִי אֶפְרַיִם אִם יֶלֶד שַׁעֲשֻׁעִים כִּי־מִדֵּי דַבְּרִי בּוֹ זָכֹר אֶזְכְּרֶנּוּ עוֹד עַל־כֵּן הָמוּ מֵעַי לוֹ רַחֵם אֲרַחֲמֶנּוּ נְאֻם־יְהֹוָה:

Leviticus 16

First aliyah

א וַיְדַבֵּר יְהֹוָה אֶל־מֹשֶׁה אַחֲרֵי מֹות שְׁנֵי בְּנֵי
אַהֲרֹן בְּקָרְבָתָם לִפְנֵי־יְהֹוָה וַיָּמֻתוּ: ב וַיֹּאמֶר
יְהֹוָה אֶל־מֹשֶׁה דַּבֵּר אֶל־אַהֲרֹן אָחִיךָ
וְאַל־יָבֹא בְכָל־עֵת אֶל־הַקֹּדֶשׁ מִבֵּית לַפָּרֹכֶת
אֶל־פְּנֵי הַכַּפֹּרֶת אֲשֶׁר עַל־הָאָרֹן וְלֹא יָמוּת כִּי
בֶּעָנָן אֵרָאֶה עַל־הַכַּפֹּרֶת: ג בְּזֹאת יָבֹא אַהֲרֹן
אֶל־הַקֹּדֶשׁ בְּפַר בֶּן־בָּקָר לְחַטָּאת וְאַיִל
לְעֹלָה:

(On Shabbat, second aliyah)

ד כְּתֹנֶת־בַּד קֹדֶשׁ יִלְבָּשׁ וּמִכְנְסֵי־בַד יִהְיוּ
עַל־בְּשָׂרוֹ וּבְאַבְנֵט בַּד יַחְגֹּר וּבְמִצְנֶפֶת בַּד
יִצְנֹף בִּגְדֵי־קֹדֶשׁ הֵם וְרָחַץ בַּמַּיִם אֶת־בְּשָׂרוֹ
וּלְבֵשָׁם: ה וּמֵאֵת עֲדַת בְּנֵי יִשְׂרָאֵל יִקַּח
שְׁנֵי־שְׂעִירֵי עִזִּים לְחַטָּאת וְאַיִל אֶחָד לְעֹלָה:
ו וְהִקְרִיב אַהֲרֹן אֶת־פַּר הַחַטָּאת אֲשֶׁר־לוֹ
וְכִפֶּר בַּעֲדוֹ וּבְעַד בֵּיתוֹ:

Second aliyah (on Shabbat, third aliyah)

ז וְלָקַח אֶת־שְׁנֵי הַשְּׂעִירִם וְהֶעֱמִיד אֹתָם לִפְנֵי
יְהֹוָה פֶּתַח אֹהֶל מוֹעֵד: ח וְנָתַן אַהֲרֹן עַל־שְׁנֵי
הַשְּׂעִירִם גֹּרָלוֹת גּוֹרָל אֶחָד לַיהֹוָה וְגוֹרָל
אֶחָד לַעֲזָאזֵל: ט וְהִקְרִיב אַהֲרֹן אֶת־הַשָּׂעִיר
אֲשֶׁר עָלָה עָלָיו הַגּוֹרָל לַיהֹוָה וְעָשָׂהוּ
חַטָּאת: י וְהַשָּׂעִיר אֲשֶׁר עָלָה עָלָיו הַגּוֹרָל
לַעֲזָאזֵל יָעֳמַד־חַי לִפְנֵי יְהֹוָה לְכַפֵּר עָלָיו
לְשַׁלַּח אֹתוֹ לַעֲזָאזֵל הַמִּדְבָּרָה: יא וְהִקְרִיב
אַהֲרֹן אֶת־פַּר הַחַטָּאת אֲשֶׁר־לוֹ וְכִפֶּר בַּעֲדוֹ
וּבְעַד בֵּיתוֹ וְשָׁחַט אֶת־פַּר הַחַטָּאת אֲשֶׁר־לוֹ:

This is what the Eternal (YHVH) said to Moses after the death of Aaron's two sons who died when they drew too near to God's presence: Tell your brother Aaron that he should not enter the Kodesh-Holy Place inside the curtain before the ark-cover at any time he chooses, lest he die; for I am able to be seen in the cloud over the ark-cover. In this manner shall Aaron enter the holy place: with a young bullock for a sin-offering and a ram for a burnt-offering.

He shall dress in the linen tunic appropriate for holy use, linen trousers shall be on his body, he shall put a linen sash around his waist, and wind a linen turban around his head; these are clothes set aside for holy use, and before he puts them on he shall wash with water. From the congregation of Israelites Aaron shall take two male goats for a sin-offering and a ram for a burnt-offering. Aaron shall then bring near in offering the bullock for his own sin-offering to seek atonement for ' himself and for his household.

He shall then take the two goats and stand them up in God's presence (before YHVH) at the entrance to the Tent of Meeting-Ohel Moed. Upon the two goats Aaron shall place lots, one lot for God (YHVH), one lot for Azazel. Aaron shall bring near in offering the goat upon which fell the lot for God (YHVH) and make it the sin-offering, while the goat upon which fell the lot for Azazel shall be stood up alive in God's presence (before YHVH) that atonement may be sought through it, to be sent away to Azazel toward the wilderness. Next Aaron shall bring near in offering the other bullock for his own sin-offering and seek atonement for himself and his household, and he shall slaughter the bullock for his sin-offering.

Let him then take a pan full of fire-coals from off the Altar, from God's presence, and two handfuls of spices finely ground for incense and bring them inside the parochet-curtain. He should then put the incense on the fire in God's presence so that a cloud of incense covers the curtain-kaporet above the ark of witness-Edut and he shall not die. Let him then take some of the bullock's blood and sprinkling it with his finger on the eastern face of the kaporet, let him sprinkle some of the blood in front of the kaporet seven times with his finger. He should then slaughter the goat for the people's sin-offering and bring its blood inside the parochet and do with its blood as he did with the bullock's blood, sprinkling it upon the kaporet and in front of the kaporet. Let him then seek atonement for the Holy Place from the impurities of the Israelites, and from their rebellious acts, whatever their wrongs may be, and let him do the same for the Tent of Meeting which abides with them in the midst of their impurities. There shall be no other person in the Tent of Meeting from the time that he goes in to seek atonement for the Holy Place until he comes out, that he may seek atonement for himself and his household and the entire congregation of Israel.

יב וְלָקַח מְלֹא־הַמַּחְתָּה גַּחֲלֵי־אֵשׁ מֵעַל הַמִּזְבֵּחַ מִלִּפְנֵי יְהֹוָה וּמְלֹא חָפְנָיו קְטֹרֶת סַמִּים דַּקָּה וְהֵבִיא מִבֵּית לַפָּרֹכֶת: יג וְנָתַן אֶת־הַקְּטֹרֶת עַל־הָאֵשׁ לִפְנֵי יְהֹוָה וְכִסָּה | עֲנַן הַקְּטֹרֶת אֶת־הַכַּפֹּרֶת אֲשֶׁר עַל־הָעֵדוּת וְלֹא יָמוּת: יד וְלָקַח מִדַּם הַפָּר וְהִזָּה בְאֶצְבָּעוֹ עַל־פְּנֵי הַכַּפֹּרֶת קֵדְמָה וְלִפְנֵי הַכַּפֹּרֶת יַזֶּה שֶׁבַע־פְּעָמִים מִן־הַדָּם בְּאֶצְבָּעוֹ: טו וְשָׁחַט אֶת־שְׂעִיר הַחַטָּאת אֲשֶׁר לָעָם וְהֵבִיא אֶת־דָּמוֹ אֶל־מִבֵּית לַפָּרֹכֶת וְעָשָׂה אֶת־דָּמוֹ כַּאֲשֶׁר עָשָׂה לְדַם הַפָּר וְהִזָּה אֹתוֹ עַל־הַכַּפֹּרֶת וְלִפְנֵי הַכַּפֹּרֶת: טז וְכִפֶּר עַל־הַקֹּדֶשׁ מִטֻּמְאֹת בְּנֵי יִשְׂרָאֵל וּמִפִּשְׁעֵיהֶם לְכָל־חַטֹּאתָם וְכֵן יַעֲשֶׂה לְאֹהֶל מוֹעֵד הַשֹּׁכֵן אִתָּם בְּתוֹךְ טֻמְאֹתָם: יז וְכָל־אָדָם לֹא־יִהְיֶה | בְּאֹהֶל מוֹעֵד בְּבֹאוֹ לְכַפֵּר בַּקֹּדֶשׁ עַד־צֵאתוֹ וְכִפֶּר בַּעֲדוֹ וּבְעַד בֵּיתוֹ וּבְעַד כָּל־קְהַל יִשְׂרָאֵל:

He shall then go forth to the Altar-Mizbeyakh which is in God's presence seeking atonement for it, taking some of the bullock's blood and the goat's blood and putting it all over the horns of the Altar. He shall sprinkle some of the blood upon it seven times with his finger to purify it and renew its holiness after the impurities of the Israelites. When he finishes seeking atonement for the Holy Place, the Tent of Meeting, and the Altar, he shall bring near the live goat. Aaron shall lay his two hands on the live goat's head and confess there all the transgressions of the Israelites and all their rebellious acts, whatever their wrongs, transferring them to the goat's head, and he shall send the animal away into the wilderness with an escort. And so the goat shall carry all the transgressions away with him to an isolated place, and the goat shall be released into the wilderness. Then Aaron shall come into the Tent of Meeting and take off the linen garments which he put on when he entered the Holy Place and leave them there. He then shall wash his body with water in the holy area, put on his regular vestments and go out to make his own burnt-offering and that of the people, seeking atonement for himself and for the people.

After Aaron shall turn the fat part of the sin-offering into smoke going up from the Altar, the person who sent the goat away to Azazel shall scour his clothes and wash his body in water, following which he may enter the camp. The goat brought for the sin-offering whose blood was used to seek atonement for the Holy Place shall be brought outside the camp, and its skin, flesh, and dung shall be burnt in the fire.

יח וְיָצָא אֶל־הַמִּזְבֵּחַ אֲשֶׁר לִפְנֵי־יְהֹוָה וְכִפֶּר עָלָיו וְלָקַח מִדַּם הַפָּר וּמִדַּם הַשָּׂעִיר וְנָתַן עַל־קַרְנוֹת הַמִּזְבֵּחַ סָבִיב: יט וְהִזָּה עָלָיו מִן־הַדָּם בְּאֶצְבָּעוֹ שֶׁבַע פְּעָמִים וְטִהֲרוֹ וְקִדְּשׁוֹ מִטֻּמְאֹת בְּנֵי יִשְׂרָאֵל: כ וְכִלָּה מִכַּפֵּר אֶת־הַקֹּדֶשׁ וְאֶת־אֹהֶל מוֹעֵד וְאֶת־הַמִּזְבֵּחַ וְהִקְרִיב אֶת־הַשָּׂעִיר הֶחָי: כא וְסָמַךְ אַהֲרֹן אֶת־שְׁתֵּי יָדָו [יָדָיו] עַל־רֹאשׁ הַשָּׂעִיר הַחַי וְהִתְוַדָּה עָלָיו אֶת־כָּל־עֲוֹנֹת בְּנֵי יִשְׂרָאֵל וְאֶת־כָּל־פִּשְׁעֵיהֶם לְכָל־חַטֹּאתָם וְנָתַן אֹתָם עַל־רֹאשׁ הַשָּׂעִיר וְשִׁלַּח בְּיַד־אִישׁ עִתִּי הַמִּדְבָּרָה: כב וְנָשָׂא הַשָּׂעִיר עָלָיו אֶת־כָּל־עֲוֹנֹתָם אֶל־אֶרֶץ גְּזֵרָה וְשִׁלַּח אֶת־הַשָּׂעִיר בַּמִּדְבָּר: כג וּבָא אַהֲרֹן אֶל־אֹהֶל מוֹעֵד וּפָשַׁט אֶת־בִּגְדֵי הַבָּד אֲשֶׁר לָבַשׁ בְּבֹאוֹ אֶל־הַקֹּדֶשׁ וְהִנִּיחָם שָׁם: כד וְרָחַץ אֶת־בְּשָׂרוֹ בַמַּיִם בְּמָקוֹם קָדוֹשׁ וְלָבַשׁ אֶת־בְּגָדָיו וְיָצָא וְעָשָׂה אֶת־עֹלָתוֹ וְאֶת־עֹלַת הָעָם וְכִפֶּר בַּעֲדוֹ וּבְעַד הָעָם:

כה וְאֵת חֵלֶב הַחַטָּאת יַקְטִיר הַמִּזְבֵּחָה: כו וְהַמְשַׁלֵּחַ אֶת־הַשָּׂעִיר לַעֲזָאזֵל יְכַבֵּס בְּגָדָיו וְרָחַץ אֶת־בְּשָׂרוֹ בַּמָּיִם וְאַחֲרֵי־כֵן יָבוֹא אֶל־הַמַּחֲנֶה: כז וְאֵת פַּר הַחַטָּאת וְאֵת שְׂעִיר הַחַטָּאת אֲשֶׁר הוּבָא אֶת־דָּמָם לְכַפֵּר בַּקֹּדֶשׁ יוֹצִיא אֶל־מִחוּץ לַמַּחֲנֶה וְשָׂרְפוּ בָאֵשׁ אֶת־עֹרֹתָם וְאֶת־בְּשָׂרָם וְאֶת־פִּרְשָׁם: כח וְהַשֹּׂרֵף אֹתָם יְכַבֵּס בְּגָדָיו וְרָחַץ אֶת־בְּשָׂרוֹ בַּמָּיִם וְאַחֲרֵי־כֵן יָבוֹא אֶל־הַמַּחֲנֶה: כט וְהָיְתָה לָכֶם לְחֻקַּת עוֹלָם בַּחֹדֶשׁ הַשְּׁבִיעִי בֶּעָשׂוֹר לַחֹדֶשׁ תְּעַנּוּ

The one who burns it shall scour the clothes, wash in water, and may then come into the camp. This shall be an eternal statute for you: In the seventh month, on the tenth of the month, you shall practice self-denial, for it is an eternal statute. You shall do no work, neither the resident nor the stranger among you. For on this day atonement shall be made for you to purify you from all your wrongs; in God's presence you shall be cleansed.

It shall be a complete Day of Renewal-Shabbat for you when you afflict yourselves, an eternal statute. The kohen-priest who is anointed and the one who is empowered to serve as kohen in place of his father shall put on linen garments set aside for holy use. He shall seek atonement for the Holy Sanctuary, the Tent of Meeting, and the Altar, on behalf of the kohanim and on behalf of the people of the congregation. And this shall be an eternal statute for you, that atonement might be granted to the Israelites from all their wrong-doings once each year. And Moses did as God commanded him.

Numbers 29:7-11

On the tenth day of this seventh month, you shall observe a sacred assembly. You shall deny your souls; you shall not work at your occupations. You shall present a pleasing offering to the Eternal, one bull of the herd, one ram, and seven yearling lambs, without blemish. The meal offering with them shall include choice flour with oil mixed in, three-tenths of a measure for a bull, two-tenths for a ram, and one-tenth for each of the seven lambs. And there shall be one goat for a sin offering, to make expiation for you. All this is in addition to the daily offerings.

אֶת־נַפְשֹׁתֵיכֶם וְכָל־מְלָאכָה לֹא תַעֲשֹׂוּ הָאֶזְרָח וְהַגֵּר הַגָּר בְּתוֹכְכֶם: ל כִּי־בַיּוֹם הַזֶּה יְכַפֵּר עֲלֵיכֶם לְטַהֵר אֶתְכֶם מִכֹּל חַטֹּאתֵיכֶם לִפְנֵי יְהוָה תִּטְהָרוּ:

Sixth aliyah (on Shabbat, seventh aliyah)

לֹא שַׁבַּת שַׁבָּתוֹן הִיא לָכֶם וְעִנִּיתֶם אֶת־נַפְשֹׁתֵיכֶם חֻקַּת עוֹלָם: לב וְכִפֶּר הַכֹּהֵן אֲשֶׁר־יִמְשַׁח אֹתוֹ וַאֲשֶׁר יְמַלֵּא אֶת־יָדוֹ לְכַהֵן תַּחַת אָבִיו וְלָבַשׁ אֶת־בִּגְדֵי הַבָּד בִּגְדֵי הַקֹּדֶשׁ: לג וְכִפֶּר אֶת־מִקְדַּשׁ הַקֹּדֶשׁ וְאֶת־אֹהֶל מוֹעֵד וְאֶת־הַמִּזְבֵּחַ יְכַפֵּר וְעַל הַכֹּהֲנִים וְעַל־כָּל־עַם הַקָּהָל יְכַפֵּר: לד וְהָיְתָה־זֹּאת לָכֶם לְחֻקַּת עוֹלָם לְכַפֵּר עַל־בְּנֵי יִשְׂרָאֵל מִכָּל־חַטֹּאתָם אַחַת בַּשָּׁנָה וַיַּעַשׂ כַּאֲשֶׁר צִוָּה יְהוָה אֶת־מֹשֶׁה: פ

Maftir (second scroll)

ספר במדבר פרק כט

ז וּבֶעָשׂוֹר לַחֹדֶשׁ הַשְּׁבִיעִי הַזֶּה מִקְרָא־קֹדֶשׁ יִהְיֶה לָכֶם וְעִנִּיתֶם אֶת־נַפְשֹׁתֵיכֶם כָּל־מְלָאכָה לֹא תַעֲשֹׂוּ: ח וְהִקְרַבְתֶּם עֹלָה לַיהוָה רֵיחַ נִיחֹחַ פַּר בֶּן־בָּקָר אֶחָד אַיִל אֶחָד כְּבָשִׂים בְּנֵי־שָׁנָה שִׁבְעָה תְּמִימִם יִהְיוּ לָכֶם: ט וּמִנְחָתָם סֹלֶת בְּלוּלָה בַשָּׁמֶן שְׁלֹשָׁה עֶשְׂרֹנִים לַפָּר שְׁנֵי עֶשְׂרֹנִים לָאַיִל הָאֶחָד: י עִשָּׂרוֹן עִשָּׂרוֹן לַכֶּבֶשׂ הָאֶחָד לְשִׁבְעַת הַכְּבָשִׂים: יא שְׂעִיר־עִזִּים אֶחָד חַטָּאת מִלְּבַד חַטַּאת הַכִּפֻּרִים וְעֹלַת הַתָּמִיד וּמִנְחָתָהּ וְנִסְכֵּיהֶם: ס

HAFTARAH FOR YOM KIPPUR MORNING

Isaiah 57:14-58:14

ספר ישעיה פרק נז

God said:

Build a road, clear a path,

Cast away all stumbling-blocks from My people's path,

For thus said the Most High and exalted,

who dwells in eternity, whose name is Holy One:

I dwell in the heights, in holy space,

But equally with those of crushed and humble spirits,

to breathe new life into the humble,

To renew the heart of those who are crushed.

Not forever will I dispute, not eternally will I be angry.

For breath unfolds from My presence, I make souls.

I smote them angrily for the sin of greed,

Angrily I slipped out of sight,

and they all turned back to the path of their own desires.

Having observed their paths, now I will heal them,

I will heal them, I will guide them,

offering a reward of solace to them and their mourners.

I who create the fruit of the lips

Say, "Shalom, shalom!" to far and near,

I, the Eternal (YHVH), will heal them.

יד וְאָמַר סֹלּוּ־סֹלּוּ פַּנּוּ־דָרֶךְ הָרִימוּ מִכְשׁוֹל מִדֶּרֶךְ עַמִּי: טו כִּי כֹה אָמַר רָם וְנִשָּׂא שֹׁכֵן עַד וְקָדוֹשׁ שְׁמוֹ מָרוֹם וְקָדוֹשׁ אֶשְׁכּוֹן וְאֶת־דַּכָּא וּשְׁפַל־רוּחַ לְהַחֲיוֹת רוּחַ שְׁפָלִים וּלְהַחֲיוֹת לֵב נִדְכָּאִים: טז כִּי לֹא לְעוֹלָם אָרִיב וְלֹא לָנֶצַח אֶקְצוֹף כִּי־רוּחַ מִלְּפָנַי יַעֲטוֹף וּנְשָׁמוֹת אֲנִי עָשִׂיתִי: יז בַּעֲוֹן בִּצְעוֹ קָצַפְתִּי וְאַכֵּהוּ הַסְתֵּר וְאֶקְצֹף וַיֵּלֶךְ שׁוֹבָב בְּדֶרֶךְ לִבּוֹ: יח דְּרָכָיו רָאִיתִי וְאֶרְפָּאֵהוּ וְאַנְחֵהוּ וַאֲשַׁלֵּם נִחֻמִים לוֹ וְלַאֲבֵלָיו: יט בּוֹרֵא נִוב [נִיב] שְׂפָתָיִם שָׁלוֹם | שָׁלוֹם לָרָחוֹק וְלַקָּרוֹב אָמַר יְהוָה וּרְפָאתִיו:

But the wicked will be like the tossing sea, finding no rest,

Its waters tossing up mud and slime;

Shalom is not, says my God, for the wicked.

כ וְהָרְשָׁעִים כַּיָּם נִגְרָשׁ כִּי הַשְׁקֵט לֹא יוּכָל וַיִּגְרְשׁוּ מֵימָיו רֶפֶשׁ וָטִיט: כא אֵין שָׁלוֹם אָמַר אֱלֹהַי לָרְשָׁעִים:

So give a full-throated cry, hold nothing back,

Raise your voice to the pitch of a shofar,

And tell My people of their rebelliousness,

Proclaim their wrongs to the house of Jacob.

True, every day they ask Me questions—

How they would love the intimate knowledge of My paths!

They pretend to be a nation which has always acted justly,

Which has not forsaken the decisions of its God.

They ask Me for decisions that would declare

them innocent,

How they would love to be near to God!

א קְרָא בְגָרוֹן אַל־תַּחְשֹׂךְ כַּשּׁוֹפָר הָרֵם קוֹלֶךָ וְהַגֵּד לְעַמִּי פִּשְׁעָם וּלְבֵית יַעֲקֹב חַטֹּאתָם: ב וְאוֹתִי יוֹם יוֹם יִדְרֹשׁוּן וְדַעַת דְּרָכַי יֶחְפָּצוּן כְּגוֹי אֲשֶׁר־צְדָקָה עָשָׂה וּמִשְׁפַּט אֱלֹהָיו לֹא עָזָב יִשְׁאָלוּנִי מִשְׁפְּטֵי־צֶדֶק קִרְבַת אֱלֹהִים יֶחְפָּצוּן:

"For what purpose have we fasted,
when You were not watching?
"Why should we have afflicted ourselves
when You seemed not to know?"
Look here: On the day you fasted you
were looking for business,
Grinding down the toilers who work under you!

Look here: You fast to dispute, to make trouble,
Pummeling everyone with wicked fists,
You're not fasting today
To raise your voice to heaven's height!
Is a fast like this the one I asked for?
A day for self-affliction, to bend the head
like a reed in a marsh,
To sprawl in sackcloth on the ashes?
Is this what you call a fast,
A day to seek the favor of God?

Is not this the fast I ask for:
To unlock the shackles of evil,
To loosen the thongs of the yoke,
To send forth crushed souls to freedom,
To tear every yoke in two!
To tear up your loaves for the hungry,
To bring the poor wanderer home,
When you see the naked, clothe them,
When you see your own flesh and blood, do not turn aside!

Then your light will burst forth like the morning,
And new flesh will soon cover your wounds:
Your reputation for justice will precede you
And the glory of God will follow close behind.
Then when you call, the Eternal One (YHVH) will respond,
As soon as you cry out, God will say, "Here I am!"

ג לָמָּה צַּמְנוּ וְלֹא רָאִיתָ עִנִּינוּ
נַפְשֵׁנוּ וְלֹא תֵדָע הֵן בְּיוֹם צֹמְכֶם
תִּמְצְאוּ־חֵפֶץ וְכָל־עַצְּבֵיכֶם
תִּנְגֹּשׂוּ:

ד הֵן לְרִיב וּמַצָּה תָּצוּמוּ וּלְהַכּוֹת
בְּאֶגְרֹף רֶשַׁע לֹא־תָצוּמוּ כַיּוֹם
לְהַשְׁמִיעַ בַּמָּרוֹם קוֹלְכֶם: ה הֲכָזֶה
יִהְיֶה צוֹם אֶבְחָרֵהוּ יוֹם עַנּוֹת אָדָם
נַפְשׁוֹ הֲלָכֹף כְּאַגְמֹן רֹאשׁוֹ וְשַׂק
וָאֵפֶר יַצִּיעַ הֲלָזֶה תִּקְרָא־צוֹם וְיוֹם
רָצוֹן לַיהוָה:

ו הֲלוֹא זֶה צוֹם אֶבְחָרֵהוּ פַּתֵּחַ
חַרְצֻבּוֹת רֶשַׁע הַתֵּר אֲגֻדּוֹת מוֹטָה
וְשַׁלַּח רְצוּצִים חָפְשִׁים
וְכָל־מוֹטָה תְּנַתֵּקוּ: ז הֲלוֹא פָרֹס
לָרָעֵב לַחְמֶךָ וַעֲנִיִּים מְרוּדִים
תָּבִיא בָיִת כִּי־תִרְאֶה עָרֹם וְכִסִּיתוֹ
וּמִבְּשָׂרְךָ לֹא תִתְעַלָּם:

ח אָז יִבָּקַע כַּשַּׁחַר אוֹרֶךָ וַאֲרֻכָתְךָ
מְהֵרָה תִצְמָח וְהָלַךְ לְפָנֶיךָ צִדְקֶךָ
כְּבוֹד יְהוָה יַאַסְפֶךָ: ט אָז תִּקְרָא
וַיהוָה יַעֲנֶה תְּשַׁוַּע וְיֹאמַר הִנֵּנִי
אִם־תָּסִיר מִתּוֹכְךָ מוֹטָה שְׁלַח
אֶצְבַּע וְדַבֶּר־אָוֶן:

If from your midst you remove

The oppressive yoke, the menacing hand, the abusive words,

If you reach out to the soul of the hungry,

If you ease the soul of the bruised,

Then your light will shine forth in the darkness,

And your shadows will change into noon;

God (YHVH) will guide you forever,

Nourishing your soul like the sun,

Restoring your bones to vigor;

You will become a well-watered garden,

A spring of unfailing fresh water.

From your midst will step forth rebuilders of ruins,

They will restore the foundations of old,

You will be known as repairers of walls long breached,

People who reclaim old paths to dwell in once more.

If you restrain your feet from Shabbat violations,

From doing business on the day of My holiness,

If you call Shabbat a delight,

God's holy time worthy of honor,

Honoring it by abandoning your customary ways,

From doing business and making idle talk,

Then you will become the delight of the Spirit (YHVH)

And I shall lift you over the high places of the earth.

I shall nurture you out of the heritage of Jacob your father,

For the mouth of God has spoken.

י וְתָפֵק לָרָעֵב נַפְשֶׁךָ וְנֶפֶשׁ נַעֲנָה תַּשְׂבִּיעַ וְזָרַח בַּחֹשֶׁךְ אוֹרֶךָ וַאֲפֵלָתְךָ כַּצָּהֳרָיִם: יא וְנָחֲךָ יְהֹוָה תָּמִיד וְהִשְׂבִּיעַ בְּצַחְצָחוֹת נַפְשֶׁךָ וְעַצְמֹתֶיךָ יַחֲלִיץ וְהָיִיתָ כְּגַן רָוֶה וּכְמוֹצָא מַיִם אֲשֶׁר לֹא־יְכַזְּבוּ מֵימָיו:

יב וּבָנוּ מִמְּךָ חָרְבוֹת עוֹלָם מוֹסְדֵי דוֹר־וָדוֹר תְּקוֹמֵם וְקֹרָא לְךָ גֹּדֵר פֶּרֶץ מְשֹׁבֵב נְתִיבוֹת לָשָׁבֶת:

יג אִם־תָּשִׁיב מִשַּׁבָּת רַגְלֶךָ עֲשׂוֹת חֲפָצֶיךָ בְּיוֹם קָדְשִׁי וְקָרָאתָ לַשַּׁבָּת עֹנֶג לִקְדוֹשׁ יְהֹוָה מְכֻבָּד וְכִבַּדְתּוֹ מֵעֲשׂוֹת דְּרָכֶיךָ מִמְּצוֹא חֶפְצְךָ וְדַבֵּר דָּבָר: יד אָז תִּתְעַנַּג עַל־יְהֹוָה וְהִרְכַּבְתִּיךָ עַל־בָּמֳתֵי [בָּמֳתֵי] אָרֶץ וְהַאֲכַלְתִּיךָ נַחֲלַת יַעֲקֹב אָבִיךָ כִּי פִּי יְהֹוָה דִּבֵּר:

TORAH READING FOR YOM KIPPUR AFTERNOON

Leviticus 19:1-18

ספר ויקרא פרק יט

The Eternal (YHVH) spoke to Moses, saying: Speak to the whole Israelite community and say to them:

You shall be holy, for I, Life's Source, your God, am holy.

You shall each revere his mother and his father, and observe My Sabbaths: I, the Eternal, am your God.

Do not turn to idols or make molten gods for yourselves: I, the Eternal, am your God.

When you sacrifice an offering of well-being to the Eternal, sacrifice it so that it may be accepted on your behalf. It shall be eaten on the day you sacrifice it, or on the day following; but what is left by the third day must be consumed in fire. If it should be eaten on the third day, it is an offensive thing, it will not be acceptable. And he who eats of it shall bear his guilt, for he has profaned what is sacred to the Source of Being; that person shall be cut off from his community.

When you reap the harvest of your land, you shall not reap all the way to the edges of your field, or gather the gleanings of your harvest. You shall not pick your vineyard bare, or gather the fallen fruit of your vineyard; you shall leave them for the poor and the stranger; I, the Creator of All, am your God. You shall not steal; you shall not deal deceitfully or falsely with one another. You shall not swear falsely by My name, profaning the name of your God: I am Eternal. You shall not defraud your fellow. You shall not commit robbery. The wages of a laborer shall not remain with you until morning.

First aliyah

א וַיְדַבֵּ֥ר יְהֹוָ֖ה אֶל־מֹשֶׁ֥ה לֵּאמֹֽר: ב דַּבֵּ֞ר אֶל־כׇּל־עֲדַ֧ת בְּנֵֽי־יִשְׂרָאֵ֛ל וְאָמַרְתָּ֥ אֲלֵהֶ֖ם קְדֹשִׁ֣ים תִּהְי֑וּ כִּ֣י קָד֔וֹשׁ אֲנִ֖י יְהֹוָ֥ה אֱלֹהֵיכֶֽם: ג אִ֣ישׁ אִמּ֤וֹ וְאָבִיו֙ תִּירָ֔אוּ וְאֶת־שַׁבְּתֹתַ֖י תִּשְׁמֹ֑רוּ אֲנִ֖י יְהֹוָ֥ה אֱלֹהֵיכֶֽם: ד אַל־תִּפְנוּ֙ אֶל־הָ֣אֱלִילִ֔ם וֵֽאלֹהֵי֙ מַסֵּכָ֔ה לֹ֥א תַעֲשׂ֖וּ לָכֶ֑ם אֲנִ֖י יְהֹוָ֥ה אֱלֹהֵיכֶֽם:

Second aliyah

ה וְכִ֧י תִזְבְּח֛וּ זֶ֥בַח שְׁלָמִ֖ים לַיהֹוָ֑ה לִֽרְצֹנְכֶ֖ם תִּזְבָּחֻֽהוּ: ו בְּי֧וֹם זִבְחֲכֶ֛ם יֵֽאָכֵ֖ל וּמִֽמׇּחֳרָ֑ת וְהַנּוֹתָר֙ עַד־י֣וֹם הַשְּׁלִישִׁ֔י בָּאֵ֖שׁ יִשָּׂרֵֽף: ז וְאִ֛ם הֵֽאָכֹ֥ל יֵֽאָכֵ֖ל בַּיּ֣וֹם הַשְּׁלִישִׁ֑י פִּגּ֥וּל ה֖וּא לֹ֥א יֵֽרָצֶֽה: ח וְאֹֽכְלָיו֙ עֲוֺנ֣וֹ יִשָּׂ֔א כִּֽי־אֶת־קֹ֥דֶשׁ יְהֹוָ֖ה חִלֵּ֑ל וְנִכְרְתָ֛ה הַנֶּ֥פֶשׁ הַהִ֖וא מֵֽעַמֶּֽיהָ:

Third aliyah

ט וּֽבְקֻצְרְכֶם֙ אֶת־קְצִ֣יר אַרְצְכֶ֔ם לֹ֧א תְכַלֶּ֛ה פְּאַ֥ת שָֽׂדְךָ֖ לִקְצֹ֑ר וְלֶ֥קֶט קְצִֽירְךָ֖ לֹ֥א תְלַקֵּֽט: י וְכַרְמְךָ֙ לֹ֣א תְעוֹלֵ֔ל וּפֶ֥רֶט כַּרְמְךָ֖ לֹ֣א תְלַקֵּ֑ט לֶֽעָנִ֤י וְלַגֵּר֙ תַּֽעֲזֹ֣ב אֹתָ֔ם אֲנִ֖י יְהֹוָ֥ה אֱלֹהֵיכֶֽם: יא לֹ֖א תִּגְנֹ֑בוּ וְלֹֽא־תְכַחֲשׁ֥וּ וְלֹֽא־תְשַׁקְּר֖וּ אִ֥ישׁ בַּעֲמִיתֽוֹ: יב וְלֹֽא־תִשָּׁבְע֥וּ בִשְׁמִ֖י לַשָּׁ֑קֶר וְחִלַּלְתָּ֛ אֶת־שֵׁ֥ם אֱלֹהֶ֖יךָ אֲנִ֥י יְהֹוָֽה: יג לֹֽא־תַעֲשֹׁ֥ק אֶת־רֵֽעֲךָ֖ וְלֹ֣א תִגְזֹ֑ל לֹֽא־תָלִ֞ין פְּעֻלַּ֥ת שָׂכִ֛יר אִתְּךָ֖ עַד־בֹּֽקֶר:

153

You shall not insult the deaf, nor place a stumbling block before the blind. You shall fear your God: I am Eternal. You shall not render an unfair decision: do not favor the poor or show deference to the rich, judge your kinsman fairly. Do not deal basely with your people. Do not profit by the blood of your neighbor: I am Eternal. You shall not hate your kinsfolk in your heart. Reprove your kinsman but incur no guilt because of him. You shall not take vengeance nor bear a grudge against your people. Love your neighbor as yourself: I am Eternal.

יד לֹא־תְקַלֵּל חֵרֵשׁ וְלִפְנֵי עִוֵּר לֹא תִתֵּן מִכְשֹׁל וְיָרֵאתָ מֵּאֱלֹהֶיךָ אֲנִי יְהוָֹה: טו לֹא־תַעֲשׂוּ עָוֶל בַּמִּשְׁפָּט לֹא־תִשָּׂא פְנֵי־דָל וְלֹא תֶהְדַּר פְּנֵי גָדוֹל בְּצֶדֶק תִּשְׁפֹּט עֲמִיתֶךָ: טז לֹא־תֵלֵךְ רָכִיל בְּעַמֶּיךָ לֹא תַעֲמֹד עַל־דַּם רֵעֶךָ אֲנִי יְהוָֹה: יז לֹא־תִשְׂנָא אֶת־אָחִיךָ בִּלְבָבֶךָ הוֹכֵחַ תּוֹכִיחַ אֶת־עֲמִיתֶךָ וְלֹא־תִשָּׂא עָלָיו חֵטְא: יח לֹא־תִקֹּם וְלֹא־תִטֹּר אֶת־בְּנֵי עַמֶּךָ וְאָהַבְתָּ לְרֵעֲךָ כָּמוֹךָ אֲנִי יְהוָֹה:

The Book of Jonah

סֵפֶר יוֹנָה פֶּרֶק א

Chapter 1

The word of the Ineffable Mystery of Life (YHVH) came to Jonah, Amittai's son, saying: "Get up, go to Nineveh, the great city, and cry out to her that the evil of her inhabitants has come up before Me."

א וַיְהִי דְּבַר־יְהֹוָה אֶל־יוֹנָה בֶן־אֲמִתַּי לֵאמֹר: ב קוּם לֵךְ אֶל־נִינְוֵה הָעִיר הַגְּדוֹלָה וּקְרָא עָלֶיהָ כִּי־עָלְתָה רָעָתָם לְפָנָי:

Instead, Jonah arose to flee to Tarshish, from before the face of Ineffable Adonai, and he descended to Jaffa, found a ship going to Tarshish, paid the fare, and went down into the ship to go with its crew to Tarshish, away from the presence of Adonai.

ג וַיָּקָם יוֹנָה לִבְרֹחַ תַּרְשִׁישָׁה מִלִּפְנֵי יְהֹוָה וַיֵּרֶד יָפוֹ וַיִּמְצָא אֳנִיָּה | בָּאָה תַרְשִׁישׁ וַיִּתֵּן שְׂכָרָהּ וַיֵּרֶד בָּהּ לָבוֹא עִמָּהֶם תַּרְשִׁישָׁה מִלִּפְנֵי יְהֹוָה:

But the Eternal heaved a great wind into the sea, and such a great storm arose at sea that the ship's crew thought she was about to break in pieces. The sailors panicked, each one of them crying out to their own god, then tossing all the baggage on the ship into the sea to reduce the weight. Meanwhile Jonah had gone down into the hold of the vessel to lie down, and fell asleep. But the chief sailor approached him and said, "How can you be sleeping? Get up, cry out to your god, perhaps the god will take notice of us and we will not be lost."

ד וַיהֹוָה הֵטִיל רוּחַ־גְּדוֹלָה אֶל־הַיָּם וַיְהִי סַעַר־גָּדוֹל בַּיָּם וְהָאֳנִיָּה חִשְּׁבָה לְהִשָּׁבֵר: ה וַיִּירְאוּ הַמַּלָּחִים וַיִּזְעֲקוּ אִישׁ אֶל־אֱלֹהָיו וַיָּטִלוּ אֶת־הַכֵּלִים אֲשֶׁר בָּאֳנִיָּה אֶל־הַיָּם לְהָקֵל מֵעֲלֵיהֶם וְיוֹנָה יָרַד אֶל־יַרְכְּתֵי הַסְּפִינָה וַיִּשְׁכַּב וַיֵּרָדַם: ו וַיִּקְרַב אֵלָיו רַב הַחֹבֵל וַיֹּאמֶר לוֹ מַה־לְּךָ נִרְדָּם קוּם קְרָא אֶל־אֱלֹהֶיךָ אוּלַי יִתְעַשֵּׁת הָאֱלֹהִים לָנוּ וְלֹא נֹאבֵד:

They said to each other, "Come, let us cast lots to find out on whose account this terrible thing has happened to us." So they cast lots, and the lot fell on Jonah. So they said to him: "Please tell us, since it is on your account that this terrible thing has happened to us, what is your work? Where do you come from? What is your land? From which people are you?"

ז וַיֹּאמְרוּ אִישׁ אֶל־רֵעֵהוּ לְכוּ וְנַפִּילָה גוֹרָלוֹת וְנֵדְעָה בְּשֶׁלְּמִי הָרָעָה הַזֹּאת לָנוּ וַיַּפִּלוּ גּוֹרָלוֹת וַיִּפֹּל הַגּוֹרָל עַל־יוֹנָה: ח וַיֹּאמְרוּ אֵלָיו הַגִּידָה־נָּא לָנוּ בַּאֲשֶׁר לְמִי־הָרָעָה הַזֹּאת לָנוּ מַה־מְּלַאכְתְּךָ וּמֵאַיִן תָּבוֹא מָה אַרְצֶךָ וְאֵי־מִזֶּה עַם אָתָּה:

155

And he said to them, "I am a Hebrew, and I stand in awe of Adonai, the God of the heavens, who made the sea and the dry land." Then a great fear came upon the men and they said, "What is this you have done?" For the men now knew, since he had told them, that he was fleeing from the Eternal (YHVH). They asked him, as the sea grew ever more stormy, "What shall we do with you so the sea may be calm for us?" He told them, "Pick me up and toss me into the sea and the sea will calm down for you. For I know that it is on my account that this great storm has come upon you."

Instead, the men dug their oars into the water, trying to row back to dry land, but they failed, for the sea was growing ever more stormy around them. So they cried to Adonai, saying, "Please, Adonai, let us not lose our lives for this man, and at the same time let us not be guilty of shedding innocent blood, for it was You, the Eternal (YHVH), who desired this and made it happen this way." And as soon as they picked Jonah up and threw him into the sea, the sea stopped raging. Then a tremendous awe of Adonai came upon the men and they offered a sacrifice to Adonai and made vows.

Chapter 2

Adonai (YHVH) designated a great fish to swallow Jonah, and Jonah was in the belly of the fish three days and three nights. And Jonah prayed to Adonai (YHVH) his God from the bowels of the fish, saying:

ט וַיֹּאמֶר אֲלֵיהֶם עִבְרִי אָנֹכִי וְאֶת־יְהֹוָה אֱלֹהֵי הַשָּׁמַיִם אֲנִי יָרֵא אֲשֶׁר־עָשָׂה אֶת־הַיָּם וְאֶת־הַיַּבָּשָׁה: י וַיִּירְאוּ הָאֲנָשִׁים יִרְאָה גְדוֹלָה וַיֹּאמְרוּ אֵלָיו מַה־זֹּאת עָשִׂיתָ כִּי־יָדְעוּ הָאֲנָשִׁים כִּי־מִלִּפְנֵי יְהֹוָה הוּא בֹרֵחַ כִּי הִגִּיד לָהֶם: יא וַיֹּאמְרוּ אֵלָיו מַה־נַּעֲשֶׂה לָּךְ וְיִשְׁתֹּק הַיָּם מֵעָלֵינוּ כִּי הַיָּם הוֹלֵךְ וְסֹעֵר:

יב וַיֹּאמֶר אֲלֵיהֶם שָׂאוּנִי וַהֲטִילֻנִי אֶל־הַיָּם וְיִשְׁתֹּק הַיָּם מֵעֲלֵיכֶם כִּי יוֹדֵעַ אָנִי כִּי בְשֶׁלִּי הַסַּעַר הַגָּדוֹל הַזֶּה עֲלֵיכֶם: יג וַיַּחְתְּרוּ הָאֲנָשִׁים לְהָשִׁיב אֶל־הַיַּבָּשָׁה וְלֹא יָכֹלוּ כִּי הַיָּם הוֹלֵךְ וְסֹעֵר עֲלֵיהֶם: יד וַיִּקְרְאוּ אֶל־יְהֹוָה וַיֹּאמְרוּ אָנָּה יְהֹוָה אַל־נָא נֹאבְדָה בְּנֶפֶשׁ הָאִישׁ הַזֶּה וְאַל־תִּתֵּן עָלֵינוּ דָּם נָקִיא כִּי־אַתָּה יְהֹוָה כַּאֲשֶׁר חָפַצְתָּ עָשִׂיתָ: טו וַיִּשְׂאוּ אֶת־יוֹנָה וַיְטִלֻהוּ אֶל־הַיָּם וַיַּעֲמֹד הַיָּם מִזַּעְפּוֹ: טז וַיִּירְאוּ הָאֲנָשִׁים יִרְאָה גְדוֹלָה אֶת־יְהֹוָה וַיִּזְבְּחוּ־זֶבַח לַיהֹוָה וַיִּדְּרוּ נְדָרִים:

פרק ב

א וַיְמַן יְהֹוָה דָּג גָּדוֹל לִבְלֹעַ אֶת־יוֹנָה וַיְהִי יוֹנָה בִּמְעֵי הַדָּג שְׁלֹשָׁה יָמִים וּשְׁלֹשָׁה לֵילוֹת: ב וַיִּתְפַּלֵּל יוֹנָה אֶל־יְהֹוָה אֱלֹהָיו מִמְּעֵי הַדָּגָה:

"I have cried out in my distress to Adonai and God has answered me, from the Sheol's belly I have pleaded, and You have heard my voice. You had cast me into the depths—into the heart of the seas—the flood surrounded me, all your rolling waves broke over me.

"I said to myself: I am cast adrift from Your sight, will I ever look again at Your Holy Temple? Water surrounded me, I was gasping for breath, the deeps closed in on me, my head was tangled in weeds,

"I sank to the bottom of the mountains, the earth was drawing the bars against me forever, but You brought up my life from the pit, Adonai my God. When the breath of life was fading from within me, I invoked the presence of Adonai, my prayer entered into Your Presence, to the Temple of Your Holiness.

"Those who heed the vaporous falsehood of idols forsake Your love. But, with thankful voice, I shall make an offering to You; what I have vowed I will complete. Liberation belongs to Adonai!"

Then Adonai spoke to the fish, who vomited Jonah onto the dry land.

Chapter 3

The word of Adonai came to Jonah a second time, saying: "Get up, go to Nineveh, the great city, and proclaim to her the cry which I told you." And Jonah got up and went to Nineveh according to the word of Adonai, for Nineveh was a great city in God's sight, requiring three days to walk across it.

ג וַיֹּאמֶר קָרָאתִי מִצָּרָה לִי אֶל־יְהֹוָה וַיַּעֲנֵנִי מִבֶּטֶן שְׁאוֹל שִׁוַּעְתִּי שָׁמַעְתָּ קוֹלִי: ד וַתַּשְׁלִיכֵנִי מְצוּלָה בִּלְבַב יַמִּים וְנָהָר יְסֹבְבֵנִי כָּל־מִשְׁבָּרֶיךָ וְגַלֶּיךָ עָלַי עָבָרוּ:

ה וַאֲנִי אָמַרְתִּי נִגְרַשְׁתִּי מִנֶּגֶד עֵינֶיךָ אַךְ אוֹסִיף לְהַבִּיט אֶל־הֵיכַל קָדְשֶׁךָ: ו אֲפָפוּנִי מַיִם עַד־נֶפֶשׁ תְּהוֹם יְסֹבְבֵנִי סוּף חָבוּשׁ לְרֹאשִׁי:

ז לְקִצְבֵי הָרִים יָרַדְתִּי הָאָרֶץ בְּרִחֶיהָ בַעֲדִי לְעוֹלָם וַתַּעַל מִשַּׁחַת חַיַּי יְהֹוָה אֱלֹהָי: ח בְּהִתְעַטֵּף עָלַי נַפְשִׁי אֶת־יְהֹוָה זָכָרְתִּי וַתָּבוֹא אֵלֶיךָ תְּפִלָּתִי אֶל־הֵיכַל קָדְשֶׁךָ:

ט מְשַׁמְּרִים הַבְלֵי־שָׁוְא חַסְדָּם יַעֲזֹבוּ: י וַאֲנִי בְּקוֹל תּוֹדָה אֶזְבְּחָה־לָּךְ אֲשֶׁר נָדַרְתִּי אֲשַׁלֵּמָה יְשׁוּעָתָה לַיהֹוָה:

יא וַיֹּאמֶר יְהֹוָה לַדָּג וַיָּקֵא אֶת־יוֹנָה אֶל־הַיַּבָּשָׁה:

פרק ג

א וַיְהִי דְבַר־יְהֹוָה אֶל־יוֹנָה שֵׁנִית לֵאמֹר: ב קוּם לֵךְ אֶל־נִינְוֵה הָעִיר הַגְּדוֹלָה וּקְרָא אֵלֶיהָ אֶת־הַקְּרִיאָה אֲשֶׁר אָנֹכִי דֹּבֵר אֵלֶיךָ: ג וַיָּקָם יוֹנָה וַיֵּלֶךְ אֶל־נִינְוֵה כִּדְבַר יְהֹוָה וְנִינְוֵה הָיְתָה עִיר־גְּדוֹלָה לֵאלֹהִים מַהֲלַךְ שְׁלֹשֶׁת יָמִים:

As soon as Jonah began entering the city on his first day's walk he called out: "Another forty days and Nineveh is overthrown!" The residents of Nineveh believed God and proclaimed a fast. From the greatest to the smallest they dressed in sackcloth. When the matter reached the king of Nineveh he got up from his throne, removed his cloak, covered himself with sackcloth and sat in ashes. He issued a proclamation in Nineveh: "By decree of the king and his notables, as follows: Neither humans nor animals, neither cattle nor sheep shall taste anything; they shall not graze and they shall not drink water. Humans and animals shall cover themselves with sackcloth, they shall cry out to God with all their evil ways and from the violence they have done. Who knows whether God will turn back and relent, turning from His wrath, so that we shall not perish?"

Then God (Elohim) saw by their actions that they have turned back from their evil ways, and God renounced the punishment which had been planned for them, and did not do it.

Chapter 4

However, to Jonah this appeared to be a great wrong, and he was angry. He prayed to Adonai and said, "Please, Adonai, isn't this what I said when I was on my own land? This is why I fled originally to Tarshish, for I know that You are a gracious and merciful God, long-suffering and abundant in lovingkindness, and compassionate about that which is wrong. So now, Adonai, please take my life from me, for dying is better for me than living."

And Adonai said, "Is it better that you be angry?"

ד וַיָּחֶל יוֹנָה לָבוֹא בָעִיר מַהֲלַךְ יוֹם אֶחָד וַיִּקְרָא וַיֹּאמַר עוֹד אַרְבָּעִים יוֹם וְנִינְוֵה נֶהְפָּכֶת: ה וַיַּאֲמִינוּ אַנְשֵׁי נִינְוֵה בֵּאלֹהִים וַיִּקְרְאוּ־צוֹם וַיִּלְבְּשׁוּ שַׂקִּים מִגְּדוֹלָם וְעַד־קְטַנָּם: ו וַיִּגַּע הַדָּבָר אֶל־מֶלֶךְ נִינְוֵה וַיָּקָם מִכִּסְאוֹ וַיַּעֲבֵר אַדַּרְתּוֹ מֵעָלָיו וַיְכַס שַׂק וַיֵּשֶׁב עַל־הָאֵפֶר: ז וַיַּזְעֵק וַיֹּאמֶר בְּנִינְוֵה מִטַּעַם הַמֶּלֶךְ וּגְדֹלָיו לֵאמֹר הָאָדָם וְהַבְּהֵמָה הַבָּקָר וְהַצֹּאן אַל־יִטְעֲמוּ מְאוּמָה אַל־יִרְעוּ וּמַיִם אַל־יִשְׁתּוּ: ח וְיִתְכַּסּוּ שַׂקִּים הָאָדָם וְהַבְּהֵמָה וְיִקְרְאוּ אֶל־אֱלֹהִים בְּחָזְקָה וְיָשֻׁבוּ אִישׁ מִדַּרְכּוֹ הָרָעָה וּמִן־הֶחָמָס אֲשֶׁר בְּכַפֵּיהֶם: ט מִי־יוֹדֵעַ יָשׁוּב וְנִחַם הָאֱלֹהִים וְשָׁב מֵחֲרוֹן אַפּוֹ וְלֹא נֹאבֵד:

י וַיַּרְא הָאֱלֹהִים אֶת־מַעֲשֵׂיהֶם כִּי־שָׁבוּ מִדַּרְכָּם הָרָעָה וַיִּנָּחֶם הָאֱלֹהִים עַל־הָרָעָה אֲשֶׁר־דִּבֶּר לַעֲשׂוֹת־לָהֶם וְלֹא עָשָׂה:

פרק ד

א וַיֵּרַע אֶל־יוֹנָה רָעָה גְדוֹלָה וַיִּחַר לוֹ: ב וַיִּתְפַּלֵּל אֶל־יְהֹוָה וַיֹּאמַר אָנָּה יְהֹוָה הֲלוֹא־זֶה דְבָרִי עַד־הֱיוֹתִי עַל־אַדְמָתִי עַל־כֵּן קִדַּמְתִּי לִבְרֹחַ תַּרְשִׁישָׁה כִּי יָדַעְתִּי כִּי אַתָּה אֵל־חַנּוּן וְרַחוּם אֶרֶךְ אַפַּיִם וְרַב־חֶסֶד וְנִחָם עַל־הָרָעָה: ג וְעַתָּה יְהֹוָה קַח־נָא אֶת־נַפְשִׁי מִמֶּנִּי כִּי טוֹב מוֹתִי מֵחַיָּי:

ד וַיֹּאמֶר יְהֹוָה הַהֵיטֵב חָרָה לָךְ:

Then Jonah went out of the city and sat on the east side, where he made himself a sukkah and sat under it in the shade to see what would happen to the city. And Adonai, who is God, designated a gourd to grow over Jonah to shade his head and protect him from his discomfort, and a great relief came upon Jonah because of the plant. Then God appointed a worm in the early morning the next day, striking at the gourd, which withered away. When the sun rose God appointed a hot east wind, with the sun striking Jonah's head till he felt faint, and he felt like dying, saying, "It is better for me to die than to live." And God said to Jonah, "Is anger about the gourd better for you?" And he said, "Angry enough to die."

And Adonai said, "You had compassion for the gourd, which you did not work to raise; one night it was there, the next it was gone. Should I not have compassion upon the great city Nineveh, with 120,000 people who don't know right from left, not to mention all the cattle?"

Micah 7:18-20

Who is a God like You, forgiving iniquity and forgiving the wrongdoings of the remnant of Your people, not holding onto anger forever, but delighting in lovingkindness. Your mercy will return to us, our wrongdoings will be gone, our sins cast into the sea. Your truth will be shown to Jacob, love to the children of Abraham, as was promised to our ancestors in the beginning days of our people.

ה וַיֵּצֵא יוֹנָה מִן־הָעִיר וַיֵּשֶׁב מִקֶּדֶם לָעִיר וַיַּעַשׂ לוֹ שָׁם סֻכָּה וַיֵּשֶׁב תַּחְתֶּיהָ בַּצֵּל עַד אֲשֶׁר יִרְאֶה מַה־יִּהְיֶה בָּעִיר: ו וַיְמַן יְהֹוָה־אֱלֹהִים קִיקָיוֹן וַיַּעַל | מֵעַל לְיוֹנָה לִהְיוֹת צֵל עַל־רֹאשׁוֹ לְהַצִּיל לוֹ מֵרָעָתוֹ וַיִּשְׂמַח יוֹנָה עַל־הַקִּיקָיוֹן שִׂמְחָה גְדוֹלָה: ז וַיְמַן הָאֱלֹהִים תּוֹלַעַת בַּעֲלוֹת הַשַּׁחַר לַמָּחֳרָת וַתַּךְ אֶת־הַקִּיקָיוֹן וַיִּיבָשׁ: ח וַיְהִי | כִּזְרֹחַ הַשֶּׁמֶשׁ וַיְמַן אֱלֹהִים רוּחַ קָדִים חֲרִישִׁית וַתַּךְ הַשֶּׁמֶשׁ עַל־רֹאשׁ יוֹנָה וַיִּתְעַלָּף וַיִּשְׁאַל אֶת־נַפְשׁוֹ לָמוּת וַיֹּאמֶר טוֹב מוֹתִי מֵחַיָּי: ט וַיֹּאמֶר אֱלֹהִים אֶל־יוֹנָה הַהֵיטֵב חָרָה־לְךָ עַל־הַקִּיקָיוֹן וַיֹּאמֶר הֵיטֵב חָרָה־לִי עַד־מָוֶת:

י וַיֹּאמֶר יְהֹוָה אַתָּה חַסְתָּ עַל־הַקִּיקָיוֹן אֲשֶׁר לֹא־עָמַלְתָּ בּוֹ וְלֹא גִדַּלְתּוֹ שֶׁבִּן־לַיְלָה הָיָה וּבִן־לַיְלָה אָבָד: יא וַאֲנִי לֹא אָחוּס עַל־נִינְוֵה הָעִיר הַגְּדוֹלָה אֲשֶׁר יֶשׁ־בָּהּ הַרְבֵּה מִשְׁתֵּים־עֶשְׂרֵה רִבּוֹ אָדָם אֲשֶׁר לֹא־יָדַע בֵּין־יְמִינוֹ לִשְׂמֹאלוֹ וּבְהֵמָה רַבָּה:

ספר מיכה פרק ז

יח מִי־אֵל כָּמוֹךָ נֹשֵׂא עָוֹן וְעֹבֵר עַל־פֶּשַׁע לִשְׁאֵרִית נַחֲלָתוֹ לֹא־הֶחֱזִיק לָעַד אַפּוֹ כִּי־חָפֵץ חֶסֶד הוּא: יט יָשׁוּב יְרַחֲמֵנוּ יִכְבֹּשׁ עֲוֺנֹתֵינוּ וְתַשְׁלִיךְ בִּמְצֻלוֹת יָם כָּל־חַטֹּאתָם: כ תִּתֵּן אֱמֶת לְיַעֲקֹב חֶסֶד לְאַבְרָהָם אֲשֶׁר־נִשְׁבַּעְתָּ לַאֲבֹתֵינוּ מִימֵי קֶדֶם:

Torah and Haftarah Readings

David

Blessings Before the Haftarah

Blessed are You, God our God, Ruler of the universe, who has selected faithful prophets and takes delight in their words which were spoken in truth.

בָּרוּךְ אַתָּה יהוה אֱלֹהֵינוּ מֶלֶךְ הָעוֹלָם,
אֲשֶׁר בָּחַר בִּנְבִיאִים טוֹבִים,
וְרָצָה בְדִבְרֵיהֶם הַנֶּאֱמָרִים בֶּאֱמֶת.

Blessed are You, Adonai, who delights in the Torah, Moses, the people Israel, and the prophets of truth and righteousness.

בָּרוּךְ אַתָּה יהוה,
הַבּוֹחֵר בַּתּוֹרָה וּבְמֹשֶׁה עַבְדּוֹ,
וּבְיִשְׂרָאֵל עַמּוֹ, וּבִנְבִיאֵי הָאֱמֶת וָצֶדֶק.

Blessings After the Haftarah

Blessed are You, Adonai our God, the Majesty of the universe, Rock of all ages, righteous in all generations. You are the faithful God who says and performs, who speaks and fulfills, whose words are true and righteous. We have faith in You, God our God, and in Your words which will be fulfilled. You are a faithful and compassionate God and Ruler.

בָּרוּךְ אַתָּה יהוה אֱלֹהֵינוּ
מֶלֶךְ הָעוֹלָם, צוּר כָּל הָעוֹלָמִים,
צַדִּיק בְּכָל הַדּוֹרוֹת,
הָאֵל הַנֶּאֱמָן הָאוֹמֵר וְעֹשֶׂה,
הַמְדַבֵּר וּמְקַיֵּם, שֶׁכָּל דְּבָרָיו אֱמֶת וָצֶדֶק.
נֶאֱמָן אַתָּה הוּא יהוה אֱלֹהֵינוּ,
וְנֶאֱמָנִים דְּבָרֶיךָ, וְדָבָר אֶחָד
מִדְּבָרֶיךָ אָחוֹר לֹא יָשׁוּב רֵיקָם,
כִּי אֵל מֶלֶךְ נֶאֱמָן (וְרַחֲמָן) אָתָּה.

Blessed are You, Adonai, the God, who is faithful in fulfilling the Way of words.

בָּרוּךְ אַתָּה יהוה, הָאֵל הַנֶּאֱמָן בְּכָל דְּבָרָיו.

Be merciful unto Zion, for it is the dwelling of our life, and may You soon in our own day save the city that grieves in spirit.

רַחֵם עַל צִיּוֹן
כִּי הִיא בֵּית חַיֵּינוּ,
וְלַעֲלוּבַת נֶפֶשׁ תּוֹשִׁיעַ
בִּמְהֵרָה בְיָמֵינוּ.

Blessed are You, Adonai, who causes Zion to rejoice with her children.

בָּרוּךְ אַתָּה יהוה, מְשַׂמֵּחַ צִיּוֹן בְּבָנֶיהָ.

Torah and Haftarah Readings

Bring us joy through Your servant Elijah,
and delight us with the establishment of the
Messianic order of David, Your anointed.
May no stranger occupy his throne
and may no usurper inherit his glory.
For You have promised that his light
will never be extinguished.
Blessed art Thou, the Shield of David.

We thank and bless You, Adonai our God,
for the Torah and for our worship
and for the prophets, [for this Sabbath day]
and for this Day of Remembrance,
which You, Adonai our God,
give us [for holiness and for rest]
for glory and delight.

May Your name be continuously praised
by the mouth of every living being forevermore.
Your word is truth and endures forever.

Blessed are You, Adonai, Sovereign over all
the earth who hallows [the Sabbath and] Israel
and this Day of Remembrance [Day of Yom
Kippur].

שַׂמְּחֵנוּ יהוה אֱלֹהֵינוּ בְּאֵלִיָּהוּ הַנָּבִיא עַבְדֶּךָ,
וּבְמַלְכוּת בֵּית דָּוִד מְשִׁיחֶךָ,
בִּמְהֵרָה יָבֹא וְיָגֵל לִבֵּנוּ,
עַל כִּסְאוֹ לֹא יֵשֵׁב זָר וְלֹא יִנְחֲלוּ
עוֹד אֲחֵרִים אֶת כְּבוֹדוֹ,
כִּי בְשֵׁם קָדְשְׁךָ נִשְׁבַּעְתָּ לּוֹ,
שֶׁלֹּא יִכְבֶּה נֵרוֹ לְעוֹלָם וָעֶד.
בָּרוּךְ אַתָּה יהוה, מָגֵן דָּוִד.

עַל הַתּוֹרָה, וְעַל הָעֲבוֹדָה,
וְעַל הַנְּבִיאִים, (וְעַל יוֹם הַשַּׁבָּת הַזֶּה,)
וְעַל יוֹם הַזִּכָּרוֹן הַזֶּה,
שֶׁנָּתַתָּ לָנוּ יהוה אֱלֹהֵינוּ,
(לִקְדֻשָּׁה וְלִמְנוּחָה,) לְכָבוֹד וּלְתִפְאָרֶת.

עַל הַכֹּל יהוה אֱלֹהֵינוּ,
אֲנַחְנוּ מוֹדִים לָךְ, וּמְבָרְכִים אוֹתָךְ,
יִתְבָּרַךְ שִׁמְךָ בְּפִי כָל חַי תָּמִיד
לְעוֹלָם וָעֶד וּדְבָרְךָ אֱמֶת וְקַיָּם לָעַד.

בָּרוּךְ אַתָּה יהוה, מְקַדֵּשׁ (הַשַּׁבָּת וְ)
יִשְׂרָאֵל וְיוֹם הַזִּכָּרוֹן (וְיוֹם הַכִּפּוּרִים).

Torah and Haftarah Readings

Songs and Readings

Artwork: Ben Shahn, Bach

Akhat Sha'alti

Akhat Sha'alti Mey'et haShem Otah Avakeysh,
Shivti, b'Veyt Adonai Kol y'Mey Khayai,
laKhazot b'Noam, b'Noam HaShem,
u-1'Vaker b'Heykhalo.

אַחַת שָׁאַלְתִּי מֵאֵת יהוה אוֹתָהּ אֲבַקֵּשׁ
שִׁבְתִּי בְּבֵית יהוה כָּל יְמֵי חַיַּי
לַחֲזוֹת בְּנֹעַם יהוה
וּלְבַקֵּר בְּהֵיכָלוֹ.

One thing do I ask from the Eternal,
that I be allowed to live in the House of Adonai
all the days of my life,
to see God's pleasantness,
and to visit the Great Hall.

Psalm 27:4

VaAnakhnu Lo Neydah

VaAnakhnu Lo Neydah Ma Na'aseh
Ki Alekha Eyneynu.
Z'khor Rakhamekha HaShem
vaKhasadekha Ki meyOlam Heymah.

וַאֲנַחְנוּ לֹא נֵדַע מַה נַּעֲשֶׂה
כִּי עָלֶיךָ עֵינֵינוּ.
זְכֹר רַחֲמֶיךָ יהוה
וַחֲסָדֶיךָ כִּי מֵעוֹלָם הֵמָּה.

We do not know what to do,
our eyes look to You,
recalling Your compassion and Your love,
always there.

Chronicles II 20:12, Psalm 25:6

Eylekha

Eylekha HaShem Ekrah v'Eyl HaShem Etkhanan.
Sh'ma HaShem v'Khaneyni, HaShem Hehyey Ozer Li.

אֵלֶיךָ יהוה אֶקְרָא וְאֶל יהוה אֶתְחַנָּן.
שְׁמַע יהוה וְחָנֵּנִי, יהוה הֱיֵה עֹזֵר לִי.

I call to You, God. I plead to the Source of All.
Listen, O God, and be gracious unto me. Help me.

Psalm 30:9,11

Songs and Readings

Modeh Ani

Dusk, when shadows fall,
We see the sun go down,
We see it all.
Dawn, when sun breaks through,
We see it new,
We see it new.

Rise and make your way.
Rise and make the day.
The world is given you;
Its beauty you renew,
And you must choose it,
Use it

Well, look to the well.
Follow its mystery
And you will "see."
Flow, the water flows,
And where it goes,

We all shall be.

Rise and make your way.
Rise and make the day.
The world is given you;
Its beauty you renew,
And you must choose it,
Use it well.

                    Betsy Combs

Morning Has Broken

Morning has broken like the first morning
Blackbird has spoken like the first bird
Praise for the singing, praise for the morning
Praise for the springing fresh from the Word.

Sweet the rain's new fall sunlit from heaven
Like the first dew fall on the first grass
Praise for the sweetness of the wet garden
Sprung in completeness where His feet pass.

Mine is the sunlight, mine is the morning
Born of the one light Eden saw play
Praise with elation, praise every morning
God's re-creation of the new day.

                    Eleanor Farjeon

Awaken, Arise ...

Awaken, arise ...
to the wholeness of your spirit.
Awaken, arise ...
to the beauty of your soul.

Hitor'ri Hitor'ri   הִתְעוֹרְרִי הִתְעוֹרְרִי
Ki Va Oreykh   כִּי בָא אוֹרֵךְ
Kumi Ori.   קוּמִי אוֹרִי.

                    Hannah Tiferet Siegel

Blessed are You, Eternal One, Sovereign of the Universe,
who sanctified us with commandments and instructed us
to wrap ourselves in fringed garments.

בָּרוּךְ אַתָּה יהוה
אֱלֹהֵינוּ מֶלֶךְ הָעוֹלָם
אֲשֶׁר קִדְּשָׁנוּ בְּמִצְוֹתָיו, וְצִוָּנוּ
לְהִתְעַטֵּף בַּצִּיצִת.

Ki Imkha M'kor Khayim, b'Orkha Nireh Ohr.
The Source of Life is with you, in Your Light we will see
Light.

כִּי עִמְּךָ מְקוֹר חַיִּים,
בְּאוֹרְךָ נִרְאֶה אוֹר.

Life

May the sound of children be your music,
May your blessings be the ones you earn.
May your days be filled with sun.
May you deeply love someone.
May that someone love you in return.

Chorus:

> Life – May yours be long and loving.
> Peace – May you enjoy its blessings.
> Joy – May it be yours to savor.
> Love – May it be yours forever.

May your only sorrows be the small ones.
May they leave you stronger when they go.
May the love of friends be yours.
May you live with open doors.
May you feel the love within you grow.

Chorus

May your smallest moment be a full one.
May your life be all that it can be.
May you come to love yourself,
And hold that love above yourself,
And hold that love for all the world to see.

Chorus

Tom Paxton

Circle Chant

Circle round for freedom.
Circle round for peace.
May all of us imprisoned
circle for release.

Circle for the planet.
Circle for each soul.
For the future of our children,
keep the circle whole.

Linda Hirschhorn

Shir LaShalom

Tnu lashemesh laalot	תְּנוּ לַשֶּׁמֶשׁ לַעֲלוֹת
Laboker l'ha'ir	לַבֹּקֶר לְהָאִיר.
Hazaka shebat'filot	הַזַּכָּה שֶׁבַּתְּפִלּוֹת
Otanu lo tachzir.	אוֹתָנוּ לֹא תַּחֲזִיר.
Mi asher kava nero	מִי אֲשֶׁר כָּבָה נֵרוֹ
Uve'afar nitman,	וּבֶעָפָר נִטְמַן,
Bechi mar lo ya'iro,	בְּכִי מַר לֹא יְעִירוֹ,
Lo yachziro lechan.	לֹא יַחֲזִירוֹ לְכָאן.
Ish otanu lo yashiv	אִישׁ אוֹתָנוּ לֹא יָשִׁיב
Mibor tachtit afel,	מִבּוֹר תַּחְתִּית אָפֵל,
Kan lo yo'ilu lo simchat hanitsachon	כָּאן לֹא יוֹעִילוּ לֹא שִׂמְחַת הַנִּצָּחוֹן
Velo shirey halel!	וְלֹא שִׁירֵי הַלֵּל!
Lachen, rak shiru shir lashalom,	לָכֵן, רַק שִׁירוּ שִׁיר לַשָּׁלוֹם,
Al tilchashu t'fila!	אַל תִּלְחֲשׁוּ תְּפִלָּה!
Mutav tashiru shir lashalom	מוּטָב תָּשִׁירוּ שִׁיר לַשָּׁלוֹם
Bitse'aka g'dola!	בִּצְעָקָה גְדוֹלָה!
T'nu lashemesh lachador	תְּנוּ לַשֶּׁמֶשׁ לַחֲדֹר
Miba'ad laprachim.	מִבַּעַד לִפְרָחִים.
Al tabitu le'achor	אַל תַּבִּיטוּ לְאָחוֹר,
Hanichu laholchim.	הָנִיחוּ לַהוֹלְכִים.
Se'u eynayim betikva	שְׂאוּ עֵינַיִם בְּתִקְוָה
Lo derech kavanot.	לֹא דֶּרֶךְ כַּוָּנוֹת.
Shiru shir la'ahava	שִׁירוּ שִׁיר לָאַהֲבָה
Velo lamilchamot!	וְלֹא לַמִּלְחָמוֹת!
Al tagidu: yom yavo	אַל תַּגִּידוּ: יוֹם יָבוֹא–
Havi'u et hayom	הָבִיאוּ אֶת הַיּוֹם!
(Ki lo chalom hu)	(כִּי לֹא חֲלוֹם הוּא)
Uvechol hakikarot	וּבְכָל־הַכִּכָּרוֹת
Hari'u lashalom!	הָרִיעוּ לַשָּׁלוֹם!
Lachen, rak shim...	לָכֵן, רַק שִׁירוּ...

Ya'akov Rotblit

Shir LaShalom—Song of Peace

Let the morning sun so bright
shine and lead the way—
We'll no longer see its light
no matter how you pray.

When someone's light blows out and dies
he's buried in the grave—
He can't awake by mournful cries and shouts
that he was brave.

No one now can bring you back
from our deep darkened cave—
No, it won't help us
if you sing the fighting songs
that tell us to be brave.

So only sing now songs of peace—
Don't softly say a prayer.
So only sing now songs of peace—
Just shout it loud and clear.

translated by Sue Roemer

Y'hi Shalom

Shalom Rav l'Ohavey Torahtekha
V'Eyn l'Amo Mikhshol.
Y'Hi Shalom b'Kheyleykh
Shalvah b'Arm'notayikh.

שָׁלוֹם רָב לְאֹהֲבֵי תוֹרָתֶךָ
וְאֵין לָמוֹ מִכְשׁוֹל.
יְהִי שָׁלוֹם בְּחֵילֵךְ
שַׁלְוָה בְּאַרְמְנוֹתָיִךְ.

May there be Shalom for the lovers of our Teaching
for they will learn hard times go by.
May there be peace, Shalom within yourself
Safety in all places you reside.

Psalm 119:165, 122:7

All We Ask

Lo Amut Ki Ekhyeh vaAsaper Maasey Yah.
Kol Shen'vakeysh Lu Y'hi.
Lo baKhayil v'Lo baKoakh Ki Im b'Rukhi.
Kol Shen'vakeysh Lu Y'hi.

לֹא אָמוּת כִּי אֶחְיֶה וַאֲסַפֵּר מַעֲשֵׂה יָהּ.
כֹּל שֶׁנְּבַקֵּשׁ לוּ יְהִי.
לֹא בְחַיִל וְלֹא בְכֹחַ כִּי אִם בְּרוּחִי.
כֹּל שֶׁנְּבַקֵּשׁ לוּ יְהִי.

Lu Y'hi, Lu Y'hi
Ana Lu Y'hi
Kol Shen'vakeysh Lu Y'hi.

לוּ יְהִי, לוּ יְהִי
אָנָּא לוּ יְהִי
כֹּל שֶׁנְּבַקֵּשׁ לוּ יְהִי.

Ohr Zaruah laTzaddik u-l'Yishrey Lev Simkha.
Kol Shen'vakeysh Lu Y'hi.

אוֹר זָרֻעַ לַצַּדִּיק וּלְיִשְׁרֵי לֵב שִׂמְחָה.
כֹּל שֶׁנְּבַקֵּשׁ לוּ יְהִי.

Ureh Vanin l'Vanekha Shalom Al Yisrael.
Kol Shen'vakeysh Lu Y'hi.

וּרְאֵה בָנִים לְבָנֶיךָ שָׁלוֹם עַל יִשְׂרָאֵל.
כֹּל שֶׁנְּבַקֵּשׁ לוּ יְהִי.

I will not die, but I will live and speak of God's works.
   All that we ask, let it be.

Not by power nor by might but by My spirit...

Light is sown for the just and joy for the upright in heart...

May your children's children see peace upon all Israel...

Verses from Psalms 118:17, 97:11, 128:6, and Zechariah 4:6
Music adapted from Lu y'Hi by Naomi Shemer.

170

The Fiddler

Here on the world's edge at this hour I have
Wondrously settled my life.
Behind me in a boundless circle
The All is silent, only that fiddler fiddles.
Dark one, already I stand in convenant with you,
Ready to learn from your tones
Wherein I became guilty without knowing it.
Let me feel, let there be revealed
To this hale soul each wound
That I have incorrigibly inflicted and remained in illusion.
Do not stop, holy player, before then!

Martin Büber

Each Rose

Each rose is an island
of the promised peace,
the eternal peace.
Inside the petals
of each rose dwells
a sapphire bird called
"And They Shall Beat Their Swords."
And it seems so
close, the light
of that rose, so close
its scent, the silence
of its leaves, so close
that island—just take
a boat and go out
into a sea of flames.

Zelda
translated by Barbara Goldberg and Moshe Dor

Requests

I want beautiful trees—
and not wars!
and a coat of many colors
and not uniforms
for all my dear ones;
I want rain
and green furrows
and houses
full of babies;
a calendar of alliances
and a "brotherhood plaza"
and lightning and thunder—
in the sky;
and bountiful rains
on earth
and a pink crocus
in the ravines;
and pinecones
on a scented bed
of pine needles—
and bulbul birds rejoicing
among leafy orchards
and sails of peace
on the Mediterranean;
and white chrysanthemums
in the parks, their fall maneuvers;
and red balls rolling
along the paths
and the sleeves
of babies' garments signaling tranquility
on clotheslines.

Esther Raab
translated by Catherine Harriett Shaw and Moshe Dor

Songs and Readings

Selections from the Midrash

A Man

Rabbi Meir used to say:
Whence do we know that even a Gentile who engages in the Torah is like a High Priest?
We learn it from: "Ye shall therefore keep My statutes, and Mine ordinances, which if a man do,
he shall live by them" (Lev. 18:5).
"Priests, Levites, and Israelites" was not said, but "a man";
thus you may learn that even a Gentile who engages in the Torah
—lo, he is like a High Priest.

The Gates

There is no creature the Blessed Holy One rejects, but God accepts them all.
The gates are open at every hour, and all who wish to enter, may enter.
Therefore it is said: "My doors I opened to the wanderer" (Job 31:32)
—meaning the Holy One of Blessing suffers his creatures.

For All To See

The Torah was given in public, for all to see, in the open.
For if it had been given in the land of Israel, Israel would have said to the nations of the world,
You have no share in it;
therefore the Torah was given in the wilderness, in public, for all to see, in the open,
and everyone who wishes to receive it, let him come and receive it.

Heaven and Man

The Blessed Holy One, continued to appease Moses
and said to him:
"Am I not as your Father, and you as my children,
you my brothers, and I your brother;
you my friends, and I your friend;
you my lovers, and I your lover?
Have I allowed you to lack?
All that I ask you is this, as I have examined myself and found eleven qualities,
so all I ask of you is eleven qualities;
and they are:
'He that walketh uprightly, and worketh righteousness,
And speaketh truth ...'" (Psalm15:2-5).

The Blessed Holy One, continued to appease Moses
and said to him:
"Do I at all favor an Israelite or a Gentile,
a man or a woman, a man-servant or a maid-servant?"
But whoever who keeps a commandment, the reward is on the heels.
Hence it was said:
"He/she who honors heaven more, heaven's honor is more,
and his/her own honor is more, as well.
He/she who honors heaven less, and honors himself/herself more,
heaven's honor continues the same, but his/her own honor is less."

Selections compiled and translated by Nahum Glatzer
and adapted by the editor.

SOURCES AND ACKNOWLEDGEMENTS

Illustrations

front cover — Banner by Rosana Azar and members of Kehila Chadasha. Used by permission of the Kehila.

back cover — Medallion by Robert Pearlman. Used by permission of the artist.

title page — "Zodiac" by Susan Leviton. ©1986 Susan Leviton, Harrisburg, Pennsylvania . Used by permission of the artist.

p 2 — Saul Raskin, "Sabbaths for Rest, Holidays for Joy," *Between God and Man*, p 88. Used by permission of the artist.

p 15 — Ben-Zion, "Man with Raised Arms," *Iron Sculpture*, no. 20. Used by permission of Lillian Ben-Zion, New York, NY.

p 26 — Joan Geller, drawing of tree with deer. © 1992 Joan Geller, Bethesda, Maryland. Used by permission of the artist.

p 32 — Ben Shahn, drawing of guitar and flute.

p 35 — Ben Shahn, drawing of crown, untitled, *Alphabet of Creation*. © Estate of Ben Shahn/Licensed by VAGA, New York, NY.

p 56 — Ben Shahn, drawing of hands forming the symbol of the Kohanim, untitled, *Alphabet of Creation*. © Estate of Ben Shahn/Licensed by VAGA, New York, NY.

p 66 — Ben Shahn, "Second Alphabet," *His Graphic Art*, p 81. © Estate of Ben Shahn/Licensed by VAGA, New York, NY.

p 68 — Saul Raskin, "Cantor Praying Before Service," *Between God and Man*, p 94. Used by permission of the artist.

p 72 — Joan Geller, drawing of star with flowers. © 1992 Joan Geller, Bethesda, Maryland. Used by permission of the artist.

p 82 — Ben-Zion, "Kohen Blessing of the Priests," *Iron Sculpture*, no. 91. Used by permission of Lillian Ben-Zion, New York, NY.

p 88 — Ben Shahn, "Today is the Birthday of the World," *His Graphic Art*, p 94. © Estate of Ben Shahn/Licensed by VAGA, New York, NY.

p 90 — Saul Raskin, "Hebrew Rhapsody," *Between God and Man*, p 92. Used by permission of the artist.

p 93 — Ben-Zion, "Rabbi," *Iron Sculpture*, no. 118. Used by permission of Lillian Ben-Zion, New York, NY.

p 96 — Ben Shahn, "Tablets of the Law with Lion," *His Graphic Art*, p 120. © Estate of Ben Shahn/Licensed by VAGA, New York, NY.

p 98 — Ben-Zion, "Moses and the Tablets," *Iron Sculpture*, no. 90. Used by permission of Lillian Ben-Zion, New York, NY.

p 103 — Ben-Zion, "Praying Prophet," *Iron Sculpture*, no. 2. Used by permission of Lillian Ben-Zion, New York, NY.

p 106 — Ben Shahn, "Trees," *Ben Shahn Drawings* (Kennedy, 1979), no. 39. © Estate of Ben Shahn/Licensed by VAGA, New York, NY.

p 109 Ben Shahn, "Wheat Field," *Collected Prints*, no. 62. © Estate of Ben Shahn/Licensed by VAGA, New York, NY.

p 112 Ben Shahn, "Warsaw 1943," *Complete Graphics Works*, no. 54. © Estate of Ben Shahn/Licensed by VAGA, New York, NY.

p 115 Ben Shahn, "Hands (Shape of Content)," *The Drawings of Ben Shahn* (Kennedy, 1970), no. 32. © Estate of Ben Shahn/Licensed by VAGA, New York, NY.

p 117 Ben-Zion, "Preacher," *Iron Sculpture*, no. 114. Used by permission of Lillian Ben-Zion, New York, NY.

p 118 Ben-Zion, "Man a Victim of His Own Devices," *Iron Sculpture*, no. 30. Used by permission of Lillian Ben-Zion, New York, NY.

p 120 Saul Raskin, "When You Intend to Approach the Creator," *Between God and Man*, p 101. Used by permission of the artist.

p 126 Ben-Zion, "Praying Man," *Iron Sculpture*, no. 35. Used by permission of Lillian Ben-Zion, New York, NY.

p 132 Ben Shahn, drawing of man blowing shofar, untitled, *Alphabet of Creation.* © Estate of Ben Shahn/Licensed by VAGA, New York, NY.

p 134 Joan Geller, drawing of torah shield, © 1992 Joan Geller, Bethesda, Maryland. Used by permission of the artist.

p 140 Ben-Zion, "Sacrifice of Isaac," *Iron Sculpture*, no. 44. Used by permission of Lillian Ben-Zion, New York, NY.

p 160 Ismar David, "Jonah," *The Five Megilloth and Jonah.* © 1969 Ismar David. Reprinted by permission of the publisher, The Jewish Publication Society.

p 164 Ben Shahn, "Bach," *His Graphic Art*, p 95. © Estate of Ben Shahn/Licensed by VAGA, New York, NY.

p 169 Ben Shahn, "Man Playing Cithara," *Complete Graphics Works*, no. 251. © Estate of Ben Shahn/Licensed by VAGA, New York, NY.

Sources for Illustrations

Alphabet of Creation, by Ben Shahn. Pantheon Books, New York: 1954. Artwork © Estate of Ben Shahn/Licensed by VAGA, New York, NY.

Ben Shahn Drawings, Kennedy Galleries, New York: 1979. Artwork © Estate of Ben Shahn/Licensed by VAGA, New York, NY.

Ben Shahn: His Graphic Art, by James Thrall Soby. George Braziller, Inc., New York: 1957. Artwork © Estate of Ben Shahn/Licensed by VAGA, New York, NY.

Ben Zion Iron Sculptures, Lillian Dubin and Tabita Shalem, eds., Alpine Fine Arts Collection Ltd, New York: 1986.

Between God and Man: Hebrew Rhapsody in 100 Drawings, by Saul Raskin. Printed by Academy Photo Offset, New York, no date.

The Collected Prints of Ben Shahn, Philadelphia Museum of Art, Philadelphia: 1967. Artwork © Estate of Ben Shahn/Licensed by VAGA, New York, NY.

Sources and Acknowledgements

The Complete Graphics Works of Ben Shahn, by Kenneth W. Prescott. Quadrangle/The New York Times Book Co., New York: 1973. Artwork © Estate of Ben Shahn/Licensed by VAGA, New York, NY.

The Drawings of Ben Shahn, Kennedy Galleries, New York: 1970. Artwork © Estate of Ben Shahn/Licensed by VAGA, New York, NY.

The Five Megilloth and Jonah, by Ismar David. The Jewish Publication Society, Philadelphia: 1969.

Quotations, Poetry and Songs

p 3   "Head of the Year," poem by Myra Sklarew. © Myra Sklarew, Yaddo, N.Y. Used by permission of the author.

p 3   "Changes," song by Phil Ochs. Reprint permission granted by the Hal Leonard Corporation, Milwaukee, WI.

p 4   A. J. Heschel, excerpts from *Who Is Man?*, pp 88-89. © 1965. Used by permission of Stanford University Press, www.sup.org.

p 5   "Fill Our Days," poem by Danny Siegel, *The Lord is a Whisper at Midnight*. Used by permission of the author.

p 7   "V'ahavta," poem by Marge Piercy. From *The Art of Blessing The Day* by Marge Piercy. © 1999 Middlemarsh, Inc. Used by permission of Alfred A. Knopf, a division of Random House, Inc.

p 13   A. J. Heschel, excerpt from *The Earth is the Lord's*, p 109. © 1949 Abraham Joshua Heschel. Copyright renewed © 1977 Sylvia Heschel. Reprinted by permission of Farrar, Straus and Giroux, LLC.

p 17   A. J. Heschel, excerpt from *The Insecurity of Freedom*, p 84. © 1966 Abraham Joshua Heschel. Copyright renewed © 1994 Sylvia Heschel. Reprinted by permission of Farrar, Straus and Giroux, LLC.

p 19   "Sometime," poem by Yehudit Kaffri, tr. by Ann Darr and Moshe Dor, *After the First Rain*. Reprinted by permission of Dryad Press from *After the First Rain: Israeli Poems on War and Peace*, edited by Moshe Dor and Barbara Goldberg, 1999, co-published by Syracuse University Press (Syracuse, NY) and Dryad Press (Takoma Park, MD).

p 27   A. J. Heschel, excerpt from *God in Search of Man*, p 105. © 1955 Abraham Joshua Heschel. Copyright renewed © 1983 Sylvia Heschel. Reprinted by permission of Farrar, Straus and Giroux, LLC.

p 27   "You are a Consolation to Your Creatures," poem by Danny Siegel, *The Lord is a Whisper at Midnight*. Used by permission of the author.

p 31   "Painting a Morning Panorama," poem by Danny Siegel, *The Lord is a Whisper at Midnight*. Used by permission of the author.

p 33   A. J. Heschel, excerpts from *Who Is Man?*, pp 113, 118. © 1965. Used by permission of Stanford University Press, www.sup.org.

p 34   A. J. Heschel, excerpts from *Quest for God*, p 39. © Sylvia Heschel. Used by permission of Sylvia Heschel, New York, NY.

A. J. Heschel, excerpts from *Man Is Not Alone*, p 16. © 1951 by Abraham Joshua Heschel. Copyright renewed © 1979 by Sylvia Heschel. Reprinted by permission of Farrar, Straus and Giroux, LLC.

"In the Garden of Shechina," poem by Hanna Tiferet Siegel. © Hanna Tiferet Siegel, Hanover, New Hampshire. Used by permission of the author.

Sources and Acknowledgements

p 43 "Blessings," poem by Marge Piercy. From *The Art of Blessing The Day* by Marge Piercy, © 1999 Middlemarsh, Inc. Used by permission of Alfred A. Knopf, a division of Random House, Inc.

p 48 A. J. Heschel, excerpt from *Quest for God*, p 151. © Sylvia Heschel. Used by permission of Sylvia Heschel, New York, NY.

p 49 A. J. Heschel, excerpt from *Man Is Not Alone*, p 99. © 1951 Abraham Joshua Heschel. Copyright renewed © 1979 Sylvia Heschel. Reprinted by permission of Farrar, Straus and Giroux, LLC.

p 50 Martin Büber, excerpts from *Ten Rungs: Hasidic Sayings*, p 82. Used by permission of The Balkan Agency, Amherst, MA, Agent for the Estate of Martin Büber.

p 51 Nahum Glatzer, excerpts from *Hammer on the Rock: A Short Midrash Reader*, p 50, with adaptations by the editor. Used by permission of Judith Glatzer Wechsler, Cambridge, MA.

p 52 A. J. Heschel, excerpt from *The Insecurity of Freedom*, p 84. © 1966 Abraham Joshua Heschel. Copyright renewed © 1994 Sylvia Heschel. Reprinted by permission of Farrar, Straus and Giroux, LLC.

p 57 "Number My Days This Way," poem by Danny Siegel, *The Lord is a Whisper at Midnight*. Used by permission of the author.

p 71 "Dust in the Wind," song by Kerry Livgren. Reprint permission granted by the Hal Leonard Corporation, Milwaukee, WI.

p 73 "Life of Nature," poem by Mordecai Kaplan, *The Sabbath Prayer Book*. © 1945 by the Jewish Reconstructionist Foundation. Reprint permission granted by Reconstructionist Press, Elkins Park, PA.

p 76 "Trajectories of Time," poem by Gustav Buchdahl. Used by permission of the author.

p 80 "Laugh at My Dreams," poem by Saul Tchernikhovsky. In the public domain. (*).

Martin Büber, excerpt from *On Judaism*, p 29. Used by permission of the publisher under "fair use" for reprints.

Martin Büber, excerpt from *Ten Rungs: Hasidic Sayings*, p 113. Used by permission of The Balkan Agency, Amherst, MA, Agent for the Estate of Martin Büber.

p 81 "Jerusalem of Gold," by Norman Newell, and Naomi Shemer-Saphir. © 1967 (Renewed) Chappell & Co., Ltd. All rights on behalf of Chappell & Co., Ltd. Administered by Chappell & Co. All rights reserved. Used by permission. Warner Bros. Publications U.S. Inc., Miami, Florida 33014.

p 91 "Eyli, Eyli," song by Hannah Senesch. In the public domain. (*).

p 91 "Every Day is a Day of Atonement," by Saul Ansky. Excerpt from *The Dybbuk and Other Writings*, (trans. Werman). Used by permission of Yale Univerisity Press , New Haven, CT.

p 92 "Meditation: Kol Nidre," poem by Morris Silverman, *High Holiday Prayer Book,* with adaptations by the editor. © 1951 by The Prayer Book Press of Media Judaica, Inc., Bridgeport, CT. Used by permission of The Prayer Book Press.

p 104 "Show Us How to Fashion Holiness," poem by Danny Siegel, *The Lord is a Whisper at Midnight*. Used by permission of the author.

p 104 Nahum Glatzer, excerpt from *Hammer on the Rock: A Short Midrash Reader*, p 89, with adaptations by the editor. Used by permission of Judith Glatzer Wechsler, Cambridge, MA.

p 108 "We Remember Them," poem by Sylvan Kamens and Jack Riemer, *Mahzor Hadash*. © 1977, 1978 by The Prayer Book Press of Media Judaica, Bridgeport, CT. Used by permission of The Prayer Book Press.

Sources and Acknowledgements

p 113 "Unter Di Khurves Fun Poyln," song by Itsik Manger. In the public domain. (*).

p 114 "A Mother's Will," *Ethical Wills*, p 76. © Jack Riemer. Reprinted by permission of Jack Riemer.

p 115 A. J. Heschel, "Too Late," reprinted in *The Challenge of Shalom*, p 152. © Sylvia Heschel. Used by permission of Sylvia Heschel, New York, NY.

p 115 "The Messiah Came to Europe," poem by Herman Taube, *Between the Shadows*. Used by permission of the author.

p 116 "Vakht Oyf," song by David Edelstat. In the public domain. (*).

p 116 "Partisanen Lied," song by Hirsch Glick. In the public domain. (*).

p 117 "Ani Ma-Amin," Hebrew song. Traditional.

p 121 "Di Zun Vet Aruntergeyn," song by Moshe Halpern. In the public domain. (*).

p 125 "Ne'ilah," poem by Herman Taube, *Between the Shadows*. Used by permission of the author.

p 126 "A Prayer," poem by Herman Taube, *Between the Shadows*. Used by permission of the author.

p 127 "Rad HaLaila," Israeli folk song. Traditional.

p 128 "Jerusalem of Gold," (see p 81).

p 128 "Erev Ba," Israeli folk song. Traditional.

p 166 "Modeh Ani," song by Betsy Combs. © 1991 by Betsy Combs. Used by permission of the composer.

p 166 "Morning Has Broken," words by Eleanor Farjeon. © 1957, Eleanor Farjeon. Reprinted by permission of Harold Ober Associates Incorporated, New York, NY.

p 166 "Awake and Arise," poem by Hannah Tiferet Siegel. Used by permission of the author.

p 167 "Life," song by Tom Paxton. Reprint permission granted by the Hal Leonard Corporation , Milwaukee, WI, on behalf of Cherry Lane Music.

p 167 "The Circle Chant," song by Linda Hirschhorn. Used by permission of the composer.

p 168 "Shir HaShalom," song by Ya'akov Rotblit and Ya'ir Rosenblum, tr. Sue Roemer. © the author and ACUM (www.acum.org.il). Used by permission. Translation used by permission of the translator.

p 171 "Each Rose," poem by Zelda, tr. Barbara Goldberg and Moshe Dor, *After the First Rain*. Reprinted by permission of Dryad Press from *After the First Rain: Israeli Poems on War and Peace*, edited by Moshe Dor and Barbara Goldberg, 1999, co-published by Syracuse University Press (Syracuse, NY) and Dryad Press (Takoma Park, MD).

p 171 "The Fiddler," poem by Martin Büber, tr. Maurice Friedman. Translation used by permission of Maurice Friedman.

p 172 "Requests," poem by Esther Raab, tr. Catherine Harnett Shaw and Moshe Dor, *After the First Rain*. Reprinted by permission of Dryad Press from *After the First Rain: Israeli Poems on War and Peace*, edited by Moshe Dor and Barbara Goldberg, 1999, co-published by Syracuse University Press (Syracuse, NY) and Dryad Press (Takoma Park, MD).

p 173-4 Nahum Glatzer, excerpts from *Hammer on the Rock: A Short Midrash Reader*, pp 40, 47, 74, 79, with adaptations by the editor. Used by permission of Judith Glatzer Wechsler, Cambridge, MA.

Sources and Acknowledgements

Sources for Quotations, Poetry and Songs

Saul Ansky, translated by Golda Werman, *The Dybbuk and Other Writings,* Yale University Press, New Haven CT: 2002.

Martin Büber, *On Judaism*, ed. Nahum Glatzer, Schocken Books, New York: 1967.

Martin Büber, *Ten Rungs: Hasidic Sayings*, Schocken Books, New York: 1968.

Moshe Dor and Barbara Goldberg, eds., *After the First Rain: Israeli Poems on War and Peace*, Syracuse University Press in association with Dryad Press, Syracuse, NY: 1998.

Nahum Glatzer, ed., *Hammer on the Rock: A Short Midrash Reader*, Shocken Books, New York: 1962.

Sydney Greenberg and Jonathan D. Levine, eds., *Mahzor Hadash: A New High Holiday Prayer Book,* The Prayer Book Press of Media Judaica, Bridgeport, CT: 1978.

Abraham Joshua Heschel, *Who Is Man?* Stanford University Press, Stanford: 1965.

_____, *God in Search of Man*, Jewish Publication Society, Philadelphia: 1955.

_____, *The Earth is the Lord's,* Jewish Publication Society, Philadelphia: 1962.

_____, *Man is Not Alone,* Jewish Publication Society, Philadelphia: 1951.

_____, *The Insecurity of Freedom,* Jewish Publication Society, Philadelphia: 1966.

_____, *Man's Quest for God*, Charles Scribner's Sons, New York: 1954. Reprinted as *Quest for God,* Crossroad Publishing, New York: 1982.

Mordecai Kaplan, *Sabbath Prayer Book*, Jewish Reconstructionist Foundation, New York: 1945.

Marge Piercy, *The Art of Blessing the Day: Poems with a Jewish Theme.* Alfred A. Knopf, New York: 1999.

Murray Polner and Naomi Goodman, eds., *The Challenge of Shalom*, New Society Publications, Philadelphia: 1994.

Jack Riemer and Nathaniel Stampfer, eds., *Ethical Wills: A Modern Jewish Treasury*, Schocken Books, New York: 1983.

Danny Siegel, *The Lord is a Whisper at Midnight*, The Town House Press: 1985.

Morris Silverman, ed., *High Holiday Prayer Book*, The Prayer Book Press of Media Judaica, Bridgeport, CT: 1951.

Herman Taube, *Between the Shadows*, Dryad Press and the Jewish Folk Arts Society, College Park, Maryland: 1986.

(*) We acknowledge Tara Publications and Workmen's Circle for their efforts in preserving our musical heritage.